U.S.-SOVIET RELATIONS IN THE ERA OF DÉTENTE

Also of Interest

†*The Soviet Union in World Politics*, edited by Kurt London

†*The Armed Forces of the USSR*, Harriet Fast Scott and William F. Scott

Verification and SALT: The Challenge of Strategic Deception, edited by William C. Potter

†*The Domestic Context of Soviet Foreign Policy*, edited by Seweryn Bialer

†*Securing the Seas: The Soviet Naval Challenge and Western Alliance Options*, Paul H. Nitze, Leonard Sullivan, Jr., and the Atlantic Council Working Group on Securing the Seas

The Angolan War: A Study in Soviet Foreign Policy in the Third World, Arthur Jay Klinghoffer

†*China, the Soviet Union, and the West: Strategic and Political Dimensions in the 1980s*, edited by Douglas Stuart and William T. Tow

Atlas of Soviet Affairs, Robert N. Taaffe and Robert Kingsbury

†*The Soviet Union in the Third World: Successes and Failures*, edited by Robert H. Donaldson

†*World Power Trends and U.S. Foreign Policy for the 1980s*, Ray S. Cline

Arms Control and Defense Postures in the 1980s, edited by Richard Burt

†*The War System: An Interdisciplinary Approach*, edited by Richard A. Falk and Samuel S. Kim

The Military Balance 1980–1981, International Institute for Strategic Studies

†Available in hardcover and paperback

About the Book and Author

U.S.-Soviet Relations in
the Era of Détente
Richard Pipes

Americans tend to view peace as a normal state, occasionally interrupted by war, which should be ended as quickly as possible to return to "normalcy." The Soviet Union, according to eminent Harvard historian Richard Pipes, may have a very different view of both peace and war, believing that peace is merely an interlude between wars, perhaps a time to arm and plan for the next war. The implications of these differing views for understanding détente, he says, are vast. The United States may well be totally misinterpreting Soviet intentions in détente.

This volume is a collection of eight of Dr. Pipes's most important papers on Soviet foreign policy, concentrating on the constants that form the bedrock of Soviet policy, its psychological, historical, and cultural foundations, its techniques, and the Soviet variant of a policy of détente. Dr. Pipes is convinced that a "grand strategy" underlies the foreign and military policies of the Soviet Union and that the roots of that strategy are deeply embedded in Russian history.

Dr. Pipes's papers reflect his perceptions of the Soviets' relationship with the rest of the world. That his assertions may be correct is shown by a recent presidential directive indicating that the United States is beginning to see that the USSR may indeed have a strategy for winning a nuclear war, while past U.S. actions have been based on a firm belief that the Soviets were convinced that neither superpower could do more than assure mutual destruction.

Richard Pipes is Baird Professor of History at Harvard University and is a prominent writer on the Soviet Union. He was director of Harvard's Russian Research Center from 1968 to 1973 and served in various consulting capacities in Washington, D.C., during the 1970s.

U.S.-SOVIET RELATIONS IN THE ERA OF DÉTENTE

RICHARD PIPES

WESTVIEW PRESS / BOULDER, COLORADO

Copyright © 1981 by Richard Pipes

Published in 1981 in the United States of America by
  Westview Press, Inc.
  5500 Central Avenue
  Boulder, Colorado 80301
  Frederick A. Praeger, Publisher

Second printing, 1982

Library of Congress Cataloging in Publication Data
Pipes, Richard.
    U.S.-Soviet relations in the era of détente.
    Includes bibliographical references and index.
    1. United States—Foreign relations—Russia. 2. Russia—Foreign relations—United States. 3. Détente. I. Title.
E183.8.R9P48   327.73047   80-27121
ISBN 0-86531-154-4
ISBN 0-86531-155-2 (pbk.)

Printed and bound in the United States of America

Contents

Preface ix

1. Russia's Mission, America's Destiny 1

2. Some Operational Principles of Soviet Foreign
    Policy 19

3. America, Russia, and Europe in the Light
    of the Nixon Doctrine. 47

4. Détente: Moscow's View. 63

5. Détente: A Discussion with George R. Urban 107

6. Why the Soviet Union Thinks It Could Fight
    and Win a Nuclear War 135

7. Soviet Global Strategy. 171

8. Militarism and the Soviet State 195

Index. 215

Preface

Linguists identify a category of words that they call "false friends." They apply this term to words that are alike in appearance and sound but that mean different things in different languages. The treachery of "false friends" was vividly brought home to me years ago when I was learning Russian and discovered that *zapomnit'*, which in my native Polish meant "to forget," in Russian meant "to remember."

The essays that follow were written during the decade of détente, a diplomatic term that in political application has proven to be the falsest of friends. When given fresh currency by de Gaulle around 1958, it was used to describe the first step of a process that was to lead through *"entente* to cooperation" between the eastern and western halves of Europe. For de Gaulle, détente's main by-product was to have been the dissolution of the two great military blocs—NATO and the Warsaw Pact— with the resultant restoration of political independence to continental Europe. In Germany, where it was adopted in the guise of *Ostpolitik,* détente came to stand for the abandonment of the Hallstein Doctrine (with its insistence on national reunification) in exchange for opportunities to engage in diplomatic and economic relations with Eastern Europe. In both instances, détente was invoked as a device to broaden the room for political maneuverability.

This was not the case with the so-called "superpowers." The United States had begun cautiously to edge toward a relaxation of tensions with the USSR in the mid-1950s when Stalin's heirs first hinted at abandoning the "cold war" in favor of "peaceful

coexistence." The meetings held at Camp David in 1959 between President Eisenhower and Nikita Khrushchev inaugurated
an American-Soviet dialogue that, even if it did not produce
immediately any concrete results, helped to improve the diplomatic climate. During the next decade, however, genuine rapprochement between the two countries was precluded by the
Vietnam War, in the course of which Moscow provided massive
military assistance to America's enemies. Even so, the 1960s
saw a steady thaw that prepared the ground for the series of
treaties and accords that under President Nixon were formally
to commit the United States to the policy of détente.

The main impetus driving the two powers toward better relations was the specter of nuclear war. At the time of the Camp
David encounter, the United States and the Soviet Union each
were in possession of thermonuclear warheads and the vehicles
for their delivery against each other's territory. Both also had
underway crash programs to greatly enlarge their arsenals of
nuclear warheads and delivery vehicles. Unregulated armament
programs carried out in an atmosphere charged with hostility,
such as had prevailed in the era of the "cold war," threatened
total devastation. Common sense dictated that the powers
capable of inflicting such destruction on each other, and on
much of the world besides, at the very least should attempt to
set procedures for regulating their differences as well as limiting
the construction of nuclear weapons. This view, adopted by the
leadership of the two countries, lent their détente a much
grander purpose than was the case with de Gaulle's and Brandt's
more modest initiatives.

But even within the confines of that shared premise, significant differences separated Washington from Moscow. As is true
of every predominantly commercial society known throughout
history, the American public and the American government regard money spent on defense as money wasted—that is, capital
withheld from the productive sectors of the economy that
create jobs and from social programs that help raise living
standards. When confronted with a direct assault on its territory,
the United States spares no effort to respond in an appropriate
fashion. Indeed, under such provocation it is likely to overcom-
pensate in order to end the threat in the quickest possible time

and return to "normalcy." Its difficulty lies in its carrying out the kind of prosaic peacetime defense effort that goes on year after year without yielding visible results, in the course of which the very face of the enemy becomes blurred and the threat seems to dissolve. Leaders of commercial democracies must respond to these realities, and they are prone to seize on any reasonable pretext that will allow them to reduce defense expenditures. This is especially true of those who administer modern welfare states in which an ever greater share of the national product is regularly "transferred" to social programs and put to use to win votes.

In the Soviet Union, of course, the situation is quite different. The leadership there confronts no electoral contests; nor is it restrained by public pressures for social welfare to limit defense expenditures. As I argue in the concluding essay of this collection, militarism is deeply imbedded in the theory and practice of Russian Communism. In its eyes, peace is not the "normal" condition, the sea level to which the turbulent waters return after occasional storms, but, in Lenin's words, an interlude, a "breathing space" for war. Even so, the Soviet leadership had its own compelling reasons to engage in détente with the United States. These had largely to do with the complications introduced into the conduct of Soviet foreign policy by the appearance of nuclear weapons. The leadership of a country driven by historical traditions, internal exigencies, and ideology relentlessly to expand faced the uncomfortable fact that there now existed nuclear weapons threatening incalculable destruction in war and that the United States, the main "citadel" of the "capitalist" camp, happened to enjoy an overwhelming preponderance of them. These facts made it most inadvisable to engage in aggressions of the direct, frontal kind that had been pursued by Stalin. Western opinion fails to appreciate the extent to which Soviet thinking about foreign and military matters since 1945 has been dominated by the reality of nuclear weapons. Whereas to us they are nothing but a nightmare, to the leaders of the Soviet state they are both a nightmare and an opportunity. Having concluded early that these weapons will dominate the battlefield of the future, they have structured their military establishment around the Strategic Rocket Forces, as well as developed a general political strategy suited for the age of fission and fusion warheads. This strategy calls for indirect aggression coupled with a concurrent program of vigorous military (especially nuclear) construction. Détente was meant to secure Lenin's "breathing space" in which this plan could be carried out.

It seems to me that the concrete tactics the Soviet leadership hoped to implement as part of the détente strategy may be summarized under two headings.

1. The dangerous policy of direct confrontations with the United States and its allies was to be abandoned in favor of less risky flanking movements carried out, preferably by proxy forces, by way of the Third World, where lie important bases and raw materials. This policy would enable the USSR gradually to increase its pressures on the Western alliance while promising to promote divisions within the enemy camp as each of its members gave priority to its national or regional interests in preference to the alliance's common global commitments.

2. The USSR hoped to undertake, at the same time, a major rearmament program for possible World War III by projecting a peaceful image to weaken the Western defense effort while attracting foreign capital and technology with which to modernize the industrial base serving the Soviet military. They also sought persuasive nuclear superiority with which to obtain compliance, preferably by use of threat, but also by war if necessary.

On the face of it, these Soviet objectives may appear incompatible. It is difficult to see why the West should be expected to provide the Soviet Union with economic assistance to help modernize its armed forces for an ultimate confrontation and stand idly by while it engages in hostile action in the Third World. Nevertheless, the United States accepted these rules of the game, at least initially. In seeking to reduce America's global role after Vietnam, the Nixon and Ford administrations, as well as Congress, were not overly troubled by Russia's penetration into the Third World. At the same time, American business, eager to enter the Soviet market, showed no concern for the long-term political and military implications of capital and technology exports to the Soviet Union. In May 1972 in Moscow, the two countries signed a document called "Basic Principles of Relations," which outlined a grandiose program of cooperation. They pledged themselves to "do their utmost to avoid military confrontations and to prevent the outbreak of nuclear war," "always [to] exercise restraint in their mutual relations," and to "be prepared to negotiate and settle differences by peaceful means." As if these promises were not enough, they affirmed that "efforts to obtain unilateral advantage at the expense of the other, directly or indirectly, [were] inconsistent" with these goals. Their "ultimate objective" was stated to be "the achievement of general and complete disarmament." This was nothing less than the promise of permanent peace, a new Holy Alliance. But whereas the first alliance had been concluded tongue in cheek to humor a Russian tsar in the grip of mysticism, the declaration of basic principles seems to have been taken seriously, at any rate on the American side.

The Soviet Union violated the spirit and letter of these accords almost at once. Prior to October 1973 it connived with Syria and Egypt to launch a surprise attack on Israel, a country with which the United States had very close relations. While military operations were in progress, it exhorted the Arab countries to embargo oil to the West; and when Egypt was on the verge of being dealt a humiliating defeat by Israel, it presented the United States with an ominous ultimatum. Early in 1975, the Soviet Union assisted North Vietnam in violating the peace accords signed in Paris and in occupying South Vietnam, which the United States had a moral obligation to protect. Later that year, it assisted Cuban troops in establishing in Angola a pro-Communist regime. None of these differences was negotiated. In each case the Soviet Union sought to obtain unilateral advantage at the expense of the United States, and in one instance it produced an ugly confrontation. Equally disturbing was the fact that notwithstanding SALT I and the promise of an effort at "general and complete disarmament," the Soviet regime was continuing to pour ever larger resources into armaments. In the strategic field there was evidence, conclusive to some, that the Soviet Union was striving for a first-strike capability. All those developments—quite consistent with the Soviet view of détente—had the effect of disillusioning the American public, which was conditioned by the extravagant claims of its leaders to expect an age of peace and cooperation. The Soviet invasion of Afghanistan in December 1979 served only as the last nail driven into the coffin of détente.

It would be difficult to find in the United States today, even among people strongly committed to improved U.S.-Soviet relations, advocates of the kind of sweeping promises once conveyed by détente. The system that was to usher in a " new era" in international relations has collapsed and vanished almost without a trace, except perhaps in Europe where, as noted, it has been attended by more modest expectations. The United States still has to formulate a policy toward the Soviet Union that, avoiding the frenzies of containment and the mirages of détente, would engage it in the kind of global "grand strategy" that Moscow pursues as a matter of course.

* * *

Being by intellectual commitment and by profession an historian, I had long avoided becoming involved in politics. My more active political involvement coincided with the birth of détente. From the outset, I was disturbed that the people who in 1969 took charge of American foreign policy seemed to be utterly ignorant of the nature of the Soviet regime with which they were about to enter into major accords. Worse than that, they did not even see the need to be better informed. The architects of U.S. détente—President Nixon and Henry Kissinger—initiated a policy that posited as its ultimate objective a complete reorientation in the world outlook of the Soviet regime, and they did so without familiarizing themselves either with Russian history or with Communist theory.

Russia has behind it some 650 years of continuous statehood. It also happens to be a country in which the central government has traditionally played an exceptionally active role in directing national life. Not surprisingly, it has developed strong habits of political conduct. Communist ideology is of more recent vintage, but it, too, has a history of more than a century of continuous evolution in the course of which intelligent and well-informed theorists have elaborated an array of strategies and tactics to suit various circumstances. All this was brushed aside as an irrelevant complication in favor of high-sounding platitudes about "convergence," "web of interests," and the like. I have never been able to determine satisfactorily whether the Nixon-Kissinger approach to the Soviet Union was inspired by intellectual indolence, naiveté, political calculation, or personal vanity. But the answer is not all that important. The result—a foreign policy based on ignorance of one's antagonist and therefore inherently inept—is the same whichever is correct.

The first essay in this book deals with the cultural-historical background that lies behind the political outlooks of the United States and Russia. It was originally delivered at the December 1969 meeting of the American Historical Association in Washington, D.C. Détente at that time was only a vague idea, and I hoped, by calling attention to the deep-seated differences in the ways American and Soviet societies perceive the world, to warn about the obstacles on the way to genuine rapprochement between the two countries. I understand that after its publication in *Encounter* magazine in October 1970, this paper was distributed to the staff of the National Security Council. If so, it produced no apparent effects on the conduct of policy.

The essay, however, attracted the attention of Senator Henry Jackson who was then leading an almost solitary campaign against President Nixon's Soviet policy. At his invitation I joined, as a consultant, the Senate's Committee on Government Operations, and in 1971 wrote for it "Some Operational Principles of Soviet Foreign Policy." This essay contains in embryo most of the ideas I subsequently developed on the subject of Soviet foreign and military strategy. Published when the expectations of détente were at their height, it exerted no influence whatsoever.

In 1973 Richard B. Foster, director of the Strategic Studies Center in Washington (a branch of the Stanford Research Institute—SRI) invited me to join his organization. My task was to study Soviet Grand Strategy, a subject entirely ignored in Washington where those who mattered in those days decided that the Soviet Union was an ordinary state that pursued its "national interest" and seized, as they presented themselves, all opportunities for enhancing its own power. I wrote for SRI two large papers. "America, Russia, and Europe in the Light of the Nixon Doctrine," published in 1974, sought to call attention to the flaws inherent in the short-lived "doctrine" named after the current president. "Détente: Moscow's View," written in 1974 and published in 1976, was a more ambitious attempt to interpret this concept as the Soviet leaders might perceive it under the influence of their particular experiences and aspirations.

By that time, détente was beginning to fall out of favor. George Urban, an English journalist and one of the most skilled practitioners of the art of interviewing, published a symposium of critical opinion on the subject, in which he included a lengthy dialogue with me.

Of all my writings, none has created as much of a stir as the one that Norman Podhoretz (editor of *Commentary* magazine, where it appeared in July 1977) gave the title "Why the Soviet Union Thinks It Could Fight and Win a Nuclear War." The background of this paper is as follows. By 1976 it was beginning to trouble some informed people that the high hopes of nuclear arms limitations raised by the so-called Interim Agreement were not being realized, inasmuch as the Soviet Union was proceeding to develop and deploy a panoply of new strategic systems that could lead it beyond parity. Questions were raised about whether the Soviet Union indeed shared the dominant U.S. strategic doctrine of "mutual assured destruction" or instead strove for a first-strike capability. Doubts of this kind spread among the members of the President's Foreign Intelligence Advisory Board (PFIAB), a body composed of accomplished scientists, businessmen, and retired military and charged with supervising the country's intelligence operations. The board was especially perturbed that the CIA's National Intelligence Estimates (NIEs) for many years running had been underestimating both the intensity and the scope of ongoing Soviet strategic programs, a failing which, if it persisted, could endanger United States security.

At PFIAB's initiative, George Bush, then director of the CIA, agreed in the summer of 1976 to an experiment in "competitive analysis." While the group in charge of drafting the current NIE on Soviet Strategic Objectives (designated for this purpose as Team A) went about its business, another group (Team B), composed entirely of outside experts, was to be given access to the same data. The purpose of the experiment was to see whether or not, using identical information, Team B would arrive at similar conclusions. I was asked to chair Team B. My expertise was not in the field of weaponry, but I was to provide the broader political dimension to the understanding of the Soviet nuclear effort—that is, to set the latter in the broader context of Soviet political and military strategy. The more narrowly technical responsibilities of Team B were assumed by a small group of experts that included Paul Nitze, who had once served as deputy secretary of defense; retired General Daniel O. Graham, the one-time director of the Defense Intelligence Agency; and Professor William van Cleave, a member of the SALT I negotiating team.

The report of Team B, submitted to George Bush in December 1976, was classified and has remained so to this day. But an account of the exercise appeared promptly in the press, causing much excitement and controversy. Urged to say something on the subject for the public at large, I wrote an article for *Commentary* in which, relying exclusively on unclassified sources, I stressed the differences separating American and Soviet approaches to nuclear weapons. Many readers were unhappy with what I had to say—some because my interpretation of Soviet nuclear doctrine challenged their emotionally held conviction that rational men had to view nuclear warfare as irrational, others because they confused my reporting of Soviet views with the advocacy of these views. Four years later, however, my ideas appear far less radical than they did at time of publication. In fact, it has now become widely accepted that the Soviet military view the utility of strategic weapons differently and that, therefore, one can no longer assume a community of interest with the USSR in this matter.

The two concluding essays develop important points only hinted at in my other publications. "Soviet Global Strategy" is a succinct (too much so, perhaps) statement of why and how the Soviet Union pursues a Grand Strategy. "Militarism and the Soviet State" calls attention to the unique role that military force plays in the Communist mentality, theory, and practice.

It means to dispel hopes that the USSR can be readily induced to participate in a peaceful resolution of disagreements and conflicts.

Clearly, I cannot subscribe today to everything that I have put on paper over an eleven-year period. In one essay, I over-estimated the trouble the Chinese would cause the Russians; but who could have anticipated that a great and civilized nation would run amok in the name of "cultural revolution"? In another, written before I had studied the subject at any depth, I adopted the consensus view and ignored the Soviet commit-ment to nuclear superiority. I also do not subscribe today to the view I expressed in my talk with George Urban that the internal structure of the Soviet state is not a matter of prime concern for the course of U.S.-Soviet relations. On the whole, however, I find my papers to be internally consistent and to have with-stood the test of time. When published, they were generally labeled "controversial"—a term that I found from experience to be favored by those who dislike someone's conclusions but do not know how to refute them. Today, these essays are cer-tainly much more within the mainstream of opinion. This devel-opment, to my mind, vindicates the historical method as superior to the sociological, comparative, and all other methods that minimize or ignore the specific elements in the environment and experience of nations in favor of abstract models or "ideal types."

Apart from some minor stylistic improvements, the texts of the papers are reproduced exactly as they had originally appeared and in chronological order. In a few places where the infor-mation either proved to have been incorrect or could be brought up to date I have made the requisite changes, but I was careful always to set them off in brackets.

Richard Pipes

U.S.-SOVIET RELATIONS IN THE ERA OF DÉTENTE

ONE

Russia's Mission, America's Destiny
The Premises of U.S. and Soviet Foreign Policy

This paper was prepared for a meeting of historians in Washington, D.C., in December of 1969. It was to have been accompanied by a second paper that took a different point of view, stressing the common interests of the two countries, and George Kennan was to have commented upon it. Unfortunately, the writer of the other paper was forced to abandon the project, and at the last moment Mr. Kennan was unable to come, so I wound up having the floor to myself.

The *détente* in American-Russian relations since Stalin's death to which the world at large owes its relative peace, has tended to obscure basic differences not only in the long-term interests of the two powers, but also in their whole manner of looking at foreign affairs. Although it is fashionable to credit the *détente* to alleged "convergences" in the development of the two countries, it is probably more realistic to attribute it to a stalemate in their diplomatic and military rivalry. A stalemate in such a conflict is bound to be temporary, and must not be allowed to deceive by concealing what remain very fundamental and deep-seated differences in the way the two rivals regard the world outside their respective borders. Historically viewed, these can be traced to two sources: the two countries' notion of the world and their place in it, as shaped by inherited

Reprinted by permission from *Encounter* (London), XXXV, No. 4 (October 1970), 3–11.

religious and philosophic traditions; and their notion of the political process as formed by experience in domestic government.

The conception which Americans and Russians have of their respective place in the world has one feature in common. Each country, though in a different sense, is an offshoot of European civilization, and yet each—again, on different grounds—rejects this civilization. This negative feature establishes a certain superficial resemblance between Americans and Russians and, on the level of individual human contact, permits a rapport often lacking in the relations of either with Europeans proper. Less sophisticated champions of the convergence theory often point to this fact as evidence that the two nations must, in time, come together. But to the historian in this case the similarities are less impressive than the differences. Specifically, that which Americans and Russians reject in European civilization is more significant than the insistence of each on having created a new and distinct civilization.

The Xenophobic View

As Peter Chaadaev pointed out in his *Philosophical Letters* (1829–1831), Russia cut herself off from the rest of Europe when she chose to receive her Christianity from Constantinople rather than from Rome. From Byzantium, Russia absorbed a singularly conservative, anti-intellectual, and xenophobic ethos. The Byzantine Church insisted more emphatically than the Latin on orthodoxy, because it viewed Christianity as a perfect achievement, once and for all realized through Christ's martyrdom. Conservatism was imbedded in its whole conception of the church as the trustee of Christ's legacy, anti-intellectualism in the attendant fear that all independent thinking endangered the foundations of the church, and xenophobia in the conviction that those who did not belong to it—deviant Christians above all—would suffer damnation.

The Russian version of Orthodox Christianity exaggerated further these attitudes, because the Russian clergy (especially during the Moscow period) was both less educated and more isolated than the Greek and therefore inclined to have an even higher opinion of itself. The collapse of Byzantium did nothing to shake this faith. Like Jews after the destruction of Jerusalem, Russians interpreted the fall of Constantinople to mean that the Byzantines had been punished for their betrayal of the true faith (specifically, by their agreement in the 1530s to reunite with the Catholic Church at the councils of Florence and Ferrara). This belief made Russians more determined than ever to avoid contact with foreigners, and, in the splendid solitude in which they had been left as the last remaining state professing the Orthodox faith, to protect its purity.

This religiously conditioned view of the world outside one's walls heavily influenced the foreign dealings of the Moscow state. There is nothing surprising in this influence, considering that the monarchy and church in Moscow lived in a condition of mutual dependence that verged on the symbiotic. Like Imperial China or Tokugawa Japan, Moscow felt no need to enter into regular diplomatic relations with foreign powers, though it was not averse to receiving their envoys and occasionally even dispatching embassies to them. Foreign missions arriving in the sixteenth- and seventeenth-century Moscow were held under conditions of virtual house arrest and escorted out of Russia the instant their task was accomplished. The Moscow government's feeling about foreigners is well illustrated by the symbolic ceremony of washing hands which the Tsar performed after dismissing an embassy, using a discreetly covered pitcher and basin placed for this purpose by his throne.[1]

Moscow's scorn for the external world, for the world of the non-Orthodox, is no less reflected in the vacuous reports submitted by its envoys on return from foreign travels. One searches in vain in these *stateinye spiski* for evidence of curiosity about foreign institutions and customs, so pronounced in the literature left behind by Western travellers to Russia of that time. Or, to be more precise, there are signs of curiosity but it has the nature of bewilderment and amusement, rather than of serious interest. Muscovite envoys visiting Renaissance Italy, Reformation Germany, or Elizabethan England saw nothing of interest to report, since nothing they experienced there had had any relevance to the cosmos as they envisaged it.

*   *   *

Even before the accession of Peter the Great, this rigid posture toward foreigners began to relax, because no matter how the church felt about contact with infidels and heretics, the monarchy could not very well defend it and the realm from Catholics, Lutherans, and Moslems unless it adopted the latest military techniques from its adversaries. With Peter the secularization of the monarchy was completed and the traditional policy of isolation abandoned. At the beginning of the eighteenth century, Russia joined the European state system and by entering into alliances with its members became an active partner in balance of power diplomacy. The sheer immensity of the Russian Empire—as Russians under Peter liked to boast, their territory equalled the visible surface of the full moon—always caused a strain on European diplomacy, because such a giant was difficult to fit into the intricate structure built on the equilibrium principle. And so we have the French complaining in 1735, when the first Russian troops appeared on the Rhine to help Austria in the War of the Polish Succession, that "barbarians" have lodged in the heart of Europe, and Castlereagh eighty years later referring to the thoroughly Frenchified Alexander I as a "Kalmuck prince." But that was only when the Russians were on the other side. The same French and British warmly welcomed the Russian battalions when they were needed to restore the European balance in their own favor.

Imperial Russia gladly, almost eagerly, played the game. She tried hard to become a regular member of the great powers' club and to follow its rules, often to the detriment of her own national interests, as Slavophile publicists were wont to point out.

But in retrospect the adherence of imperial Russia to the European state system appears to have been more precarious than contemporaries realized. What had seemed an irreversible trend in Russian history, turned out to be but an episode. The conventional foreign policy which the imperial government pursued was that of a Westernized court leaning on a Westernized gentry. It expressed the views of a new élite which had broken with the Muscovite traditions and expected great benefits for Russia from close involvement in the affairs of Europe. It was not the policy of what became known in the mid-nineteenth century as the "democratic intelligentsia," who wished the government to devote all its attention and resources to the resolution of domestic ills. Even less was it a policy favored by the ordinary citizenry—the peasants, artisans, industrial workers, merchants, shopkeepers, lower functionaries (public and private), and the clergy. These lower orders had been barely touched by Westernization. Their culture remained rooted in that of old Moscow; that is, they continued to reject all of non-Orthodox civilization, as represented by foreign countries and state systems and by Russia's own Westernized élite.

Had Russia escaped revolution, the non-Westernized bulk of its population in all likelihood would have become Westernized and Russia would have joined the international state system for good, as happened with Japan. The October Revolution prevented this from occurring. By rejecting the political, economic, and social institutions of the old régime, the Bolsheviks, unconsciously and inadvertently, also cut Russia off from Western culture from which these had been drawn. Once the smoke of the Civil War was cleared, it became apparent that in October 1917 much more had been dethroned than the monarchy and private property: with them disappeared the Westernized élite which for two centuries had served as Russia's link with the West, and through it, with the world at large.

Under Stalin, the country's administration fell into the hands of elements, drawn largely from an amorphous petty bourgeoisie, which throughout the imperial period had been forced to sit on the sidelines, excluded from the seats of power—elements characterized by resentment, conservatism, anti-intellectualism, and xenophobia. The élite which has controlled Russia for the past fifty years may well be irreligious and even militantly atheist: but having come to power on what is in effect an anti-Western program, it has no other culture to fall back on except that of Muscovy. These people instinctively think of themselves as a nation sui generis, unique and unrelated to any other, part of no state system or international community, the only guardians of true Orthodoxy, once Christian, now Communist. Like their Muscovite ancestors, they see nothing to be learned from foreigners save technology, especially when it has military application.

Reading the recent memoirs of Stalin's daughter, a historian receives a jolt from her account of a conversation with Suslov. She had requested a passport so that she could carry to India the ashes of her recently deceased husband, and ran into difficulties. "What is it that attracts you so much abroad?" Suslov, apparently genuinely puzzled, wanted to know. "Why, my family and I never go abroad, and don't even feel like going. It is not interesting!"[2] Shades of boyars and priests whose beards he had clipped and whose properties he had despoiled, exacting revenge on Peter the Great! He had thought life abroad so interesting that for a time he worked there as an ordinary laborer.

Strangers and Sinners

Contempt for that which lies outside one's national boundaries is not unfamiliar in the United States, but it is not characteristic of those who make national policy, and certainly not of those who have responsibility for the making of American foreign policy. The external world on which Americans are most likely to turn their backs is that which the language of historiographic shorthand calls "feudal"—the world of privilege and authority resting on inherited wealth in land. It is a selective and a qualified rejection whose criteria are drawn from a major strain of European culture, namely the ethos of the mercantile and manufacturing classes first articulated (as Werner Sombart has shown) in the Italian city states of the late Middle Ages and subsequently adopted by the European bourgeoisie at large. The United States has assimilated this ethos mainly through the agency of English liberalism. In Europe it never gained exclusive domination, because there it had to contend with strong anti-liberal, anti-bourgeois traditions of the Church and aristocracy.[3] In the United States where, for all practical purposes, there was neither Church establishment nor a true aristocracy to dampen business exuberance, what had been the ethos of a class promptly turned into the ideology of a nation.

American isolationism does not rest on an exclusivist, Manichean outlook rooted in a community-oriented religion; instead, it is rooted in a religion extolling the individual conscience and free will. Individualistic and voluntarist, it assumes that nations, like persons, are capable of finding the true path. The American habit of injecting morality into diplomacy descends (genetically speaking) from the moralist obsession of the liberal middle class, especially the English. Behind it lies the passion which had moved Wilberforce to agitate against slavery, Cobden against foreign tariffs, and Gladstone against Turkish atrocities. It derives from the religious-philosophical conviction that there is a right and a wrong in every action and that man must constantly make a choice between the two. The refusal to grant diplomatic recognition to a wicked government is a logical extension of the principle of private conduct that one must not associate with depraved persons. If England itself has not followed this practice, it is only because the management of its foreign relations has been customarily entrusted to patricians who lack such moral qualms.

Neither in the old, conservative isolationism of America, nor in its new, radical strain does xenophobia play a prominent part. American isolationists like to think that nations, like individuals, must solve their own problems. Those that display self-reliance, courage in the face of adversity, a commitment to equality of opportunity for its citizenry, the American is instinctively prepared to like. The admiration which the so-called "New Left" professes for Cuba or North Viet Nam is based on many of the same values that lay behind the extravagant sympathy that the Old Right expressed for Finland. This outlook clearly implies involvement in affairs of the world at large, and a sense of belonging—if not, indiscriminately, to all humanity, then at least to that segment of it which shares the American ideal of self-perfectibility. It is an isolationism qualitatively different from that sense of exclusiveness pervading the Muscovite and Soviet ruling élites, which tends to confound nationality and historic mission: as different as Liberal Protestantism is from Greek Orthodoxy from which the two isolationisms, respectively, derive.

*   *   *

So much for the broad context within which foreign policy is conducted. Now, as to the choice of means, the following generalization may be suggested: that Russian diplomatic methods have been shaped by the experience acquired in administering a vast multi-national empire, whereas the American ones are best explained by the country's predominantly commercial and manufacturing background.

The Russian State emerged on the fringe of an extensive but loosely constructed and chronically unstable Turco-Mongolian empire. In order to form a national state, Moscow not only had to impose its authority on rival Russian principalities, but also to repel, subdue, and integrate the Turco-Mongol and Finnic populations with which it was surrounded. As a result, in Russia the process of nation-building took place concurrently with that of empire-building. The two processes, so distinct in the history of Western states, cannot in the case of Russia be readily distinguished either chronologically or geographically. In the second half of the sixteenth century, after it had captured Kazan but long before it had completed the self-imposed mission of "gathering the Russian lands," Moscow already administered a sizeable colonial population of Tatars and peoples of the Finno-Ugrian race. To these, in the seventeenth century, were added the natives of Siberia and the Ukrainian Cossacks, in the eighteenth the nomads of Central Asia, the Crimeans, Ukrainians, Belorussians, Poles, Jews, and the Baltic nationalities, and in the nineteenth, the Finns, Caucasians and Moslems of Turkestan.

To say that the Moscow state avoided entering into regular diplomatic relations with foreign powers does not, therefore, mean that it had no foreign dealings. Even before the accession of Peter, the Russian government had at its disposal a great amount of foreign expertise, but this it had acquired from administering subject peoples, both Western and Oriental, not from dealing on equal terms with other sovereign states. The *Posol'skii Prikaz* ("Office of Ambassadors") knew much less, relatively speaking, how to handle foreigners than did the Bureaus or *prikazy* of Kazan, Siberia, and Little Russia, which were charged with administering immense territories inhabited by peoples of alien races and religions. In some measure, the same held true of the imperial period during which the Ministries of War and of the Interior had more extensive day by day contacts with non-Russians than did the Ministry of Foreign Affairs.

The implications of this historical fact are not far to seek. A country whose governing apparatus has learned how to deal with foreign peoples from what are essentially colonial practices is not predisposed to think in terms of "a stable international community" or of "the balance of power." Its instincts are to exert the maximum force and to regard absorption as the only dependable way of settling conflicts with other states, especially those adjoining one's borders. There is little need here of theory, because the options available concern tactics rather than strategy or objectives.

To anyone acquainted with the rich literature on the international relations of the Western powers it must come as a surprise to learn that there is no definitive or even merely comprehensive history of Russian foreign policy. The literature on the theory of Russian foreign policy is so meagre that it may be said not to exist at all. That Russians have felt no need to compile the record of their external relations or to investigate its principles is in itself a significant fact, illustrative of their general attitude toward the outside world.

In analyzing the conduct of Russian foreign policy another peculiarity of Russian history must be taken into account, namely that its [state organization] had always been highly élitist. For reasons which cannot be gone into here, throughout Russia's history its governments have administered the country by means of a service class which, in return for services rendered, it rewarded not only with money, offices, and land, but also with rights withheld from the rest of the population. Indeed, one of the reasons why Russian rulers have always been so reluctant to grant their citizenry what other European countries have long come to regard as elementary civic rights lies in the use they have made of such rights as privileges: in other words, as instruments of government. In the Moscow state and in Imperial Russia until the emancipation of the serfs in 1861, the service class (known as *dvorianstvo,* a kind of gentry) had a virtual monopoly on the country's main source of productive wealth, bonded labor. Furthermore, it enjoyed exemption from taxes and corporal punishment, as well as other important privileges enumerated in the celebrated Charter of the Nobility issued by Catherine the Great in 1785. The privileges of the Soviet service class (the Communist party apparatus and the managerial groups working for it) have not as yet been codified but they are no less real for that. Among them is access to scarce consumer goods, living quarters, and sources of objective information, and the right to travel abroad.

Because of the traditionally close relationship between government and its service class, Russia, past and present alike, fits better the Marxist model of a class society than does any other European country.[4] We have here a state in which those who rule enjoy economic powers and legal rights enabling them effectively to defend their privileged position against challenges from below and from outside. The harmony between economic base and political and ideological superstructure is, in the case of the Soviet régime, nearly perfect. In such a country "national interest" tends to fuse completely with the interest of the privileged service class. Foreign policy—as well as internal policy—aims not so much at the improvement of the condition of the nation, but at safeguarding and expanding the privileges of its service élite. It is a "statist" foreign policy, par excellence, vastly different from not only the liberal ideal envisioned by an Adam Smith or Turgot, but also from the more narrowly nationalist one of a Friedrich List.

A good illustration of the close inter-dependence between Russia's internal colonial experience and its manner of dealing with foreign powers is the interesting use which its governments have frequently made of privilege as a device of foreign policy. It had been an old practice in pre-revolutionary Russia to suppress or, if possible, prevent and neutralize nationalist opposition in conquered areas by extending the privileges enjoyed by the Russian élite to that of the conquered peoples. In the seventeenth century, for example, Moscow effectively emasculated resistance in what had been sovereign Tatar principalities by the simple device of enacting a law restricting the ownership of serfs to Christian landlords. The consequence was mass conversion of Moslem notables. Granted the privileges of the Russian *dvoriane,* they promptly and tracelessly dissolved among them.[5] A similar result was obtained in the eighteenth century along the southern border by admitting into the ranks of the Russian gentry the Cossack elders, the most vociferous champions of Ukrainian "liberties." Characteristically, Russians experienced some of their greatest administrative difficulties on territories of the defunct Polish-Lithuanian Commonwealth, in no small measure because here the nobility had enjoyed even greater privileges than those the Russian conquerors had to offer. Unable to seduce the Catholic nobles to its side, the monarchy bade for support of the Catholic peasantry, according it land allotments and rights of self-governance considerably in excess of those enjoyed by the peasants of Russia proper.

Thus, in the course of their extended colonial experience, Russians have acquired much skill in manipulating social privilege and social conflict to their own advantage. This skill was put to use internationally by the Comintern between the wars and by the Soviet government in its zone of occupation in Eastern Europe after World War II. Neither Stalin nor his successors ever regarded the countries of Eastern Europe as sovereign states: to them, in the calculations made in their political sub-conscious, these were all along as yet undigested parts of the Russian domain, exactly as Kazan, Siberia, or the Ukraine had once been for Tsarist governments. In an effort to subdue and integrate them, recourse was had to the old and tried method of creating privileged but dependent élites. By entrusting power and granting privileges to a completely new class, whose status is conditional on the survival of Communism, i.e., on Soviet backing, Soviet Russia has managed to contain (up to a point, to be sure) the powerful nationalist sentiments in these countries. It may well be that the old and tried methods will no longer work, applied to countries with live traditions of statehood. But the point is that Russian governments know no other. Had all these historical factors been kept in mind during World War II, there would have been less disappointment in the West with Russia's failure "to live up to the Yalta agreement," whose very language was alien to its historical experience.

Aversion to balance-of-power politics is another one of those qualities which Americans and Russians share. This negative factor made it possible for the two powers, so different in their political backgrounds, to reach in the mid-1950s agreement on two-power cooperation: an arrangement for which the Russians have coined the euphemism "peaceful co-existence," but which in reality represents an old-fashioned and straight-forward agreement on spheres of influence. In a manner of speaking this arrangement, too, rests on an equilibrium of power. But this fact is not acknowledged by the leaders of either country, who prefer to believe that it derives from a special understanding which they enjoy by virtue of their capacity instantaneously to destroy one another.

The Penchant for Stability

Here once again, however, the similar proves to be dissimilar. In the Russian case, antipathy to balance-of-power politics derives from an inherent distaste for the whole concept of a stable state system. In the case of the United States, it represents yet another instance of an anti-feudal and moralistic way of thinking. Classical balance-of-power politics, as practiced by European diplomats from the mid-seventeenth century onwards, entailed secret diplomacy, palace intrigues, bribery in the guise of subsidies, trading of territories and their inhabitants, alliance with countries whose form of government one did not approve. In short, it meant *Realpolitik,* politics shorn of morals, something the American conscience has always found repugnant in the extreme.[6]

But if one abstracts from American pronouncements on foreign policy and turns to American practices, one discovers quickly enough that the United States is as deeply committed to balance-of-power politics abroad as it is to "checks and balances," its constitutional equivalent, at home.[7] It is probably true to say that no country has ever exceeded the United States in its loyalty to that principle which on the conscious level it finds itself unable to accept. The principle of "interventionism," so frequently invoked that some historians regard it as the quintessence of American foreign policy, is, after all, little more than a particular application of the balance-of-power principle. It merely calls for engagement after the equilibrium has been upset rather than before. It is corrective rather than preventive action, but its purpose is exactly the same. (Outside the Western hemisphere, of course, which is a very special case.) In Viet Nam, the decision to intervene with American troops seems to have posited that once an equilibrium had been reached on the field of battle under which neither side could aspire to victory, a negotiated settlement would automatically follow. Apparently, when this policy was devised it was not contemplated that the other side might not subscribe to the balance-of-power philosophy and refuse to play the game. Perhaps the most striking illustration of America's faith in the efficacy of the balance-of-power principle is the decision to allow the Soviet Union to attain parity in nuclear weapons. The hope behind this gamble seems to be that once a nuclear equilibrium between the two powers has been obtained, a dynamic and therefore potentially explosive situation will defuse and turn static. It would be difficult to find in the whole history of international relations another instance of a country, in effect, deliberately reducing its advantage over a rival for the sake of attaining an equilibrium—doing, as it were, the job of balancing on his behalf. Even the British insisted on preserving a clear-cut superiority over the Germans in the naval race at the turn of the century for which they attempted to lay down the ground rules.

Clearly, we are dealing here with a deeply ingrained conviction. At the lowest psychological substratum, it seems to derive from the mechanistic outlook which forms so prominent an ingredient of American culture. It is an outlook which conceives reality in terms of physical bodies acting on each other in accord with definable laws and in terms of measurable quantities of force. The remarkable American propensity to indulge in abstractions, to translate objects made of flesh and blood into faceless "movements" and palpable pains into esoteric "problems" capable of being "solved"; the American love for the vocabulary of mechanics ("framework of thought," "social dynamics," "structure of society," and so on)—this is one of the several qualities that Americans under 30 share with their elders. How could such a people resist the "balance-of-power" philosophy, no matter how repugnant some of its implications may be to the other side of its culture, the middle-class, moralistic liberalism? For the whole conception of the balance of power is, of course, a by-product of the science of mechanics, and was originally conceived as an effort to regulate relations between states on the same rules which Galileo, Kepler, and

Newton had discovered to determine relations between physical bodies.

The Mechanics of Chaos

The balance-of-power philosophy, however, is attractive to a country with a predominantly business ethos not only or even primarily because it is scientific and therefore calculable, but also because it seems to provide the key to the creation of conditions in which trade and manufacture can best flourish. Obviously, business desires stability. It wants an environment in which political activity—by its very nature volatile and unpredictable—has been reduced to a minimum, that is one in which political entities are brought to a condition resembling bodies at rest. The American constitution is constructed on this principle, and Americans, like most people, tend to view the constitution of the world in the light of their own. Usually the transposition is unconscious; but sometimes, as, for example, in the case of Professor Frank Tannenbaum's astonishing suggestion that the relations between all sovereign states be modelled on the system regulating relations between the federal states of the United States of America, it is explicit.[8] The commercial ethos and mechanistic philosophy complement one another admirably.

One could cite numerous examples to illustrate this generalization, but a single one must suffice: the criterion which the United States is most prone to invoke when confronted with the question whether to extend or deny support to another foreign power.

The official version of U.S. foreign policy holds that the United States, being the leader of what is known as the "Free World," befriends and supports those governments which give proof of their dedication to the principles of liberty.[9]

Even if it is palpably evident that there is a substantial and qualitative difference in the degree of freedom available to citizens of the two blocs, it is obvious that the United States does not and cannot choose its allies on so vague a criterion as liberty. If it did, it could not maintain friendly relations with the governments of Spain, South Korea, and South Viet Nam.

At the same time, the mirror image of the official explana-tion which holds that fear for its wealth and foreign invest-ments drives the United States to defend the status quo through-out the world and therefore to support conservative causes and régimes, is no more persuasive. Time and again, the United States has extended support to movements and governments of radical and nationalist complexions, among them Com-munist Yugoslavia and nationalist Indonesia. In the Middle East, after being repeatedly frustrated in its efforts to come to terms with the Arab states, most of them conservative in their outlook, it has settled on Israel, by any standard the most pro-gressive country in the area.

The reason for this seeming inconsistency is that the United States is guided in its alliances not so much by criteria of politi-cal and social ideology or by short-term economic calculations as by broader consideration of stability. There is a tendency in the United States to assume that governments which keep their people free and prosperous are stabler than those which do not; and, all things being equal, the United States would prefer to ally itself with democratic and consumer-oriented governments. But when it is forced to choose between one government which is democratic and unstable, and another which is undemocratic but stable, the United States, as a rule, will settle for the latter. The unspoken assumption of its policy is that countries which have attained internal stability—no matter whether by conser-vative or radical means—are less likely in their external relations to behave in an unpredictable manner. They are, consequently, better to do business with: for, like the planets, their move-ments can be calculated and charted in advance, which is not the case with meteors.

It is on these grounds that the United States can cooperate simultaneously with Franco and with Tito, one an ex-ally of Hitler, the other of Stalin. It is for this reason, too, that it pre-fers to have dealings with the Soviet Union, a country poten-tially more of a threat to its security but to all appearances stable, than with China which seems in permanent turmoil. In the late 1940s the United States supported the Indonesian nationalists—revolutionaries with a suspect ideology—against the conservative, free-enterprise Dutch, because, having concluded that "de-colonialization" had become unavoidable, it preferred speeding it along to risking protracted civil war in South-east Asia. And finally, Israel (where the United States has insignificant investments) is more attractive, at least in some measure, because of its internal stability than the sometimes feudal, sometimes fascist, but always volatile Arab states (where it has investments in the billions).

There is one more difference in the historical background of the two countries which calls for comment. The economic experience of the United States is primarily commercial, that of the Soviet Union agrarian. (Even today, nearly one-half of the present population of the U.S.S.R. lives on the land, and most of the remainder consists either of peasants who had moved to the cities or of peasants' children.) Now in commercial activity both sides expect to profit: a trade in which one side gains all and the other only loses is a contradiction in terms. A dispute between traders concerns the division of profits, each party being aware that its gain is conditional on the other party earning something as well. Commerce is therefore by its very nature conducive to compromise. Nations raised on it instinctively seek a common ground for agreement, that exact point at which the other side might be prepared to make a deal.

This is not the case with nations preoccupied with the exploitation of resources. The production of goods—whether raw or manufactured—does not, of itself, teach the art of compromise. Disputes over land or any other resources are such that what one side gains the other loses, and it is entirely possible for one to gain all. Industry, on which some sociologists and economists count to create a common style of life throughout the world, from this point of view resembles agriculture more than trade. A country can readily make a transition from raising foodstuffs to manufacturing without changing its habits and mentality. Such a change occurs only when goods are traded. It is not the production of goods, in other words, but their exchange that infuses the habits of civilized life, that teaches individuals and nations alike to respect the rights of others on the ground that their well-being is the precondition of one's own prosperity. Such commercial experience Russia badly lacks; nor will it acquire it under the present system. No matter how much Russia "industrializes," until it begins to trade in earnest within and without, it will not learn to understand the value of compromise and the need for seeking a common ground of agreement.

*   *   *

There is little comfort in these reflections for anyone who believes that somehow, by a magic marriage of good will and enlightened self-interest, the foreign policies of the United States and Russia will come to coincide. The notion of what is "good" and what is "self-interest" is not the same for those who make policy in the two countries. The condition of international equilibrium existing since the mid-1950s, which so far has provided a precarious peace, does not result from the acceptance by the Communist leadership of the principle of an international community of interest. As seen from there, the cosmos consists not of majestic planets revolving according to the laws of nature, each in its allotted orbit, in the midst of which man has been placed to prove his worth. The vision there—when it is not completely drowned in cynicism—is one of chaos in which wondrous and terrible things happen, and God, in the guise of History, renders implacable Final Judgment.

Notes

1. V. O. Kliuchevskii, *Skazaniia inostrantsev o moskovskom gosudarstve* [Foreign accounts of the Muscovite state] (Petrograd, 1918), 61.

2. S. Alliluyeva, *Only One Year* (1969). Suslov performs in the present administration the same function that Pobedonostsev had performed for Alexander III.

3. As Thomas Masaryk once observed in response to the charge that Americans are materialistic: "Yes, it is true that Americans chase after dollars: the only difference between them and us, Europeans, is that we chase after pennies. . . ." But that, of course, makes all the difference.

4. This fact, incidentally, helps explain the remarkable popularity enjoyed by Marx's ideas in Russia long before the country had developed sizeable industry and a working class.

5. Among the better known descendants of this assimilated Tatar

nobility are Karamzin, Turgenev, and Rakhmaninov.

6. And still does: Senator Fulbright, having learned recently that the United States had paid the Philippines, South Korea, and Thailand to send troops to Viet Nam, called the practice "the ultimate in corruption" (*Evening Star,* Washington, D.C., November 19, 1969). He ignores that this "ultimate" had long been reached and exceeded by Britain, which for centuries had subsidized allies to enable them to participate in its wars.

7. Hans Morgenthau makes this point: *In Defense of the National Interest* (New York, 1951), 5–7.

8. Frank Tannenbaum, *The American Tradition in Foreign Policy* (Norman, Okla., 1955).

9. The term "Free World" has recently fallen into disrepute, especially among the young who profess to see no difference sufficiently wide between the two blocs to justify calling the one "Free" and the other unfree or "Totalitarian." One can perhaps rescue this useful term by defining the "Free World" to mean that part of the world where one can say, openly and without fear of punishment, that it does not exist.

TWO

Some Operational Principles
of Soviet Foreign Policy

*In 1972 Senator Henry Jackson asked me to prepare a longer
paper on Soviet foreign policy that would develop the ideas
presented in a summary fashion in my testimony before the
Senate Committee discussing the ABM Treaty. The article that
follows is the result. In retrospect I am rather pleased with my
forecast, presented in the concluding two paragraphs, that
Soviet foreign policy in the immediate future would become
less cautious and more militaristic.*

Perhaps the best way to define the scope of this essay is nega-
tively, by stating what it is not. Our purpose is not to lay bare
the motives of Soviet foreign policy or its ultimate aspirations.
These topics lie at the heart of the matter, of course, and cannot be entirely ignored; but, belonging as they do to the realm
of national and elite psychology they are best set aside for
separate treatment.

Nor will our concern be with the narrower subject of Soviet
techniques of negotiation. Although diplomats trained in the
traditional school have good reason to look upon Russian (or,
more precisely, Communist) methods of negotiating as in a class
of their own, it is doubtful whether such methods actually
exist.[1] Frustrations experienced in negotiating with Com-

Memorandum Prepared at the Request of the U.S. Senate Subcommittee on National
Security and International Operations of the Committee on Government Operations
(Washington, D.C., 1972). Published subsequently in Michael Confino and Shimon
Shamir, eds., *The Soviet Union and the Middle East* (New York, 1973).

munists derive from the fact that the latter often engage in talks in order not to reach an agreement but to attain some other, incidental objective, such as ascertaining how strong is their opponents' determination on a given issue, splitting hostile alliances, or influencing world opinion. When they intend to use negotiations in this manner, Communist diplomats indeed display an intransigence which can be mollified only by full acceptance of their terms, that is, by surrender of the principle of compromise which is the quintessence of negotiation.

However, whenever they happen to be interested in a settlement, Communist diplomats act in a traditional manner, efficiently and undeterred by difficulties. One need only recall the speed with which in 1939 the Soviet Union concluded its non-aggression treaty with Germany, or the relative ease with which the Communist bloc settled its outstanding difficulties with the West immediately after Stalin's death, once the new party leadership in Russia had concluded that a détente was in order. Responding to Eisenhower's "deeds not words" speech of April 16, 1953, in which the President called for a resolution of several major problems, among them Korea, Vietnam, and Austria, Communist diplomats negotiated in reasonable time mutually agreeable terms on issues which only a short time earlier had seemed to defy all solution. As a result, in July 1953 there was an armistice in Korea, in June 1954 an armistice in Indochina, and in May 1955 a long overdue treaty with Austria. It certainly is no coincidence that shortly after President Nixon had announced he intended to pay a state visit to China, hoary disagreements affecting the status of West Berlin melted away and a workable draft of a four-power agreement could be hammered out. All of which suggests that if the West often faces excruciating difficulties negotiating with the Communists the fault lies not in different negotiating techniques. The Communists employ distinct methods of diplomatic intercourse only when they have in mind objectives other than negotiation and agreement.

One way to describe what we will be talking about is to borrow terms from the vocabulary of military science. The language of Soviet politics is permeated with militarisms: even the most pacific spheres of government activity become "fronts" which

have to be "stormed," all-out "offensives" are launched to conquer internal difficulties, and even peace itself becomes the object of a "struggle." The martial language is appropriate, for, as
will be noted shortly, Soviet theory does not distinguish sharply
between military and political forms of activity, regarding both
as variant ways of waging conflict which it regards as the essence
of history. "Strategy" and "tactics" are useful in this connection, and have been employed. But even more accurate is a
third term from the vocabulary of Soviet military theory, "the
art of operations" (*operativnoe isskustvo*). Its origin apparently
goes back to the 1890s, but it acquired special relevance in the
1920s, when Soviet experts, analyzing the record of World
War I and of the Russian Civil War, concluded that neither
"strategy" nor "tactics" adequately described warfare waged
with mass armies under industrial conditions. They then created
the concept "art of operations" to bridge the two. Since that
time this concept has occupied an honored place in Soviet military thinking, and, indeed, some Soviet authorities credit Russian victories in World War II to its systematic application. If
tactics describes the employment of troops on the battlefield,
and strategy the overall disposition of all of one's forces, the
"art of operations" denotes the fluid and dynamic element in
military planning by virtue of which individual tactical moves
are coordinated over a period of time to promote the ultimate
strategic objective, defeat of the enemy.

According to Soviet theorists, under conditions of prolonged
modern warfare, victory requires a succession of interdependent
operations, based on solid logistic support and synchronized
to produce on the enemy mounting pressure which, attaining
unbearable levels, eventually causes him to collapse. In the literature on the subject, there are just enough hints to indicate that
the "art of operations" is derived mainly from analysis of the
campaigns waged in World War I by General Ludendorff, whose
masterful conduct of "total" war seems to have exercised a
greater influence on Communist political practices than the
writings of Karl Marx and Friedrich Engels combined. "The
purpose of operations is the destruction, the complete annihilation of the vital forces of the enemy," states a recent Soviet
handbook on the subject, paraphrasing an authority of the

1920s, "its method is the uninterrupted attack; its means, prolonged operational pursuit, which avoids pauses and stops, and
is attained by a succession of consecutive operations, each of
which serves as the transitional link toward the ultimate goal,
accomplished in the final, closing operation."[2] The whole
concept, with its stress on coordinated, uninterrupted assault
intended to bring mounting pressure on the enemy, admirably
describes what is probably the most characteristic feature of
Soviet foreign policy.

The subject is of great importance and deserves the kind of
careful study given to Soviet military practices. Soviet foreign
policy involves a great deal more than diplomacy: diplomacy is
one of its minor instrumentalities and Soviet diplomats resemble
more the bearers of white flags sent to cross combat lines than
the staff officers or the combatants. But it is also more than
mere military bluster. One cannot isolate from the total arsenal
of Soviet foreign policy any one weapon and by neutralizing its
sting hope to halt its thrust. To understand this policy one must
understand its mode of operations. The purpose of this paper is
to shed some light on this remarkably ignored subject.

The Art of Operations

In an essay on creativity, Arthur Koestler observed that
seminal ideas are born from bringing two premises belonging to
two different mental fields to bear upon each other.[3] Using this
approach, Marxism may be said to owe its influence to a successful fusion of sociology with economics, and Freudianism to the
grafting of medicine onto psychology. With this definition in
mind, we may ascribe the significance of Leninism as an ideological force in the twentieth century to an innovative linking
of politics with warfare—in other words, to the militarization of
politics which Lenin was the first statesman to accomplish.

For psychological reasons which need not be gone into here,
Lenin was most attracted in the writings of Marx and Engels
not by the liberal and democratic spirit strongly in evidence
there, but by the idea of class war. Peter Struve, who knew him
well in his early political career, says that Lenin took to Marx's
theory mainly because he found in it "the doctrine of class war,

relentless and thoroughgoing, aiming at the final destruction and extermination of the enemy."[4] Class war, of course, was and remains the common property of all socialist and anarchist movements of modern times. But to Lenin, more than to any other prominent radical of his period, it was a real, tangible thing: a daily, hourly struggle pitting the exploited against the exploiters and (after November 1917) what he defined as the "camp of socialism" against that of "capitalism" or "imperialism." What to Marx and Engels was a means, became for him an end. His preoccupation as theorist was always with the methods of waging political warfare: anything that did not in some way bear on that subject, he regarded as harmful, or at best, as useless. All his thinking was militant. He was the first public figure to view politics entirely in terms of warfare, and to pursue this conception to its inexorable conclusion. Lenin read Clausewitz rather late in life (1915), but he immediately found him a most congenial writer. He referred to him often, praising him as a thinker whose ideas, as he once put it, have become "the indispensable acquisition of every thinking man."[5] As one might expect, he especially admired Clausewitz's insistence that war and politics were not antithetical means of conducting relations among states but alternatives, chosen according to what the situation required. On one occasion, Lenin told a friend that "political tactics and military tactics represent that which the Germans call *Grenzgebiet* [adjoining areas]," and urged Communist party workers to study Clausewitz to learn the applications of this principle.[6]

These historical and biographical facts require mention because the Soviet leadership in power since November 1917 has been thoroughly imbued with the spirit of Leninist politics. The reason lies not in the innate force of Lenin's ideas or the ability of any idea to be bequeathed intact from one generation to another. It lies in the fact that the Soviet leadership of today finds itself in a situation in all essential respects identical with the one Lenin had left on his death, that is, devoid of a popular mandate or any other kind of legitimacy to justify its monopoly of political power except the alleged exigencies of class war. The regime is locked in; and even if it wanted to extricate itself from its predicament by democratizing it could not do so because of the staunch opposition of the bureaucratic establishment to genuine political reform. The closed character of Russia's ruling elite, its insulation from the inflow of fresh human types and ideas by means of the principle of co-optation assures a high degree of ideological and psychological continuity. In this respect, the Soviet elite resembles a self-perpetuating religious order rather than what one ordinarily thinks of as a governing class. The growth of productivity, the rise in living standards, the spread of education, and the sundry other factors which some Western observers count on in time to liberalize the Soviet system have no bearing either on the internal position of the ruling elite or on its political outlook. Only a major upheaval—such as a prolonged and unsuccessful war, or a prolonged and unresolved feud among the leaders—could alter the situation.

The Soviet government conducts a "total" foreign policy which draws no principal distinction between diplomatic, economic, psychological, or military means of operation. It also does not differentiate in any fundamental respect between domestic and foreign relations. This accounts for the virtual absence in the Soviet Union of a literature devoted to the theory of foreign relations. Every policy decision, after all, is made in the Politburo of the party. As a rule, the Soviet Minister of Foreign Affairs (the incumbent, Andrei Gromyko, included) is not a member of the Politburo—a fact which suggests what importance attaches to his office.[7] The Soviet Union maintains a Ministry of Foreign Affairs with its diplomatic corps because other countries with which it deals happen to do so. It does not, however, charge the Ministry with the formulation of foreign policy. All important foreign policy decisions are made in the Politburo and often even carried out by its own departments [the Secretariat]. The role of the Ministry is further whittled down by the practice increasingly to entrust foreign policy matters to organs of the police and intelligence. The KGB, through its "Foreign Directorate" (First Main Administration), and with the assistance of organs of military intelligence (GRU), may well have a greater voice in Soviet foreign policy, especially as it concerns the so-called Third World, than the Ministry of Foreign Affairs. Alexander Kaznacheev, a one-time Soviet diplomat stationed in Rangoon, states that among his hundred or more colleagues in the embassy, fewer than one-fifth actually worked for the Ministry and were responsible to the Ambassador; the remainder was employed by other agencies, mostly engaged in intelligence activities and reporting directly to Moscow.[8] In contending with a foreign policy of such an unorthodox kind, the United States has had to charge its own Central Intelligence Agency with a variety of responsibilities exceeding its formal mandate. These activities have recently been restrained, to the visible relief of the KGB and other operational intelligence agencies of the Soviet Union which prefer to have this particular field all to themselves. The steady shift of the epicenter of US foreign policy management from the Department of State to the White House is probably part of the same process which earlier had led to the broadening of the CIA's functions, namely the need somehow to counter "total" Soviet policy with a "total" policy of one's own.

The Correlation of Forces

When we say that Soviet policy is inherently militant we do not mean to imply it is necessarily belligerent. In the context of an ideology which regards armed conflict as only one of several instruments at the politician's disposal, militancy can assume a great variety of expressions. If those who take a "soft" line in regard to Soviet Russia tend to err in their estimate of Soviet motives and aims by making them appear more reasonable than they in fact are, the "hard" liners err only a little less seriously in their judgment of Soviet procedures, overestimating the role of warfare and neglecting other means of waging battle which Russia employs. In the decade that followed the end of World War II, American policy toward the Soviet Union, anchored as it was in the "hard" position, concentrated so exclusively on the Soviet military threat that when in 1954–1955 Russian strategy changed and "peaceful coexistence" replaced the head-on assault attempted under Stalin, American policy was thrown into a confusion from which it still has to recover.

Militancy rather means maintaining one's citizenry in the state of constant war-like mobilization, and exerting relentless pressure outside Russia's borders. The means used differ, depending on the circumstances.

One of the basic ingredients in the formulation of Soviet foreign policy is what Russian theoreticians call the "correlation of forces" (*sootnoshenie sil*). By this term is meant the actual capability of the contending parties to inflict harm on each other, knowledge of which allows one to decide in any given situation whether to act more aggressively or less, and which of the various means available to employ. The concept is used in the analysis of the internal conditions of a foreign country in which Russia has an interest, (in which case it refers to the power relationship of social classes) as well as to international affairs where the parties are sovereign states or multinational blocs. Analyses of the "correlation of forces" are by no means an academic exercise. Under Khrushchev, when rivalry with the United States assumed new and dangerous forms, Soviet publications were filled with learned inquiries into the power balance between the Western and Eastern blocs, and there is every reason to believe that then, as now, such studies seriously influence policy. "Force," of course, is a vague and relative concept, and Russian analysts almost always overestimate quantity (e.g., land, population, and productivity figures) at the expense of quality (e.g., fighting spirit, cultural factors, or the caliber of leadership). Still, mindful of the Russian proverb: "If you don't know the ford, don't step into the river," they do not plunge into contests blindly; they rarely gamble, unless they feel the odds are overwhelmingly in their favor.

Russian leaders regard military force as a weapon to be used only in extreme contingencies when there is no alternative and the risks involved appear minimal. There are many reasons to account for this caution, the main one probably being lack of confidence in their own troops, especially when engaged outside Soviet borders. They much prefer to use military force as a means of blackmail. The reluctance to commit their military forces abroad distinguishes Soviet expansionism from the German, and it would be a mistake to hope to contain it by excessive reliance on methods which might indeed have stopped Hitler in the 1930s.

The militancy of Soviet foreign policy rests on the unspoken assumption that the Soviet Union can assail the enemy at a time and a place, and in a manner of its own choosing. It is so strongly permeated with the offensive spirit that contingency plans in the event of failure and enemy counter-attack seem rarely to be drawn up, if only because even to contemplate retreat opens one to accusation of defeatism. The Russians are quite prepared to pull back when resistance on any one sector of the enemy front turns out to be stronger than anticipated: there are always other sectors which are less staunchly defended and where one's force can be applied to better advantage. But when the opponent chooses to strike back, they are surprisingly vulnerable. The inability of the Russians, in the summer of 1941, to stop Hitler from penetrating deep into their country was in no small measure due to a failure to prepare for defensive war. In the Cuban missile imbroglio of 1962, the response in Moscow to decisive American counter-measures was panic. (How embarrassing to the Soviet government may be judged from the fact that Khrushchev's famous cable of October 26 to President Kennedy still has not been released. Considering that much more embarrassing revelations concerning the US government have been made public in recent years, such solicitude for Russian feelings seems out of place.) Nor did the Soviet leadership seem to have anticipated the outbreak of the Israeli-Arab war of 1967 which its own actions had done a great deal to provoke. If, so far, the government of Soviet Russia has not been required to pay a heavier price for the failure to anticipate blows, it is only because their opponents usually have been content with a reversion to the status quo ante and did not press their advantage.

Militancy is so deeply entrenched in the mentality of the Soviet elite, it follows so naturally from the character of its personnel and its relationship to the population at large, that it is doubtful whether the best way to ease East-West tensions is by attempting a piecemeal resolution of specific disagreements. Those who urge so in the name of pragmatism are in fact motivated by impatience. In the case of East-West tension, specific disagreements are not the cause but the consequence. The Second World War, too, after all, was not fought over Danzig.

The Uses of Threat

On February 23, 1942, on the occasion of the twenty-fifth anniversary of the founding of the Red Army, Stalin issued an Order of the Day in which he listed five "constant principles" that win wars. They were, in order of importance, first and foremost "stability of the home front," followed by second, morale of the armed forces, third, the quantity and quality of the divisions, fourth, military equipment, and fifth, ability of the commanders.[9] That Stalin should have attached such significance to morale, and in particular to the morale of the civilian population, is not surprising considering that the Bolsheviks came to power in Russia because the "home front," unable to withstand the strains of war, had collapsed. Given his admiration for Hitler, Stalin might even have come to believe that German defeat in World War I, too, had been caused by the failure of the civilian population to support the front-line troops. In this pronouncement, we have a valuable clue to that element in military and political operations which the maker of Soviet Russia and his heirs regard as crucial.

It has long been an axiom of military theory that the ideal battle is won before a single shot has been fired, by the victor depriving the enemy of the will to resist. Demoralization has been practiced with particular success by Napoleon, and German military theorists, following the example he has set, have striven with great determination to duplicate his feats. For all their admiration for the German military and willingness to learn from them, the Russians, however, have been slow to apply this particular principle to politics. The foreign policy of the Soviet Union in the first quarter of a century of its existence was ponderous and unimaginative. Soviet leaders seem first to have learned how to unnerve the opponent without actually fighting (or as a prelude to fighting) from observing the brazen manner in which Hitler, alternating threats with inducements, had managed to paralyze England and France. The effect on colonial peoples of Axis victories has often been noted; but it was probably no smaller on Soviet Russia which shared with the colonial nations a sense of awe toward the great powers of the West. Stalin has expressed on a number of occasions respect for

Nazi methods, but always with one reservation: Hitler was overconfident, he underestimated the enemy, he did not know when to stop. The Cold War which he himself launched in 1946 represented, in effect, a replay of Hitler's game but with careful attention to the "correlation of [forces]."

The quality common to Nazi and post-1946 Soviet methods of waging political warfare is the practice of making limited, piecemeal encroachments on Western positions to the accompaniment of threats entirely out of proportion to the losses the West is asked to bear. The threats are coupled with all kinds of inducements which make non-acquiescence [seem] even more absurd. The Soviet Juridical Dictionary, in its definition of threat as a criminal offense, inadvertently provides a useful description of its uses as a political weapon: Threat (*ugroza*), it says, is a "distinct type of psychic influence on the victim for the purpose of compelling him to commit one action or another, or to refrain from committing them, in the interest of the threatener. . . . Such threats . . . can serve to paralyze the victim's will. . . ."[10] In the case of international politics, the primary target of threats is public opinion. Their function is to disorient it to the point where it refuses to follow the national leadership and by passive or active resistance forces the government to make one concession after another.

Threats can be of a direct and an indirect kind. Khrushchev specialized in the former, cultivating the public stance of a violent and unpredictable man whom it would be unwise to provoke—a ploy of which Hitler was the first to make masterful use. Sometimes Khrushchev liked to drop hints what Russia would do if thwarted—hints so vaguely worded as to be open to differing interpretations. At other times he spelled out his threats with brutal frankness, as for example, when he spoke of "country-busting." The present Soviet administration, though not immodest in making its capacity at punishing adversaries clear, prefers to appear as a mature world power, aware what awesome responsibility possession of nuclear weapons imposes on it. But it is not averse to taking advantage of the "irresponsibility" ploy by shifting blame on its friends and allies, which it occasionally depicts as wildly emotional, hoping, by this device, to enlist Western support for its policies. This gambit has been used repeatedly in recent years in the Middle East. A recent dispatch from London by United Press International, for example (and it is one of many), credits anonymous East European diplomatic sources with the intelligence that the Soviet Union fears Egypt could involve it in a Middle Eastern war against its wishes. Russia—so the dispatch continues—is, of course, doing all it can to restrain President Sadat, but since its own prestige is at stake "precipitate Egyptian war action could drag Moscow into hostilities despite Russian intentions."[11] The implied conclusion is that the United States in order to avoid general war in which it might have to confront the Soviet Union, should compel Israel to comply with Egyptian terms. Such "leaks," reported by the Western press as if they were news, have for Soviet Russia the same value as direct threats but they cost it even less, allowing it to blackmail in the name of third parties.

Until it had the bomb and the means of delivering it across continents, the Soviet Union was unable credibly to threaten military action as Hitler had done in 1933–1939 and therefore could not wage global Cold War in an effective manner. Stalin had ordered the manufacture of atomic and hydrogen bombs but without having a clear understanding of their uses: he probably thought he had to have them to be able to face the United States as an equal. His attempts at paralyzing the West into submission were ultimately a failure because his threats carried no conviction. The benefits to be derived from nuclear blackmail were first grasped by Khrushchev and the military who had helped him unseat the more cautious Malenkov. Almost immediately upon coming to power, Khrushchev instigated a major deception intended to convince the United States that he had at his disposal more nuclear weapons and better means of delivering them than in fact was the case. First came Aviation Day of July 1955 when small units of Bisons, apparently flying in circles over Moscow, suggested to Western observers that Russia already had a respectable fleet of strategic bombers. Two years later came the Sputnik, and an even more incredible deception concerning the number of Soviet ICBM's.[12] These stratagems helped undermine the traditional sense of invulnerability to external attack of the United States and persuade it that the only viable alternative to mutual nuclear destruction was accommodation with the Soviet Union. This proposition was not explicitly stated but hinted at. It was President Eisenhower and his advisors who first spelled out the principles that there was "no alternative to peace," that "war had become unthinkable" and that, therefore, negotiation was the only feasible way of settling all disagreements with the Soviet Union. The Geneva Conference of 1955 and the Camp David meeting of 1959 formalized this understanding. Since, as will be pointed out, the Soviet Union enjoys great advantages in negotiations with Western powers, the acceptance by the West of these principles represented a considerable Russian victory. It set the rules for the conduct of operations against the West in a fashion favorable to the Soviet side.

In one sense, the policy of threats initiated by Khrushchev has not worked: even nuclear blackmail has not made the United States and its allies give up their principal positions, such as NATO and West Germany's membership in it. But the policy has had considerable effect on Western public opinion. Ever since the Soviet Union has acquired the ability to inflict heavy punishment on Western countries a paralysis of the will has set in. The leadership stands firm but it can no longer wholly depend on the citizenry, and this condition sooner or later must reflect itself in national policies. While encouraging these tendencies toward isolationism and *embourgeoisement* in the West, the Soviet leadership in its internal policies seeks to steel the Soviet population and by depriving it of the good things of life to keep it lean, hungry, and alert.[13]

Appeals to Foreign Groups

In seeking to influence foreign opinion, Soviet leaders rely on sociological methods of analysis to differentiate the various social and ethnic groupings and determine where each is most vulnerable. We are dealing here with a practical application of political sociology learned from Marx with which the founders of the Soviet state had gained experience while still in the underground. The method is certainly not infallible: it serves better to spot weaknesses than strengths. Even so, it is vastly superior to that rather amateurish manner with which some Western powers approach foreign affairs. Five years ago, when the United States committed half a million men to fight a ground war in Vietnam not a single American university had a chair devoted to Vietnamese history. (There still is none at the time of writing, for that matter.) It is simply unthinkable that the Soviet Union would ever plunge into a major foreign intervention without acquiring beforehand a solid store of historical, economic, political, social, and cultural information on the country in question, and from it obtain at least some idea who are its potential friends and who its enemies there, and how to deal with them. A large part of the research in Soviet institutes devoted to the social sciences and of academic and cultural exchanges is intended to provide the government with such information. Although Russians enjoy a reputation for abstract theorizing and Americans for pragmatism, in the formulation of foreign policy the reverse holds true. The Russians are not likely to undertake any action on the basis of highly generalized assumptions: they usually arrive at decisions on the basis of concrete, factual data in which everything bearing on the "correlation of forces" is given the most careful scrutiny.

Before World War II, Soviet propaganda was aimed primarily at the same underprivileged groups which traditionally had been the object of socialist propaganda: the working class and colonial peoples, above all, followed by other discriminated or deprived groups. Since World War II, the appeal to the underprivileged has been gradually muted and the Soviet leadership has been increasingly courting the established and the aspiring. Why this change occurred it is difficult to say. Perhaps the lower classes had not justified the high hopes placed in them, revealing an unsuspected penchant for nationalism. Perhaps the Russians were impressed by the success which Hitler had had in manipulating the upper and middle classes in England and France. Finally, perhaps as the ruling class of Russia has itself turned into a privileged order it has come to feel greater affinity for its counterparts abroad. Whichever explanation is the correct one, there can be no doubt that in recent years Russian Communists have courted with greater vigor and success the upper third of the social strata than the bottom one.

In Western countries, the appeal is to the moneyed and managerial elite. In recent years, Soviet theorists have become increasingly sophisticated in their analyses of "capitalist" societies, recognizing the existence of various interest groups within what under Stalin had been considered a homogeneous "ruling class."[14] This information enables the Soviet government to direct appeals calculated to sway influential groups in favor of its policies and through them to apply political pressure on foreign governments. In addition, individual persons, valuable because of their connections or their influence on public opinion, are won over by appeals either to their greed or their vanity. A considerable effort is mounted to this end, an effort of whose dimensions the general public—and often its very victims—have little inkling. In the underdeveloped countries, much of the effort is aimed at the aspiring lower middle class, which is lured by the prospect of secure office jobs in the enlarged bureaucracy which would come into being under a one-party system and a centralized economy.

In this connection a few words must be said about the function of foreign Communist parties which is often misunderstood. Communist parties are not used for purposes of subversion except in the most backward areas of the world because, being open to penetration by police agents, they cannot provide the necessary security. KGB agents who have been uncovered in the West not only had no connection with local Communists but sought to appear very conventional. Nor are these parties thought of as alternate governments to take over after the existing governments have been overthrown. When, after World War II, the Soviet Union occupied Eastern Europe it did not put into positions of power local Communists but Communists trained in Moscow. Once the East European client states had been solidified, the local Communists were purged as thoroughly and with even greater vindictiveness than adherents of the so-called "bourgeois" political parties.

The principal role assigned Communist parties abroad seems to lie in the realm of legitimate political activities and opinion molding. Where they enjoy enough voter support to form significant parliamentary blocs—as in France or Italy—they can be used to tip the legislative scales in a manner favorable to the

USSR: for example, by opposing NATO or the Common Market. Where they are not strong enough to do so, they can still provide vigorous opposition to the groups in power and to some extent intimidate them. Public demonstrations are particularly useful. These are never spontaneous but they appear as such and always receive public notice. A well-organized demonstration can create a completely false impression of the actual state of opinion in a given country and sway fence-sitters. In October 1968, while a crowd of six thousand protested on Grosvenor Square against American intervention in Vietnam, only seven demonstrators showed up in front of the Soviet Embassy to protest the invasion of Czechoslovakia. In Tokyo, the masses roam the streets to protest the terms on which Okinawa is to be transferred to Japan; there is no news of demonstrations against Soviet refusal even to discuss the transfer to Japan of the Kurile Islands. In countries with a low level of literacy, the Communist press is also often used to spread the most outrageous lies aimed at discrediting individuals, parties, and states unfriendly to Soviet interests and prepared by the "disinformation" branch of the KGB. Last but not least, foreign Communist organizations are valuable to the Soviet Union for internal purposes. On any issue, the Soviet press can always cite resolutions of foreign Communist parties to convey to the Soviet public an impression of solid support abroad for Russian policies. Useful as they are, one must not overestimate the importance which the Soviet leadership attaches to foreign Communist parties. It much prefers to establish working relations with the foreign elites; and there is enough evidence on hand to indicate that when the interests of the Soviet Union require it, foreign Communist parties are readily sacrificed. They are only one element in the calculation of forces, and not the most weighty one at that.

Some Diplomatic Propaganda Techniques

In addition to appealing to specific opinion and interest groups abroad, the Soviet Union also engages in major propaganda moves on issues which it regards as of major international importance, the purpose of which is to attain concrete political advantages. These are never launched haphazardly: they are deliberate, projected over the long term, and pressed with great vigor.

The most important of those has been the cause of peace. There is no need to go into the history of the various peace campaigns initiated by Stalin and perpetuated by his successors. What merits attention is the adroit use made of the peace slogan for the benefit of Soviet foreign policy. Inside Russia, the Communist regime has succeeded for a long time in establishing the principle that any opposition to it is, ipso facto and, as it were, by definition, counter-revolutionary. Once that principle has been established, the Soviet government need not examine any claims made against itself or engage in self-justification. It may admit, in retrospect, that errors have been committed; but while the policies which might lead to these errors are in force, no questioning is allowed since to do so is tantamount to giving aid and comfort to the class enemy. From the time it has acquired nuclear weapons the Soviet Union has succeeded to a surprising extent in persuading foreign opinion that insofar as any conflict between the major powers creates the danger of world destruction, all hostility to the Soviet government and its ideology or any thwarting of its will is ipso facto and by definition tantamount to war-mongering. By this logic, "anti-Communism" is equated with "anti-humanism." Like so many weapons of political warfare, this device is double-edged; but it so happens that the other edge is never bared.

To maintain its reputation as *defensor pacis,* the Soviet Union frequently concocts imaginary threats to world peace which it then takes credit for dissipating. Soviet histories of foreign policy are filled with such incidents: for example, an alleged Turkish threat to Syria in 1957, alleged United States plots against Iraq in 1958 and 1962, and alleged Western designs against the Congo in 1960 and Cyprus in 1964. By foiling such nefarious designs of its own invention, the Soviet Union gains much credit at small expense and minimum risk. In the spring of 1967 this time-tested device backfired when an alleged Israeli plot against Syria, put forward by Soviet intelligence, for once was not quietly resolved but led to war.

An interesting and often successful technique employed by

Moscow is to turn the tables on the opponent by confusing the real issues at stake. A classic example is Soviet propaganda in the present Israeli-Egyptian dispute. To understand how this technique works it is best to abstract from the specific issues of the Israeli-Egyptian conflict and approach it in a generalized manner. Two powers—let us call them A and B—are at odds. War breaks out, country B defeats A, occupying in the process A's territory. At this juncture, in normal international practice, sooner or later negotiations begin. In the peace settlement which results, the defeated party usually has to make some concessions to the victor, among them, possibly, territorial ones. If for the defeated party A we substitute, say, France in 1870–71 or Finland in 1939–40, and for the victorious party B, respectively, Prussia and the Soviet Union, the pattern becomes clear. In both instances, the victor secured from the vanquished some territory and returned the remainder. Such too, according to the dictates of logic, precedent, and interest of the countries involved, ought to be the outcome of the 1967 War. That it is not, is due, in the first place to the unwillingness of Egypt to recognize the existence of Israel as a sovereign state. In this refusal Egypt is supported by the Soviet Union. The peculiar feature of this conflict is that whereas the real issue at stake is negotiation between the belligerents, Soviet propaganda has managed to make the main issue appear Israeli withdrawal from territories occupied in the course of the war. Thus, a matter which should be part of the final settlement of the conflict becomes a precondition of negotiations leading to a settlement. Whatever one's feelings about the substance of the Israeli-Egyptian dispute, one cannot but admire the adroit use of an intellectual confidence trick to turn the tables on an opponent and shift the burden of recalcitrance from oneself to the other party.

Soviet Estimate of the American Psyche

In dealing with the United States in particular, the Russians have worked out over the past thirty years an interesting set of approaches based on certain assumptions about American ways of thinking and feeling.

In dealing with relations between America and Russia, one cannot emphasize strongly enough the effect which their disparate economic traditions have had on their political conduct. A country like the United States whose preoccupation is commerical is inherently predisposed toward compromise: each trading transaction, after all, must hold some profit for both parties; negotiation is over the division of profits, not over the principle of mutual benefit. On the other hand, a country which makes its living primarily from the production and consumption of goods—never mind whether agricultural, extractive, or industrial—is equally predisposed toward exclusive possession and the denial of the principle of compromise.

This factor has had immense influence on the conduct of international relations of the two countries. When the United States makes a proposal to the Soviet Union, it invariably includes in it provisions designed to make it palatable to the other party; in other words, it makes concessions in advance of actual negotiations, assuming the other party will do likewise. But where the other party is a country like the Soviet Union, without a great commercial tradition and furthermore impelled by ideology toward intransigence, this assumption does not hold. The Russian position always represents the actual expectations of the Soviet government, weighted down with additional unrealistic demands to be given up in exchange for the other side's concessions. In this sense, the Russians always enjoy an immense advantage in negotiating with a country like the United States. Any compromise works in their favor insofar as the American preliminary position already includes some concessions which need not be fought for at all. Occasionally, in diplomatic talks, Russian negotiators work out with their opposite numbers from the West a compromise formula which is then sent to Moscow as representing the Western position. Clearly, when Moscow sends back its counterproposals, the Russians come out the winners. This technique of "splitting the half" theoretically gives the Russians three-quarters of the gain in any compromise solution.

Equally important though more difficult to define is the Russian play on certain elements in the American psyche. A strong residue of Protestant ethics, causes Americans to regard all hostility to them as being at least in some measure brought about by their own faults. That one can be hated for what one is rather than for what one does (to use Mr. George Kennan's formula) is difficult to reconcile with the liberal Protestant ethic which still dominates American culture. It is quite possible to exploit this tendency to self-accusation by setting into motion a steady barrage of hostile actions accompanied by expressions of hatred. The natural reaction of the victims, if they are Americans, can be and often is bewilderment, followed by guilt. Thus is created an atmosphere conducive to concessions whose purpose it is to propitiate the allegedly injured party. The roots of English appeasement of the 1930s probably lay in these psychological factors; and the Russians, imitating the Nazis, have had much success in exploiting similar methods. One need only recall the uses made of so-called American "intervention" in the Russian Civil War, as a counterpart of the Versailles *Diktat,* to see the parallel.

Adherence to Priorities

The militant spirit of the Soviet leadership, its refusal to separate sharply either peace from war or internal politics from external ones, and the participation in the making of foreign policy of several organizations, among which the Ministry of Foreign Affairs occupies a place of subordinate importance—all this creates a foreign policy which tends to be undisciplined and overactive to the point of frenzy. Soviet foreign policy consists, in the first instance, of an interminable succession of probings, which like military reconnaissance, are meant to draw enemy fire and reveal his capabilities, dispositions, and intentions. Much attention is paid in Moscow to these responses. The Soviet government undoubtedly likes the arrangement with the White House established in the 1960s by virtue of which the two parties signal to one another some of their intentions: it saves Moscow a great deal of guesswork and permits it to make appropriate dispositions of its own forces. In the past it has not always correctly interpreted American responses: overly sophisticated signals bewilder Russian leaders and can mislead them. There can be little doubt that Stalin interpreted Dean Acheson's statement that Korea was not within the American "defense perimeter" to mean just what it said. Acheson's attempt to deflect from himself responsibility for some blame in the Communist attack on South Korea is not convincing. For although it may be true, as he says, that other statesmen and military figures had made the same point before him,[15] his voice, as that of the Secretary of State and President Truman's confidant, was in Russian eyes the authoritative one. Brilliant and successful as he generally was in dealing with them, in this one instance Acheson inadvertently gave the Russians the wrong signal. President Kennedy's careful distinction between "defensive" and "offensive" weapons in response to Soviet arms shipments to Cuba, could well have suggested to Moscow lack of resolution, and encouraged it to send missiles there. [As a rule], it does not pay to be too clever with Russian politicians: they are inclined to interpret ambiguity as equivocation, equivocation as weakness, and weakness as a signal to act.

Although uncommonly activist, Soviet foreign policy is not haphazard and without direction. The record indicates that it tends at any one time to concentrate on only one major task.

The very first objective of Soviet foreign policy is to make certain that all the territory which at any time has come under Russian or Communist rule remains so: in other words, that whatever changes occur in the world map affect the holdings of the other camp. The reason why this should matter so much is complicated and only partly explainable by the need to appear to be always advancing and never retreating imposed on its adherents by historical materialism. Another and perhaps the major part of the explanation lies in the historical experience of Russia, namely in the manner by which the centralized Russian state originally came into being. The national state of Western Europe typically emerged from the suppression by the monarchy of the feudal nobility and church, and the concentration in its own hands of all public authority. While this process also occurred in Russia, there another factor came into play as well. The rulers of Moscow, aspiring to become masters of the whole country, had first to subjugate the numerous rival principalities born from the collapse of the Kievan state in the twelfth and thirteenth centuries. To do so, they had to conquer territory and incorporate it into the Muscovite domain. From the earliest, seizing land, uprooting from it all vestiges of self-government, and holding on to it, assumed for the rulers of Russia an extraordinary importance, becoming in their mind the essential attribute of sovereignty. Stalin carried this preoccupation to the lengths of an obsession: he not only made certain to recover territories (Eastern Poland, the Baltic states, and Bessarabia) which he had first obtained by virtue of his nefarious deal with Hitler, but he also insisted on recovering all the lands lost by the tsars. Sometimes the cost of holding on to conquered land is unreasonably high, as in the case of the Kurile Islands, whose retention mars Russia's relations with Japan.

Russian Communists consider the status of lands and peoples presently under their control entirely beyond discussion. In this respect, Soviet foreign policy adheres consistently to the principle "what is mine is mine, what is yours is negotiable." For evidence we need look only at Berlin. The status of Berlin after World War II was regulated by agreements made among the four Allies. Hence, any unilateral change in its status by one of the four occupying powers was illegitimate, and at the very least should have been accompanied by similar changes in the status of the other parts. Now in 1958 the Soviet Union decided to recognize East Germany as a sovereign state and gradually transferred East Berlin to its control. The Western powers both refused to recognize this act as legitimate and to follow suit by transferring sovereignty over West Berlin to the Federal Republic. The Russians for their part have not allowed the status of East Berlin to be placed on the agenda of any of the summit meetings or conferences concerning the fate of the two Germanys since 1958. At the same time, however, by applying intermittent pressure on West Berlin, and in particular by hindering its communications with West Germany, they have transformed what in fact is a problem of Berlin as a whole into a "West Berlin problem" which threatens peace and as such requires a negotiated settlement. In the recently concluded four-power agreement, the Federal Republic apparently secured better terms on Berlin than it had expected. Still, the cold fact remains that neither the Federal Republic nor the Western powers secured in it any concessions whatever on East Berlin because East Berlin was not even on the agenda. Under these conditions, the Russians have nothing to lose and always something to gain from negotiations, which helps explain their penchant for summit meetings, security conferences, and other big power encounters.

Closely connected with the insistence on holding on to land, is the quest for foreign diplomatic recognition. The importance attached to securing international legitimacy became evident from the instant Communists had seized power in Russia. Lenin's policy, which led to the signing of the Brest Litovsk Treaty in March 1918, rested on the premise that every price was worth paying as long as in return the Central Powers would recognize his regime was the legitimate government of Russia. Lenin's conduct on this occasion is regarded by Communist theoreticians as a textbook model. The implicit recognition of East Germany contained in the recently concluded four-power agreement probably outweighs in the eyes of both Russian and East German Communists the value of all the concessions which they had to make to secure it: the more so that they had no right to the things they traded in the first place. It may also be noted that the Russians find genuine satisfaction in the fact that from what otherwise was a thoroughly humiliating experience—the Cuban missile episode of 1962—they had managed to retrieve implicit American recognition of the Castro government.

The defensive element in the Soviet foreign policy is unmistakably clear: the sanctity of Communist authority, once established, is inviolate; violation means war. The West has accepted this equation, allowing the Soviet government to concentrate on offensive operations.

Since the end of World War II the Soviet offensive effort has concentrated on three consecutive targets. Between 1946 and 1953 it was Europe, where the aim was to eliminate American influence and to transform the entire area into a Soviet dependency. This attempt having failed, due to resolute American opposition, the priorities changed. In 1954–1955, Stalin's successors launched a flanking movement against the United States and Western Europe aimed at detaching the so-called Third World. The policy of what became known as "peaceful coexistence" put into effect concurrently and coupled with nuclear blackmail, was designed to keep the United States at bay while it was being contained and isolated. A brilliant success, this gambit may well have borne even more spectacular results were it not that the Chinese Communists refused to go along with it. In the 1960s, the conflict with China has increasingly attracted Russia's principal attention. In the past several years, the previous strategy of containing and isolating the United States has been replaced by one stressing the containment and isolation of Communist China.

While pursuing the primary objective of the moment, the Soviet Union does not neglect other opportunities; but by and large, mindful of the principle of "correlation of forces," its leaders maintain a clear distinction between the primary thrust and diversionary actions. The quiet manner in which they have in the 1960s liquidated their political interests in such areas of tertiary bearing on their conflict with China as West Africa and Latin America, and are presently pursuing a détente in Europe, illustrates this fact. Anyone who deals with Soviet foreign policy must also know how to distinguish the central from the incidental, and not allow himself to be misled by noisy but non-essential diversions.

Role of Intelligence Services

Not even the most cursory survey of the subject can avoid some mention of the influence which intelligence organs exercise on the formulation and execution of Soviet foreign policy. Russians are very proud of their intelligence services, being confident of their ability to penetrate the highest echelons of political and military establishments abroad. Their pride and confidence are justified. Sir William Hayter, one-time British Ambassador to Moscow, concedes that probably no important secrets are hidden from Soviet intelligence. But the uses to which information obtained by these services is put is another matter. Sir William goes on to say:

> [Soviet diplomatic agents] seem only able to gather information
> by underhand intelligence means and to be incapable of picking up

the kind of information that any normal foreigner can acquire by using his eyes and ears. Partly this is due to the distrust with which
they are trained to regard all non-Communist phenomena. Partly
it is due to their distrust of each other, which makes normal contact
with foreigners, and normal reactions to such contacts, suspect in
the eyes of the numerous agents who are watching each other in the
embassies. For whatever reasons, one has the impression that Soviet
embassies have much information about, but little real knowledge
of, the countries in which they are working.[16]

These generalizations can be broadened to include not only
the Soviet embassies but that whole vast realm of foreign
policy where the intelligence services play a major part. Intelligence organs are constitutionally unsuited to judge broader
issues of public policy and in particular to understand public
opinion. The Soviet intelligence apparatus is even less suited
for work of this kind than the others, because, accustomed as it
is to operating with virtual impunity at home, it instinctively
treats all politics as a subject of manipulation pure and simple.
There is much indication to suggest that some of the outstanding fiascoes of Soviet foreign policy in the Third World have
been caused by overconfident and ill-informed intelligence
operatives.

Even more risky have been Soviet experiences with the device of "disinformation" so dear to the heart of the KGB because so successful in the hermetically sealed environment of
Soviet Russia. On the face of it, the grand deception perpetrated
on the United States in the 1950s concerning the number of
Soviet bombers and ICBM's was an outstanding success. It
succeeded in that it caused the United States to give up the idea
of "massive retaliation" and freed the Russians to engage in all
kinds of adventures in the Third World. But in the end the deception brought the Soviet Union more harm than good because
the authors ignored its political implications. For one, it spurred
the United States to enlarge its rocket arsenal. Secondly, it
confused and angered the Chinese government which, apparently uninitiated into the secret, took Soviet boasts at
face value and interpreted Russia's failure to press its alleged
advantage over the United States as cowardice, collusion, or
both.

The Effects of the Sino-Soviet Conflict

Soviet foreign policy since the end of World War II has been predicated on the assumption that the United States, Russia's principal rival, does not covet anything that belongs to the Soviet Union and therefore will not pursue offensive operations. This conviction must first have been planted in the mind of Soviet leaders by America's refusal in the late 1940s to take advantage of its nuclear monopoly in face of rising Soviet challenges and provocations. If there were any doubts about its validity, they should have been dispelled by the hollowness of John Foster Dulles' "rollback" threat. With this assurance, the Soviet Union could launch with relative impunity the offensive operations whose outlines we have sketched. In such a contest, time clearly was on Soviet Russia's side. Its offensive operations carried out on many levels assured that it could lose nothing and gain much, while Western public opinion could be expected to exert increasing pressure on their governments to seek accommodation as an alternative to nuclear holocaust.

Today most of this policy lies in shambles. The conflict with China is a calamity of the first order for the Soviet Union, with the profoundest consequences for the conduct of its external relations. That Russian leaders and theorists do not talk much about these implications only serves to underline the gravity with which they view the matter, because, as a rule, the Soviet hierarchy is least inclined to discuss in public issues which concern it the most. The calamity derives not only in incurring the enmity of a country regarded as a trusted ally responsible for guarding Russia's eastern flank. Rather, it derives from the nature of the Chinese Communist regime and the kind of political warfare it is likely to wage against the Soviet Union. Henceforth, the comfortable premises which had permitted the Soviet Union to carry out long-term offensive operations will no longer apply. China does not recognize the inviolability of Russian possessions: indeed, it makes active territorial claims on the USSR. It cannot be intimidated by nuclear blackmail, because its population is held as firmly in the regime's grip as is the Soviet. On all issues, it does not seek the middle ground, but full satisfaction of its interests. In the Third World, it appeals to much the same constituencies. In short, it enjoys the same advantages vis-à-vis the Soviet Union that the Soviet Union for the past quarter of a century has enjoyed vis-à-vis the West.

As the tricks which have worked so well with the prudent commercial nations of the West prove unavailing against another Communist regime, Soviet Russia may well throw caution to the wind and rely increasingly on brute force. Under these conditions, militancy can indeed come to mean belligerency. The immense and uninterrupted growth of the Soviet military establishment in all its branches suggests that such a shift may already have taken place. In the perspective of history, the Indo-Pakistani war can appear as the opening round of a trial of physical strength, since behind Russia's puzzling concern for the self-determination of Bangladesh seems to lie the desire to eliminate Pakistan, China's ally on the subcontinent.

Psychologically speaking, the Soviet Union may be at that point in its history which Germany had reached around 1890: a point at which it feels predisposed to throw aside cautious probing based on the weighing of the "correlation of forces," in order to engage in "world politics" in which power is pursued for its own sake. If that happens, other operative principles in the conduct of foreign relations will have to be worked out.

Notes

1. This subject is treated by a group of experienced negotiators in Raymond Dennett and Joseph E. Johnson, eds., *Negotiating with the Russians* (Boston, 1951), and in an amusing chapter in Heinz Pächter's *Weltmacht Russland* (Oldenburg-Hamburg, 1968), 373–377.

2. *Voprosy strategii i operativnogo iskusstva v sovetskikh voennykh trudakh, 1917–1940 gg.* [Questions of strategy and the art of operations in Soviet military works, 1917–1940] (Moscow, 1965), 13.

3. *Insight and Outlook* (New York, 1949), especially Chapter XVIII, "The Eureka Process."

4. Cited in my book *Struve: Liberal on the Left, 1870–1905* (Cambridge, Mass., 1970), 134.

5. V. I. Lenin, *Sochineniia,* 3rd ed. (Moscow, 1926–1937), XXX, 333. Admiration for Clausewitz is something the Bolsheviks and the Nazis have in common.

6. V. Sorin, "Marksizm, taktika, Lenin," *Pravda*, No. 1 (January 3, 1923), 5. On another occasion, Lenin wrote: "To have an overwhelming superiority of forces at a decisive moment in a decisive place—this 'law' of military success is also the law of political success. . . ." Lenin, *Sochineniia*, XXIV, 635. Lenin's copious notes on Clausewitz are reprinted in *Leninskii sbornik*, XII (1931), 387–452.

7. [Subsequent to the writing of this essay, Gromyko became a member of the Politburo.]

8. Cited in Sir William Hayter, *Russia and the World* (London, 1970), 18, 19.

9. Cited in J. M. Mackintosh, *The Strategy and Tactics of Soviet Foreign Policy* (London, 1962), 90, 91.

10. P. I. Kudriavtsev, ed., *Iuridicheskii slovar'* [Juridical Dictionary] 2nd ed., II (Moscow, 1956), 550.

11. *Boston Evening Globe*, November 10, 1971, 15.

12. This fascinating story is described in Arnold L. Horelick and Myron Rush, *Strategic Power and Soviet Foreign Policy* (Chicago, 1966). I owe these two authors the reference cited above in note 10.

13. It is interesting to observe that whereas in the era of "peaceful coexistence" with the West the Soviet government goes out of its way to maintain in Russia the spirit of ideological militancy toward the West, during the period of amity with Nazi Germany (1939–1941) it was equally anxious in its internal propaganda to give no offense to the government of Hitler.

14. H. William Zimmerman, *Soviet Perspectives on International Relations, 1956–1967* (Princeton, N.J., 1969), 214–218.

15. Dean Acheson, *Present at the Creation* (New York, 1969), 357–358.

16. Hayter, *Russia and the World*, 24.

THREE

America, Russia, and Europe in the Light of the Nixon Doctrine

This essay and the one that follows were written while I was working as a consultant for the Strategic Studies Center of the Stanford Research Institute in Washington, D.C. It expresses my doubts about the premises underpinning the so-called Nixon Doctrine and emphasizes the need for closer relations with China.

In Solzhenitsyn's *August 1914,* among the hordes of incompetent officers leading the imperial Russian armies to their doom, one figure stands out, that of Colonel Vorotyntsev. He alone has his wits about him as he rushes from one sector of the wobbling front to another, querying generals and common soldiers, studying the topography, observing enemy dispositions, and, in the end, guiding back to Russian lines a small band of retreating soldiers. All along, Vorotyntsev sees what needs to be done with a lucidity of which those actually entrusted with the responsibility for decisions are entirely incapable; and had someone like him been in charge, Russian troops surely would not have suffered the debacle of Tannenberg. Exasperated by the obtuseness of his superiors, at one point he asks himself: *"Pochemu PONIMANIE vsegda sloitsia nizhe VLASTI?"*—Why does understanding always lie beneath authority?

Why, indeed? If I could converse with the colonel or his

Reprinted by permission from Richard B. Foster et al., eds., *Strategy for the West: American-Allied Relations in Transition* (New York, 1974), pp. 109–122.

creator, I would suggest the following answer: Because understanding, being a product of intellectual processes, concerns itself primarily with ends, with what needs to be done; authority,
on the other hand, involving as it does management of men,
belongs to the realm of applied arts, and tends to become preoccupied with means. Sometimes this preoccupation grows so
obsessive that those in power lose sight of the whole purpose to
which power has been given them. The more ambitious an
undertaking, the more people involved in it, the greater the likelihood that overconcern with the means will produce stupendous
mismanagement. (Hence Santayana's definition of fanaticism
as "redoubling one's efforts after one has forgotten one's aims.")

All of which is meant to explain my temerity in presenting
a critique of policies of statesmen whose intentions are no
worse than mine, but who also happen to have access to information that is inaccessible to me. The great merit of free public
opinion is that it acts as a corrective to statesmanship by raising questions of purpose, all too often obscured by concerns
with implementation.

The so-called Nixon Doctrine appears to be the product of
two factors: the steady growth of Soviet military power and the
concurrent decline of the American public's willingness to continue bearing a heavy load of international obligations. In some
ways these two factors are causally related, but it is safe to say
that of itself neither would have produced the kind of change
in foreign policy that the Nixon Doctrine entails. The inevita-
bility of some kind of disengagement from the [theory of con-
tainment] had become apparent even before Mr. Nixon assumed
office. In an essay published in 1968, Mr. Kissinger outlined the
principles of foreign policy which the Republican Administration has been following ever since. He called for a new world
"order," one of whose features would be a more equitable
spread of responsibilities among all the major powers:

> Our deepest challenge will be to evoke the creativity of a pluralis-
> tic world, to base order on political multipolarity even though
> the overwhelming military strength will remain with the two super-
> powers. . . . A more pluralistic world . . . is profoundly in our long-
> term interest.[1]

This basic idea became subsequently elaborated into the Nixon Doctrine which—like the historic causes giving rise to it—rests on two principles:

1. In regard to the Soviet Union, America's only serious military rival, "confrontation" is to give way to "negotiation." Rather than attempt at every point of the globe to match and frustrate Soviet challenges with countermoves of its own, as the theory of containment had demanded, the United States will concentrate on locating areas of agreement between the two superpowers. No matter how insignificant or even trivial these agreements may be from the politico-military point of view (so the theory runs), they create a climate of mutual trust conducive to the solution of major differences. Concurrently, through increased trade, the USSR is to be enmeshed in a "web of interests" through which it will gain a greater stake in world stability.

2. In order to make foreign policy burdens lighter and more acceptable to its public, the United States will insist that its allies and friends exert more effort on their own behalf. Peace— and, one hopes, freedom—are everyone's concern.[2] The United States will be willing to help those whose security is threatened, but it will no longer rush to bail them out. In particular, Western Europe and Japan must be weaned from their overdependence on U.S. military strength, and must invest a larger share of their national product in defense.

Like every statesman in our history-obsessed age, Mr. Nixon is anxious to win for himself a secure place in history books, for which reason he is given to wild exaggerations of both the novelty and the significance of his policies. Undoubtedly, the Nixon Doctrine marks a major departure from the foreign policy pursued by the United States since 1948. Whether it indeed inaugurates a "new era" in international relations, as we are insistently told, remains to be seen; such attributions are better left to the historian. As to its alleged novelty, here too the historian may be permitted a skeptical attitude. In terms of diplomatic practice, the Nixon Doctrine introduces nothing new; it merely combines two well-known and tested methods of handling international rivalries, the idea of the "concert" of great powers (the United States and the Soviet Union) and the

idea of the balance of power (the United States and the rest of
the world). The two elements of the Nixon Doctrine are not
correlated in any apparent way, with the result that the present
administration pursues two separate policies.

To raise questions about its originality or historic significance
is not to reject the Nixon Doctrine. Given the realities of the
international and domestic situation in the late 1960s, it is difficult to see how the policy of containment could have been
maintained. The only conceivable alternative—complete abandonment of world responsibilities—would have been much
worse for the United States and its friends. The conduct of
foreign policy under President Nixon has been, on the whole,
more skillful than under his immediate predecessors. The weakness of the Doctrine seems to me to lie in its theoretical underpinnings and it is these that I wish to question. Are its basic
assumptions realistic? Are they mutually compatible? A frankly
pragmatic foreign policy would be immune to such critical
analysis. A policy based on a view of a new world "order,"
one which promises to usher in a new "era," is not. Doctrines
have a tendency to acquire a life of their own, to produce
action in their own support. Such was the fate of the policy of
containment: conceived and formulated on the basis of a realistic appraisal of Communist intentions and American capabilities,
it eventually degenerated into something corresponding to
neither.

The Nixon Doctrine rests on a theoretical conception of
Communism and the Soviet regime. If one can judge by Mr.
Nixon's public pronouncements, it is his view that the adversary which he as President faces is an ideological force strongly
tinged with fanaticism. This view may be a legacy of his early
political career, launched when the anti-Communist hysteria in
the United States was at its height. It may also reflect his superficial education. Whatever the reason, there is nothing in President Nixon's speeches that indicates a rudimentary acquain-
tance with the histories of Russia and its Communist Party, or
with the political, economic, and social realities of the contemporary Soviet Union. Apparently he is unaware that the
rulers of the Soviet Union and other Communist states have a
material interest in the preservation and expansion of their

system and that therefore their commitment to it is not merely or even primarily due to an ideologically inspired set of attitudes.

Attitudes can be changed, and it is this prospect that underlies Mr. Nixon's apparently genuine optimism about future Russo-American relations. He seems persuaded that the logic of events requires the world, especially the industrialized nations headed by the United States and the Soviet Union, to draw closer to one another and to learn to cooperate in the solution of common human problems, such as the quality of the environment and the applications of science, to mention but two. However, from the reasonable premise that nations *ought* to engage in such cooperation, Mr. Nixon imperceptibly slips into the conclusion that they *will* in fact do so. He is remarkably prone to change the [subjunctive] mood of a verb into an indicative one. By means of rhetorical devices, "should" turns into "shall" in his public pronouncements, and, one suspects, in the privacy of his mind.

What makes this faulty logic doubly dangerous is that it is bolstered by a more sophisticated but no less fallacious conviction of Mr. Kissinger's that in modern times territorial expansion has become an anachronism:

> In the past, stability has always presupposed the existence of an equilibrium of power which prevented one state from imposing its will on the others. The traditional criteria for the balance of power were territorial. A state could gain overwhelming superiority only by conquest. . . . In the contemporary period, this is no longer true. Some conquests add little to effective military strength; major increases in power *are possible* entirely through developments within the territory of a sovereign state. . . . If the Soviet Union had occupied Western Europe but had remained without nuclear weapons, it would be less powerful than it is now with its existing nuclear arsenal within its present borders.[3]

Mr. Kissinger does not tell us what would be the effect on its power status if the Soviet Union had *both* its nuclear arsenal and Western Europe. One suspects that his views on the matter may have undergone some modification as a result of personal experiences with the unappeasable North Vietnamese appetite for territory. Nevertheless, the notion that expansion is no

longer profitable does underlie much of the Nixon Doctrine
in theory and in practice, reinforcing the related view of great
power conflict as out of date. Here too the conditional shades
into the affirmative apparently without the author's awareness
of the transition.

The political instinct of Mr. Nixon and the historical convictions of Mr. Kissinger lead them to the same conclusion: modern
conditions impel mankind toward cooperation and render obsolete the spirit of rivalry, aggressiveness, and expansion, as well
as the politico-military techniques derived from it. In accordance
with this premise, conflict with the Soviet Union is to be de-
emphasized and the maximum effort put into seeking out areas
of mutual agreement. Personal contacts with Soviet leaders have
amply demonstrated that they are anything but fanatical
ideologues, and have thus strengthened the President's and his
aides' belief in their responsiveness to pragmatic arguments.

Assuming that this analysis is correct, it is difficult to know
where to begin the critique of the Nixon Doctrine, so riddled is
it with misconceptions and inconsistencies. To begin with, the
equation modernity = peace goes back at least a century and a
half, to Saint-Simon and the Saint-Simonians, and, somewhat
later, Herbert Spencer, who had confidently predicted that the
age of "industrialism" would soon replace that of "militarism."
The two global wars waged not by the so-called backward but
by the most industrialized nations of the world should have laid
this appealing equation permanently to rest, but this apparently
has not happened. Much of Mr. Nixon's optimism has a pronounced Wilsonian ring, although, according to Henry Brandon,
a sympathetic historian of his administration, Mr. Nixon regards
Wilson's "idealism" with suspicion.[4] Many of his ideas concerning the need to create a new order to prevent future conflict also remind one of General Smuts and his 1919 blueprints
for the League of Nations.

Let us now turn briefly to some specific fallacies:

1. Communism is not merely or even primarily an ideology;
nor has fanaticism ever played a decisive role in it. True, Communist movements prior to seizure of power attract ideologues
and fanatics; but these are promptly gotten rid of after power
has been acquired. Lenin began to slough off his ideological

allies almost immediately after he had overthrown the Provisional Government. By accepting the extremely onerous peace terms of Brest Litovsk, he gave his recalcitrant followers an unforgettable lesson in political pragmatism. The readiness of the Soviet regime to sacrifice any element in its doctrine for the sake of preserving and enhancing its power is a fact so well established historically that one is embarrassed even to have to mention it. There has never been a political doctrine or a government with a keener sense of the realities of power relationships (*sootnoshenie sil*) than the Soviet one. The Soviet system is and always has been distinguished by extreme pragmatism. It is indeed a classic example of authority which, facing gigantic tasks of harnessing human resources, has utterly lost sight of its original aims.

2. This being the case, it is groundless to expect that the Soviet regime will turn more pragmatic. If the Soviet government has agreed to a partial détente with the United States—indeed, has initiated and insisted on it—the reason must be sought not in a growing awareness among its leaders that humanity shares a common destiny, but in factors having to do with international power relationships. The Russians, it must be emphasized, interpret the "balance of power" much more broadly than do Western strategists, who tend to restrict it to military [forces]: the former include and weigh under this rubric economic, social, and psychological factors. Thus, they may be aggressive when the military balance happens to favor their opponents (e.g., 1946–1950), and conciliatory when it is evenly distributed (the present time), factors other than military ones playing a decisive part in the calculation. The Soviet government launched the détente policy in 1956 for two reasons: because it desired a breathing spell for its population, which twenty-five years of Stalinism and World War II had left exhausted, and because it wished to extricate itself from the isolation into which Stalin's foreign policy had driven it. Since then other considerations have come into play. The primary consideration today is the conflict with China, which compels the Soviet Union to reduce tension on the Western front. Second, there are economic difficulties and the need for Western technology and credits. Paradoxically, having attained nuclear

parity, the Soviet Union has a greater interest in a détente with the United States than it had when it was vulnerable to nuclear destruction. This is a practical decision. There is no evidence whatever in Soviet statements intended for internal consumption that the Soviet Union shares President Nixon's and Mr. Kissinger's ideas about the nature of contemporary international diplomacy. The adamant refusal to call off or even to restrain the "ideological war" is not a minor issue, as the White House appears to think; it signifies that from Moscow's point of view the détente is a temporary expedient. Internally, the Soviet media ascribe the improvement in relations with the United States to a shift in the balance of power in Russia's favor. The United States is depicted, as it was in Stalin's day, as the central bastion of world imperialism and the principal backer of "fascist" regimes. There are no delusions *there* about the United States having experienced a change of heart; America's new policy is said to be the result exclusively of the realities of the power relationship. The unwillingness of the Soviet Union to participate in the "new era" of international diplomacy is clearly demonstrated by the continued jamming of the Voice of America broadcasts.[5] Because he regards Communism primarily as an ideology, Mr. Nixon prefers to disregard these facts, which he probably views as a kind of anachronism and as a practical politician tends to dismiss. If, however, he approached the Soviet Union as a congeries of institutions designed to protect the special interests of the ruling elite, he would take a much more serious view of the Soviet insistence on the right to continue the "ideological" war.

Anyone who reads the President's annual reports to Congress cannot help being struck by one glaring inconsistency. In the theoretical parts, which explain the premises of the Administration's foreign policy, everything is sunny. But as soon as it is time to deal with the specifics, dark clouds appear. It is as if we were listening to an opera, the first half of which was composed by Mozart and the second by Wagner: suddenly Pamino begins to sing the *Götterdämmerung*. The Soviet Union, which is supposed to be evolving from fanaticism to pragmatism and entering into a common partnership with the rest of the world, unaccountably arms itself at a pace and in a style which cannot be explained solely in terms of its security needs. The bewilderment of the President with this evidence is apparent in his 1972 address, where he speaks of "developments in 1971 which make it unclear whether we are witnessing a permanent change in Soviet policy or only a passing phase concerned more with tactics than with a fundamental commitment to a stable international system." Among these developments the President lists the Soviet Union's manufacture and deployment of weapons, its arms policy in the Middle East, its behavior during the India-Pakistan crisis, and "the expansionist implications of Soviet naval activities."[6] This is quite a list. Since these facts raise basic questions about Soviet intentions, one would expect some analysis of their significance to ensue. In vain. In the next paragraph of the President's 1972 speech all these doubts are brushed aside as the catalog of "positive developments" is resumed. One can only conclude that the present Administration, while aware of evidence contrary to its premises, chooses to ignore it. The result is that the two superpowers cooperate in combating heart disease and protecting walruses off the Aleutians while at the same time competing in the perfection of the most lethal kinds of weapons. The White House, bent on accentuating the positive, sees nothing worrisome in this.

Another of the glaring inconsistencies in President Nixon's foreign policy is the failure to link in any evident manner the Russo-American détente with his demands on Western Europe concerning its security. In his recent keynote address (April 23, 1973) Mr. Kissinger strongly stressed the need for Europe to contribute more to its own defense, the necessity for Europeans to rethink their defense strategy, and the importance of keeping American troops in Europe, but he said nothing about the reasons behind these requests. The enemy is never mentioned. Against whom are all these measures intended? If the Soviet Union is indeed becoming a responsible power genuinely interested in maintaining world stability, then so much emphasis on military preparedness seems misplaced. Or are these contingency measures? There is a serious gap between U.S. policy toward Russia and that toward Europe, one result of which is that Europeans do not take very seriously American exhortations about the need for a greater defense effort on their part.

The importance of Western Europe to the United States is such that, in the event of Russia's direct onslaught, the United States would certainly react in an appropriate manner. President Nixon is as much aware as his predecessors have been of the fatal consequences that would ensue if West European talent and resources were to come under Soviet control. But for this very reason a direct military attack on Western Europe by the Red Army seems highly improbable. Not only do the Russians have no wish to trigger a nuclear exchange, but they also have less apocalyptic reasons for caution: the desire to maintain good working relations with the United States; lack of experience with coordinated offensive operations on hostile foreign territory; mistrust of satellite armies, and fear of disorders in the event of military reverses. The development by the United States of "smart weapons" capable of disorganizing the enemy logistic lines without recourse to nuclear warheads further weakens the offensive capacity of the Russians in Europe. True, the Soviet Union maintains very large troop concentrations in Europe—it has chosen not to weaken them in order to build up its Chinese front—and it has shown little interest in reasonable mutual force reductions. But from this it does not follow that the Soviet High Command seriously envisages the deployment of its European troops in massive offensive operations. The primary purpose of the Soviet divisions stationed in Europe is to intimidate. They are to preclude nationalist uprisings in Eastern Europe, and to remind Western Europe that over it always hangs the threat of a devastating war.

In view of these considerations, which seem to me to have a high degree of plausibility, the heavy stress laid by Western planners on major military conflict with the Soviet Union appears misplaced. Far too much effort goes into thinking and rethinking the possible Western responses to Soviet offensive operations against Western Europe, and far too little thought is devoted to other, more probable contingencies. On the military front, for example, some action may well take the form of intervention on the periphery of Western Europe—for instance, in Yugoslavia or Greece, where external aggression could be preceded and assisted by internal subversion. Does "flexible response" provide realistic countermoves for this possibility?

For example, would NATO units credibly threaten East Germany or Czechoslovakia in order to deflect Soviet operations in the Balkans, should such be undertaken?

The West seems even less prepared to cope with what seems the most realistic threat to its integrity, namely, slow, patient, piecemeal disintegration of Western Europe by a combination of external and internal pressures. The Russian elite has unrivaled experience in uprooting neighboring powers in just such a manner: it is thus that the Russian state has traditionally extended its frontiers and managed to attain the highest rate of territorial expansion ever recorded. Anyone interested in these methods would do well to study the history of the Russian conquest of Novgorod (fifteenth century), Kazan (sixteenth century), and Poland (eighteenth century). The Ottoman Empire might well have fallen victim to the same process in the nineteenth century had it not been for resolute British action on its behalf. Nor should it be forgotten that the scramble for "concessions" in late imperial China, which only the outbreak of World War I prevented from ending in the dismemberment of that country by the great powers, had also been initiated by Russia (Manchuria, 1896 ff.). What we have here is a traditional manner of doing things, admirably suited to Russia's geopolitical situation and to its cumbersome, centralized political machine.

The first step in the eventual absorption of Europe by the Soviet Union has been taken. After a quarter century, the West has finally come to acknowledge the Russian occupation of Eastern Europe not only de facto but also de jure. The recent accords [of the Federal Republic with the Soviet Union] mean, in effect, that the West has reconciled itself to Eastern [Germany] passing permanently into the Soviet sphere of influence and joining the rest of the Soviet empire.

The next step—control of Western Europe—is, of course, incomparably more difficult to accomplish. And yet preliminary measures must soon be taken by Russia to neutralize Europe's military threat for reasons which, in the first instance, have to do with its difficulties with China.

The Soviet Union is not at all pleased with President Nixon's balance-of-power policy, and denigrates it as dangerous to world stability. Why? A "pentagonal" world, envisaged by President

Nixon, confronts Russia with the prospect of a two-front war with two potential hostile blocs: Western Europe acting in concert with the United States, and China allied with Japan. The prospect of a European-East Asian military entente, whatever its likelihood, must be a nightmare to Soviet statesmen and strategists. To counter it, the Soviet Union is vigorously pressing an alternative policy—namely, "collective security"—which it would like applied first to Europe and then to Asia. The purpose of such arrangements seems to be to prevent the formation of potential anti-Soviet blocs by the introduction of the principle that no major political or military decisions anywhere in the world can be taken without the Soviet Union's direct participation. This is one reason the Soviet Union lays such emphasis on the development of a navy, a force which has always served great powers as an instrument of "world politics."

Essentially, the Soviet Union hopes to neutralize the damage to its interests implied in the balance-of-power principle by establishing its physical (military) presence in every major strategic area of the globe and demanding a senior voice in all regional politico-military arrangements. A "collective security" pact in Europe should enable the Soviet Union to nip in the bud any designs of NATO to exert pressure on it should Russia become militarily engaged in the Far East. Similarly, an Asian "collective security" pact (Russia, America, India, Japan, etc.) could be used to isolate and contain China.

It is difficult to believe that the Soviet Union will get away with a scheme that so transparently serves its own interests and offers the others nothing in return but a limitation of options. It is impossible to see the purpose of a European "security pact" of which the Soviet Union would be an active partner. Either the Soviet Union is a threat to Western Europe, in which case it should no more participate in European security arrangements that a wolf be invited to join a self-defense organization of lambs, or it is not such a threat, in which case there is no need for collective security. Certainly the Soviet Union has no need to fear offensive actions from NATO; past experience demonstrates that NATO does not exploit Soviet difficulties. Nor does Western Europe confront a military threat from any other source than the Soviet Union. One must conclude, therefore, that the immediate purpose of Soviet collective security proposals is to guarantee a dependable western flank and to free its hands for possible action in East Asia.

Such is the immediate aim of Soviet security proposals, but beyond them lurk long-term goals which carry ominous prospects for Europe. Russian participation in the politico-military institutions regulating Western Europe—without, needless to add, corresponding opportunities being granted Western Europe in Europe's Eastern half—will provide Russia with a framework within which to initiate a process of internal disintegration of the kind mentioned above. The basic tactic would be to divide in every country the "peace" party from the "war" party, to pit one state against another (especially France against Germany), to weaken economic unity by deals with individual member states of the EEC, and, over the long run, to detach Europe from the United States.

Realism requires one to recognize that this policy has much better chances of success than one would have believed possible a decade ago. The essential point, in my opinion, is that postwar Europe has undergone a veritable social revolution which has decreased its willingness (although not its ability) to meet the kind of threat the Soviet Union poses to its political existence. Until World War II, Europe had been socially a highly stratified continent in which the lower orders, as it were, "knew their place." Consumer goods beyond the essential ones, travel, most sports, spectacles, and luxuries were outside the range of their pocketbooks and even of their vision. Leadership positions in the diplomatic and military services were reserved for descendants of the "feudal" class and the propertied groups assimilated to it. Now, with the help of American military protection and investments, this situation has undergone radical change. The rise of wages accompanying advances in industrialization and the savings made on defense outlays with the attendant lowering of costs of consumer products have given the mass of Europeans for the first time in history access to goods and activities previously considered the exclusive domain of the elite. At the same time the old "feudal" class has dwindled in influence, partly because the social democratization of Europe has diminished the awe in which it had been held traditionally. Western

Europe is in the throes of a consumer orgy which, with each passing year, diminishes its appetite for an active foreign policy and a major defense effort. The West Europeans do not seem to wish to assume the responsibility for their political and military self-preservation and, deep in their hearts, they see no need to do so, being convinced that the United States cannot afford to let them fall into Russian hands. The policy of détente toward Russia pursued by the United States reinforces this belief, and so does the Russian peace offensive.

Realistically speaking, the best chance of preventing future Russian encroachments in Europe and in Asia seems to lie in a coordination of West European and Chinese diplomacies and (eventually) military strategies. The Chinese seem fully to realize the advantages which would accrue to them from such a policy. But they are not strong enough at this time to carry any weight, nor can they assure Europe of significant relief in the event Europe should be menaced by the Russians. American diplomacy for its part seems strangely to ignore this possibility, whether because it does not wish to alarm the Russians or because it believes that such a policy is impractical. However, ultimately this line seems more promising than the notion of an "Atlantic Community" pressed on Europe by the Nixon Administration. There is a curious inability in the White House to perceive the global ramifications of foreign policy, to understand that the détente with the Soviet Union produces effects on European attitudes toward Russia, and that the opening of American-Chinese relations could in turn affect Russian behavior toward Europe. The balance-of-power element in the Nixon Doctrine cannot be made workable if an exception is made for the Soviet Union on the grounds of a special relationship between the two superpowers. If balance-of-power politics is to be pursued in earnest, then Russia must be considered a factor in it; and once that is done it will become obvious that the American-European relationship also involves China and possibly Japan.

Notes

1. Henry A. Kissinger, "Central Issues of American Foreign Policy," in Kermit Gordon, ed., *Agenda for the Nation* (Washington, D.C., 1968), 589, 599.

2. I say "one hopes" because in recent years, responding to the Soviet "peaceful coexistence" propaganda policy, the United States has allowed the cause of peace to overshadow completely that of freedom, in which the USSR, of course, has no interest. It is certainly easier to search for peace at any price than on stated conditions.

3. Kissinger, "Central Issues," 590. Emphasis added.

4. Henry Brandon, ed., *The Retreat of American Power* (New York, 1973), 21.

5. [Since these words were written, the Soviet government has ceased jamming Voice of America broadcasts, although it continues to jam Radio Liberty.]

6. *U.S. Foreign Policy for the 1970's: The Emerging Structure for Peace,* A Report to the Congress by Richard Nixon, President of the United States, February 9, 1972 (Washington, D.C., 1972), 5–6.

FOUR

Détente: Moscow's View

In 1973–74 I edited a volume of papers by several outstanding specialists on Soviet policies in Europe. The symposium sought to ascertain what the Soviet Union wanted in Europe, how it was going about getting it, and to what extent it had already achieved its objectives. My paper dealt with the first of these questions. A few years later, a Russian émigré historian wrote an interesting criticism of my views in which, while commending my estimate of Soviet intentions, he complained that I was anti-Russian. In his opinion, all of the ills of the Soviet regime are due not to Russia's historical heritage, which I stress, but to the pernicious influence of Marxist ideology. I believe him to be wrong, but his view is very widespread among conservative émigrés from the Soviet Union.

Today, there is no question of any significance which can be decided without the Soviet Union or in opposition to it.... Moreover, it is precisely our proposals . . . that are at the center of political discussions.
  —*A. A. Gromyko at the XXIVth Party Congress (1971)*[1]

Reprinted by permission from Richard Pipes, ed., *Soviet Strategy in Europe* (New York, 1976), 3–44. This essay was the subject of an exchange; see Wladislaw G. Krasnow, "Richard Pipes' Foreign Strategy: Anti-Soviet or Anti-Russian," and my response in *The Russian Review* (Vol. 38, No. 2, 180–197), reprinted in *Encounter* (London), LIV, No. 4 (April 1980), 67–75.

Soviet Historical Background

In the accounts they left behind, travelers who had visited Russia between the seventeenth and nineteenth centuries liked to stress the unusually low business ethics of the native population. What struck them was not only that Russian merchants, shopkeepers, peddlers, and ordinary *muzhiks* engaged in the most impudent cheating, but that once they were found out they showed no remorse. Rather than apologize, they shrugged the matter off by quoting a proverb which from frequent repetition became very familiar to resident Westerners: "It is the pike's job to keep the carps awake." This version of *caveat emptor*— "let the buyer beware"—not only enjoins the customer to look out for his interests but it also implies that if he is hoodwinked, the fault is entirely his, insofar as the pike (in this case the seller) has a nature-given right to gobble up unwary fish. It is a distillation of centuries of experience, a kind of folkish anticipation of Social Darwinism, to which a large majority of the Russian population (with the notable exception of the intelligentsia) has learned to adhere, whether placed by fortune in the role of pike or of its potential victim.

All people tend to some extent to base their understanding of foreign civilizations on personal experience and self-image and to assume that underneath the cloak of even the most exotic exterior there thinks the same mind and beats the same heart. But no one is more prone to work on this assumption than a person whose occupation is commerce and whose political creed is liberalism. The idea of human equality, the noblest achievement of "bourgeois" culture, is also the source of great political weakness because it denies a priori any meaningful distinctions among human beings, whether genetic, ethnic, racial, or other, and therefore blinds those who espouse it to a great deal of human motivation. Those differences that cannot be ignored, the commercial-liberal mind likes to ascribe to uneven economic opportunity and the resulting cultural lag. The most probable cause of this outlook, and the reason for its prevalence, lies in the contradiction between the "bourgeois" ideal of equality and the undeniable fact of widespread inequality. Such an outlook enables the "bourgeois" to enjoy his advantages without guilt, because as long as all men are presumed to be the same, those who happen to be better off may be said to owe their superior status to personal merit. In the United States, a country whose underlying culture is permeated with the commercial ethos and liberal ideology, this way of thinking is very common. Among the mass of the people it expresses itself in a spontaneous and rather endearing goodwill toward foreigners, accompanied by an unconscious and (to foreigners) irritating assumption that the American way is *the* way. Among the more learned, it conceals itself behind theoretical façades that appear to be supremely sophisticated but on closer inspection turn out to be not all that different from the ideas held by the man on the street. The various theories of "modernization" that have acquired vogue among American sociologists and political scientists since World War II, once they are stripped of their academic vocabulary, say little more than that when all the people of the globe have attained the same level of industrial development as in the United States, they will become like Americans.

This outlook is so deeply ingrained in the American psyche and is so instinctively and tenaciously held that it produces among U.S. legislators, diplomats, and other politicians a strong distaste for any sustained analysis of foreign civilizations, because such analysis might (indeed, almost certainly would) demand recognition of permanent cultural pluralities and thus call for an effort at learning and imagination not required by its more comforting alternative. It is probably true that only those theories of international relations that postulate a fundamental convergence of all human aspirations with the American ideal have any chance of acceptance in the United States. It is probably equally true that no major power can conduct a successful foreign policy if such policy refuses to recognize that there exist in the world the most fundamental differences in the psychology and aspirations of its diverse inhabitants.

The current policy of "détente," as practiced in Washington, is no exception to these rules. To me at least, it appears to be without theoretical underpinnings and to repose on nothing more substantial than a vaguely felt and poorly articulated faith that the march of human events follows the script written by the Founding Fathers, and that if one can only avoid general war long enough all will be well. We are told that détente is vital because the only alternative to it is a nuclear holocaust. This, however, is an appeal to fear, not to reason. When pressed further, the proponents of détente justify it with offhand allusions to the "web of interests" that allegedly enmeshes the Soviet Union with the rest of the world and gradually forces it to behave like any other responsible member of the international community—as if a metaphor were a substitute for evidence or analysis. A convincing argument in favor of the present détente policy would require a close investigation of the internal situation in the Soviet Union, as it was, is, and becomes, insofar as a basic postulate of this policy holds that its pursuit will exert a lasting influence on the mind and behavior of the men who rule the USSR. It would demand, at the very least, an inquiry into the social structure of the USSR, its various "interest groups," the Communist party apparatus, the internal agitation and propaganda as they relate to détente, Soviet public opinion, and the Soviet government's ability to maintain its internal controls. It would seek to explain the apparent contradictions between the Soviet government's professions of détente and certain contrary actions such as incitement of its population to the "ideological struggle" against the West, the pursuit of an unabated pace of armaments, and the appeals made to the Arabs in 1973 to persevere with their oil embargo. Furthermore, it would analyze the probable effects of détente on the Western alliance system, on the morale of the dissidents and the non-Russian inhabitants of the Soviet Union, and on U.S.-Chinese relations. It would try to do this and much more that is clearly relevant. But in fact little analysis of this type has been attempted, and virtually none of it has been made public.

What makes such failure inexcusable is that the other party to détente certainly has done its homework. Whatever the limitations of their understanding of the United States (and they are considerable), the leaders of the Soviet Union at least have made the mental effort to place themselves in the position of the U.S. government and public. With the help of the expertise available at such of their international research institutes as IMEMO (The Institute of World Economy and International Relations) and ISShA (Institute of the U.S.A.), they have devised a policy of détente which serves their immediate interests without jeopardizing their long-term aspirations. *They* at least know what it is they want and how to try to go about getting it, by objectively analyzing Western strengths and weaknesses. And although the results of détente to date probably have not justified the Politburo's most sanguine expectations, thanks to an effort to understand the rival power it at least has managed to extract more than it has had to concede.

The purpose of this paper is to try to show how détente is viewed by Moscow. Much attention is given to internal factors, it being my conviction that in Russia, as elsewhere, political thinking and behavior are shaped largely by the experience gained in the arena of domestic politics. The argument in favor of this postulate is that politicians make their careers within a domestic power apparatus and, as a rule, gain the right to conduct their country's international affairs only after having successfully fought their way to the top of an internal power structure. (At any rate, the contrary almost never happens.) Foreign policy is thus an extension of domestic politics: It involves the application to other countries of habits acquired at home, in dealing with one's own subjects. The approach is also historical. Experience indicates that a country's internal politics evolve more gradually and prove more resistant to change than its foreign politics. It should be apparent that this approach differs fundamentally from that underlying the present administration's approach to the Soviet Union. The administration appears to assume the primacy of international politics (that is, the decisive impact of international relations on a country's domestic politics) and to ignore historical experience in favor of a "behavioral" response to the immediately given situation.

*   *   *

The first historical fact to be taken into account when dealing with the political life of Russia is that country's peculiar governmental tradition. For economic and geopolitical reasons that cannot be gone into here, during the nearly seven centuries that have elapsed since the founding of the Moscow monarchy the Russian state has claimed and, to the extent permitted by its limited means, actually exercised a kind of "proprietary" or "patrimonial" authority over the land and its inhabitants.[2] In a regime of this type, the government and its bureaucratic-military service elite feel that the country literally belongs to them and that in their capacity as its administrators and defenders they have the right to live at its expense without owing an accounting to anyone. Although Russian history has known several "liberal" interludes—notably the reigns of Catherine II and Alexander II—when attempts were undertaken to depart from this patrimonial tradition, these proved short-lived and without lasting effects. By expropriating all the "productive wealth" and much private property besides, the Soviet regime has dramatically reverted to this tradition (even though this had not been its founders' intention). In Communist Russia, as in Muscovite *Rus'*, the government as represented by the bureaucratic and military elites owns the country. No comforts or privileges in the USSR can be acquired save by favor of the state; and none are likely to be retained unless that state remains internally frozen and externally isolated.

This basic fact of Russian history has had many consequences for the modus operandi of Russian politicians, whatever the regime and its formal ideology. One of them of special relevance to détente is the intrinsically illiberal, antidemocratic spirit of Russian ruling elites. In "capitalist" countries it is in the interest of the elite composed of property owners to restrain the powers of the state, because the state is an adversary who, by means of taxes, regulations, and the threat of nationalization, prevents it from freely enjoying its property. By contrast, in the USSR or any other state where "property" is merely conditional possession dispensed by, and held at the grace of, the state, the elite has an interest in preventing the diminution of the state's power because this would inevitably result in the mass of the population demanding its rightful share of goods. The Soviet elite instinctively dislikes democratic processes, social initiative, and private property at home as well as abroad. In its relations with foreign powers it prefers to deal on a state-to-state basis, preferably on a "summit" level, bypassing as much as possible unpredictable legislatures that represent the citizenry. Because it fears emboldening its own population, it rejects people-to-people contacts, unless suitably chaperoned. Nor is the Soviet elite averse to corrupting democratic processes in foreign countries. In its relations with the Nixon Administration, the Soviet government placed its authority squarely behind the president during his various contests with Congress. Thus, in violation of accepted international practices, during President Nixon's June 1974 visit to Moscow, Brezhnev publicly sided with him against congressional critics of his foreign policy. The Soviet government has also openly encouraged private lobbies (for example, the National Association of Manufacturers) to apply pressure on Congress on its behalf and has urged the administration in diverse unsubtle ways to bypass Congress in concluding various agreements with it. Entering into business arrangements with European governments and private enterprises, the Soviet government has been known to insist on secrecy, which, in the long run, also tends to subvert democratic procedures.[3] In countries of the so-called Third World, representatives of the USSR openly exhort local governments to strengthen the "public" sector of the economy at the expense of the private.[4] Just as the capitalist entrepreneur feels most comfortable in an environment where everybody pursues his private profit, so the Soviet elite prefers to be surrounded by regimes of the "patrimonial" type, run by elites like itself.

Second, attention must be called to the persistent tradition of Russian expansion. Its causes are to be sought not in racial or cultural propensities (as a matter of fact, Russians are not noted for imperialist fantasies and dislike leaving their homeland), but rather in the same economic and geopolitical factors that account for Russia's peculiar tradition of government. Climate and topography conspire to make Russia a poor country, unable to support a population of high density: Among such causes are an exceedingly short agricultural season, abundant rainfall where the soil is of low quality and unreliable rainfall where it happens to be fertile, and great difficulties of transport (long distances, severe winters, and so on). The result has been unusually high population mobility, a steady outflow of the inhabitants in all directions, away from the historic center of Great Russia in the taiga, a process that, to judge by the censuses of 1959 and 1970, continues unabated to this very day. The movement is partly spontaneous, partly government sponsored. It is probably true that no country in recorded history has expanded so persistently and held on so tenaciously to every inch of conquered land. It is estimated, for example, that between the middle of the sixteenth century and the end of the seventeenth, Russia conquered territory the size of the modern Netherlands *every year* for *150 years* running. Not surprisingly, it has been the one imperial power after World War II not only to refuse to give up the colonial acquisitions made by its "feudal" and "bourgeois" predecessors, but to increase them by the addition of new dependencies acquired during the war in Eastern Europe and the Far East. Nothing can be further from the truth than the often heard argument that Russia's expansion is due to its sense of insecurity and need for buffers. Thanks to its topography (immense depth of defense, low population density, and poor transport) Russia has always been and continues to be the world's most difficult country to conquer, as Charles XII, Napoleon, and Hitler each in turn found out. As for buffers, it is no secret that today's buffers have a way of becoming tomorrow's homeland, which requires new buffers to protect it. Indeed, a great deal of Soviet military activity in Western Europe in recent years has been justified by the alleged need to defend Russia's interests in Eastern Europe, which interests Russia had originally acquired with the tacit acquiescence of the West as a buffer zone. It is far better to seek the causes of Russian expansionism in internal impulses springing from primarily economic conditions and the habits that they breed.

In this connection it deserves note that the population movement, which initially took the form of spontaneous colonization and in time became increasingly dependent on conquest, has from the earliest times brought Russians into intimate contact with a great variety of nations and races. It has taught them how to handle "natives" and how to exploit to their advantage "contradictions" present in neighboring countries for the purpose of weakening and subverting them preparatory to annexation. To understand some of the techniques presently employed on a global scale by Soviet diplomacy one can do no better than study the history of Moscow's conquest of Novgorod (fifteenth century), the Golden Horde (sixteenth century), and the Polish-Lithuanian Commonwealth (eighteenth century), as well as the efforts of Imperial Russia in the nineteenth century (largely frustrated by Western countermeasures) to partition the Ottoman Empire and China. No other country has a comparable wealth of accumulated experience in the application of external and internal pressures on neighbors for the purpose of softening them prior to conquest.

The third historical factor to which attention must be called in assessing Soviet attitudes to détente is the personal background of the elite that at the present time happens to govern the Soviet Union. This group rose to positions of power in the 1930s, in the turmoil of Stalin's purges and massacres—that is, under conditions of the most ruthless political infighting known in modern history. No ruling elite in the world has had to learn survival under more difficult and brutal circumstances. This elite is the product of a process of natural selection under which the fittest proved to be those who knew best how to suppress within themselves everything normally regarded as human—where indeed the "dictator of genius" treated any expression of human qualities as personal disloyalty and usually punished it with deportation or death. No one dealing with Brezhnev and his colleagues ought to forget this fact.[5]

The fourth historical fact bearing on détente is that the elite currently ruling the Soviet Union is for all practical purposes directly descended from a peasantry. This holds true also of those of its members whose parents were industrial workers or urban petty bourgeois (*meshchane*) because a large part of Russian industry was traditionally located in the countryside, and much of the so-called urban population consisted of peasants temporarily licensed to reside in cities. Now the Russian *muzhik* is a very complicated being: The mysteries of his character form a puzzle that has engrossed some of Russia's finest literary minds. Certainly no quick characterization can hope to succeed where some of the greatest writers have tried their talents. However, as far as his social and political attitudes are concerned (and these alone matter where détente is concerned) it must be borne in mind that during the past four centuries (the brief interlude 1861–1928 apart) [a high proportion]

of Russian peasants has been serfs—that is, they had few if
any legally recognized rights, were tied to the soil, and did not
own the land they cultivated. They managed to survive under
these conditions not by entrusting themselves to the protection
of laws and customs, but by exercising extreme cunning and
single-mindedly pursuing their private interests. This experience
has left deep marks on the psyche of ordinary Russians. The
world view of such people, including those running the Communist party apparatus, is better studied from Russian proverbs
(for example, Dal's *Poslovitsy russkogo naroda*) than from the
collected works of the "coryphaei" of Marxism-Leninism. The
basic thrust of these proverbs is that life is hard and that to survive one must learn to take care of oneself and one's own,
without wasting much thought on others ("the tears of others
are water"). Force is one of the surest means of getting one's
way (*"bei Russkogo, chasy sdelaet"*—"beat a Russian and he
will make you a watch"). In personal relations, the Russian
peasant always was and probably still remains one of the
kindest creatures on earth, and nowhere can a stranger in need
feel more certain of finding sympathy and help than in a Russian
village. But these qualities of decency and empathy (unfortunately, much corrupted by the trauma of Stalinism) have
never been successfully institutionalized: They tend to vanish
the instant the Russian peasant leaves the familiar environment
of personal contacts and becomes a stranger among strangers.
When this happens, he is likely to view the world as a ruthless
fighting ground, where one either eats others or is eaten by
them, where one plays either the pike or the carp.

These various elements of historical experience blend to
create a very special kind of mentality, which stresses slyness,
self-interest, reliance on force, skill in exploiting others, and,
by inference, contempt for those unable to fend for themselves.
Marxism-Leninism, which in its theoretical aspects exerts minor
influence on Soviet conduct, through its ideology of "class
warfare" reinforces these existing predispositions.

Admittedly, history does not stand still. There are examples
on hand to indicate that deep national experiences or vastly
changed conditions can indeed alter a people's psychology. The
consciousness of a people and the mentality of its elite are

constantly affected by life around them. But in the case of Russia, all the great national experiences, especially since 1917, happened to reinforce the illiberal and antidemocratic impulses. It is surely unreasonable to expect that the increase of U.S.-USSR trade from $1 billion to, say, $5 billion a year, or agreements on joint medical research, or broadened (but fully controlled) cultural exchanges will wipe the slate clean of centuries of accumulated and dearly bought experience. Nothing short of a major cataclysm that would demonstrate beyond doubt that impulses rooted in its history have lost their validity is likely to affect the collective outlook of the Russian nation and change it, as defeat has caused the Germans or Japanese to turn away from dictatorships, and the Nazi massacres have caused the Jews to abandon their traditional pacifism. Unless and until that happens, one can ignore Russia's historical tradition only at great risk.

Détente and Soviet Policy

In order to understand how, in view of what has just been said of its outlook on life, the Soviet government initiated a policy of détente with the West, one must consider the situation in which the Soviet Union found itself after the death of Stalin.

Genealogically, détente is an offset from the "peaceful coexistence" inaugurated by the Khrushchev administration nearly twenty years ago. But "peaceful coexistence" itself was much less of an innovation in Soviet foreign policy than world opinion, anxious to have the burden of the cold war lifted from its shoulders, liked to believe. It had been an essential ingredient of Lenin's political strategy both before and after 1917 that when operating from a position of weakness one had to exploit "contradictions" in the enemy camp, and this entailed a readiness to make compacts with any government or political grouping, whatever its ideology. "Direct action" ran very much against Lenin's grain. In 1920, when he expelled the Anarchists from the Third International, the charge that he leveled against them (and that his successors of the 1950s and 1960s revived against the Chinese communists) was a dogmatic rejection of the *divide et impera* principle. Both he and Stalin made no secret of the fact that in their foreign policy dealings expediency was always the principal consideration. Hitler was barely one year in power (into which he had been carried by a viciously anticommunist campaign) when Stalin approached him in a public overture. At the XVIIth Party Congress, held in 1934, he announced his willingness to establish with Nazi Germany a relationship that today would be characterized as one of détente. Stalin declared on this occasion:

> Of course, we are far from being enthusiastic about [Hitler's] fascist regime in Germany. But it is not a question of fascism here, if only for the reason that fascism in Italy, for example, has not prevented the U.S.S.R. from establishing the best relations with that country.[6]

Inaugurating détentes (as well as calling them off) is for the USSR a relatively easy matter: There exist for such action ample historic precedent and more than adequate theoretical justification. A "soft" foreign line must, therefore, under no conditions be interpreted as prima facie evidence of a change in the basic political orientation of the Soviet Union.

Behind the "peaceful coexistence" drive inaugurated in the mid-1950s and reinforced by decisions made in the early 1970s lay several considerations. Some of these had to do with the need to overcome the disastrous consequences of Stalin's rule; others, with changes in the world situation.

The most immediate task facing Stalin's successors was the need to give the country a chance to lick its wounds after twenty years of privations, terror, and bloodletting of unprecedented dimensions. Stalin had assured himself that no opposition could endanger his dictatorship, but he did so at the cost of draining the citizenry of all vitality. In the mid-1950s the population of the Soviet Union was spiritually exhausted, as can be confirmed by those who had a chance then to visit the country.

Looking beyond these most pressing exigencies, it was thought imperative to extricate the USSR from the diplomatic-military predicament in which Stalin's postwar policies had placed it. Every attempt by Stalin to bully the West had caused the West to close ranks and build up its military potential. The net effect of Stalin's intransigent aggressiveness had been to enhance the role of the United States as leader of the noncommunist majority of humanity and, correspondingly, to isolate the Soviet Union. A different, more pliable and indirect strategy seemed to promise much better results. One had to initiate friendly relations with the freshly liberated colonies of the West, which Stalin had rudely alienated on the grounds that they were dominated by a "national bourgeoisie," allegedly tied to the apron strings of its departed colonial masters. Further, one had to establish contacts with all kinds of political groupings and movements of public opinion in the United States and Western Europe that, without being friendly to the Soviet cause, could nevertheless serve its purposes. In short, instead of following Stalin's (and Lenin's) dictum "who is not with us is against us," it was thought preferable to adopt for an indeterminate time the principle "who is not against us is with us"—a more sophisticated political strategy first devised by the Russian Social Democrats in the 1880s in their struggle against the imperial regime.

The third problem confronting Stalin's successors derived from the development of strategic nuclear weapons. Stalin had ordered his military to provide him with a nuclear arsenal, but it is doubtful whether he fully appreciated the implications and uses of nuclear weapons. His successors seem to have realized that after Hiroshima nothing would ever be the same again. War with such weapons was suicidal, and this meant that one could no longer count on mere quantitative and qualitative superiority in weapons to assure hegemony. This realization must have strengthened the resolve of the new leadership to depart from the strategy of confrontations with the West, pursued by Stalin in emulation of Hitler.

Such appear to have been the principal considerations behind the decision, taken in 1954–1955, to reverse the "hard" line pursued by Stalin since the end of the war and adopt in its place a "soft" strategy. The plan was simple and attractive: By means of a reasonably long period of relaxation of internal and international tensions to energize the Soviet population and reinfuse it with the enthusiasm of the early years of communism; to break the ring of alliances forged by the United States around the Soviet Union; to gain support of the Third

World and public opinion in the West; and in this manner to initiate a gradual shift of the international balance of power in favor of the USSR. One of the implicit assumptions of this strategy was that during the era of "peaceful coexistence" the Soviet Union would greatly improve its economic potential and, by devoting a goodly share of the growing national product to defense, would expand its military power so as to attain parity or even superiority vis-à-vis the United States. The end goal of this policy was to turn the tables on the United States and, by containing the would-be container, drive him into the corner into which he had driven the USSR during the cold war.

The Khrushchev policy succeeded up to a point. The Third World responded enthusiastically to Soviet diplomatic overtures and offers of economic and military aid. Western opinion appeared more than ready to put Stalin out of mind and accept at face value professions of the Soviet government that it had no wish to export revolutions. America's leadership remained suspicious, the more so that every now and then détente was tested by means of strong-arm methods reminiscent of the coldest cold war.[7] But by persuading President Eisenhower to acknowledge in principle the necessity of renouncing war between their two countries, Khrushchev scored a major success. He planted an idea that, once adopted, would have caused the West to give up its strongest weapon against the Soviet Union—superiority in strategic weapons—without the Soviet Union being compelled in return to forfeit political and ideological warfare, at which it excelled.

This policy's principal failure was economic. In his exuberance, a kind of throwback to the early 1930s and First Five-Year Plan when his own political career got underway, Khrushchev seems to have believed that, given a fair chance, the Soviet economy, thanks to the advantages inherent in planning, would catch up and overtake the U.S. economy. He also thought that this economic progress would accelerate the shift in the international balance of power on which he counted to achieve an ultimate isolation of the United States. But being a rather primitive, commonsensical man (judging by his memoirs), Khrushchev had little idea how much the world economy had changed since the days when he had helped Stalin with his Five-Year Plans. While he kept his eyes riveted on statistics of steel production, a technological revolution was reshaping the economies of the capitalist countries. After Khrushchev's removal, it became apparent to the new Soviet leadership that, notwithstanding the upward movement of their productive indices, Russia and its bloc were steadily falling behind the United States, Western Europe, and Japan.[8] One symptom of this fact was the decline in the Eastern bloc's participation in world trade. Between 1966 and 1973 the share of world exports of the USSR and the six "People's Democracies" declined from 11.4 to 9.0 percent; the Soviet Union's share dropped from 4.3 to 3.4 percent.[9] These figures suggested that owing to some basic flaws—technological backwardness, poor management, bad planning—the communist countries not only were not catching up with the capitalist countries but were failing to keep pace with them; and this, in turn, meant that the automatic shift in the balance of power postulated by "peaceful coexistence" would not take place either.

Tackling this matter presented formidable difficulties; and it is testimony to the courage and capacity at objective analysis of the post-Khrushchev Soviet leadership that its members acknowledged the problem and boldly set themselves to deal with it. They had two basic alternatives open to them. One was to carry out major economic reforms of the kind that had been discussed and even halfheartedly attempted in the late 1950s. This course, however, posed certain political dangers. All proposals of economic reform current in the communist bloc called for a certain degree of decentralization of economic decision making. But decentralization of the communist economy always threatens to end up in decentralization of the political process, for where the state owns the economy there can be no firm line separating economics from politics, and no effective way of ensuring that reform stays within safe limits. If there was any chance of the Politburo adopting the path of internal reform it was eliminated by the experience of Czechoslovakia in 1968, which showed how quickly and irreversibly economic reform led to a breakdown of communist controls.

So there was only the other alternative left—instead of economic reform, economic aid from abroad. It was easier to swallow the idea that all the Soviet economy needed to put it right was Western technical know-how than to concede that the fault lay with bureaucratic centralism—easier because to concede the latter point meant to put in question the Soviet system as a whole. The decision, formally ratified at the XXIVth Party Congress in 1971, must have been accompanied by anxious soul-searching. It marked one of the major turning points in the history of the Soviet Union, and only the widespread contempt for, and ignorance of, history among people who occupy themselves with Soviet affairs explains why Western opinion has not been made aware of this fact. It had been one of the principal claims of the Bolsheviks before coming to power that Russia was an economic colony of the imperialist West, and one of their proudest boasts upon assuming power was that they had freed Russia from this degrading dependence. The fact that fifty-odd years after the Revolution, the Soviet Union, in the words of Chou En-lai, has to go "begging for loans" and put "its resources for sale"[10] is a tacit admission of stupendous failure. It signifies that notwithstanding all the human sacrifices and privations of the past half century, the Soviet system has not been able to generate the resources, skills, and enterprise necessary to keep the pace set by the allegedly wasteful, crisis-ridden free economies. The humiliation is extreme. To convey what it would mean in terms of American history one would have to imagine the United States in the 1850s, threatened by Civil War, concluding that it was, after all, incapable of governing itself and requesting Britain temporarily to assume charge of its administration. The point needs emphasis because only if one realizes how agonizing the decision to seek Western economic assistance must have been for Soviet leaders can one appreciate how desperate was the need that drove them to it and gain an idea of the price the West could demand for its help. It makes one much less anxious than the present U.S. administration seems to be lest too hard bargaining on our part should cause the USSR to abandon détente.

Major Soviet Strategic Objectives of Détente

The national policy of the Soviet Union is distinguished by a high degree of strategic and tactical coordination. Because it is the same group of people—the Politburo—who bear ultimate responsibility for the totality of domestic and foreign decisions, they have no choice but to package their policies, as it were, into neat bundles, without loose ends. The kind of situation that exists in the United States where authority over people and objects is widely distributed—with the administration pulling one way and Congress another, with industry looking out for its own interests and the media for theirs—such a situation is, of course, unthinkable in the Soviet Union. Even the most sanguine believer in the "interest group" approach to Soviet politics would not go so far as to see in them an arena of untrammeled competition.

Lest the use of the terms "strategy" and "tactics" in the Soviet context arouse in the reader the suspicion that we are employing cold war terminology, it must be said at the outset that Soviet theoreticians insist that they are, in fact, thinking in strategic and tactical terms when making political decisions. The following passage, taken from a standard Soviet party manual, makes this point without equivocation:

> The measures which make up the activity of the Marxist-Leninist Party are not the result of improvisations of the party leadership. They represent the concrete expression of the *political line,* which is worked out by the party on the basis of scientific analysis of a given phase of the struggle and a given situation. In the political language to describe this line one also uses the concepts of *tactics* and *strategy.* . . .

> At the present time, Communists talk of strategy or the strategic line when referring to the party's general line, which aims at the fulfillment of the principal tasks of the given historical phase, proceeding from the existing correlation of forces among the classes. In this respect strategy differs from tactics, which defines the *current policy* and which is worked out on the basis of the party's general line for a briefer period (e.g., tactics in an electoral campaign, the attitude toward the maneuvers of right-wing socialist leaders, the approach to left socialists, etc.).[11]

One can, of course, dismiss such claims as meaningless pretense on the grounds that in the end all politics must be improvisation and that no country, the Soviet Union least of all, operates in accord with preconceived "scientific analysis." This argument is correct, but only up to a point. After all, in military affairs, where no one would deny the applicability of the concepts of strategy and tactics, it is improvisation, too, and not "science" that wins battles. Yet who would argue that one can wage war successfully without some strategic concept and tactical skill? In the end, the terms "strategy" and "tactics" always mean economy of force, whether we speak of warfare, of politics, of investment, or of athletic contests; he who seeks to attain any objective with insufficient means must employ some kind of strategic and tactical concept lest he hopelessly scatter his resources. In this sense, any strategy and any improvisation carried out within some strategic design are better than no strategy at all.

The Soviet effort at coordination of policy facilitates the task of the observer. Here we shall attempt to delineate in their broad outlines the principal tasks of the strategy and tactics of détente as they may be perceived by Moscow.

Inside the Soviet Union

Internally in the USSR the highest priority is attached to political security—that is, to preventing the idea of relaxation of tensions with the "capitalist" world from leading Soviet citizens to question the necessity of preserving the dictatorial regime. To this end, the Party's leadership has emphatically committed itself to the line that détente does not mean an end to the conflict between capitalism and socialism or any convergence between the two systems.[12]

One of the major tasks of the whole vast agitprop machinery in the USSR is to keep up the "ideological struggle" against hostile or alien ideologies and to forestall any blurring of the lines separating the two systems. Increased internal controls, symbolized by the recent promotion of the head of the KGB to the Politburo and, even more so, by the dismissal of P. N. Demichev as Secretary for Agitation and Propaganda (see below, p. 106) are manifestations of that effort.

Related is the drive to enhance Soviet Russia's military posture. We shall revert to this subject later on. Here we must merely point out that the military effort is in no small measure inspired by the fear that détente could lead to internal relaxation and thus to a dissolution of the system. It is as if Soviet leaders felt that by keeping up a steady tempo of armaments they were helping to maintain that state of tension that is required to keep the system intact.

The failure, promises notwithstanding, to give the population more consumer goods probably stems from the same motive. Consumerism, as Russian leaders had the opportunity to observe in the West, leads to a decline in public spirit and an addiction to comfort that significantly diminishes the state's ability to mobilize the citizenry.

Toward the United States

One of the highest priorities of the Soviet Union in dealing with the United States has been to gain recognition as an equal, that is, as one of two world "superpowers," and hence a country with a legitimate claim to have its say in the solution of all international problems, even those without immediate bearing on its national interests. Recognition of this status is essential because only by establishing itself in the eyes of the world as an alternate pole to that represented by the United States can the Soviet Union hope to set in motion the shift in the world balance of power that is the long-term aim of its foreign policy. To achieve and maintain this status, the USSR requires an immense up-to-date military establishment with a devastating destructive capability, for in Moscow's eyes to be a "superpower" means nothing more or less than to have the capacity to face the United States down in a nuclear confrontation.

It is very much in the interest of the USSR to induce the United States to renounce or at least limit (regulate) the use of those instruments of power politics at which it enjoys a pronounced advantage, and to do so without offering reciprocal concessions. This means, in the first place, reducing to the maximum extent possible the threat posed by the American strategic nuclear arsenal. The various agreements into which the United States has entered with the USSR for the purpose of controlling and limiting the use of nuclear weapons certainly have not been accompanied by concessions on the part of the Soviet Union to restrain those instruments of power politics at which it is superior, namely, subversion and ideological warfare— and in this sense, such agreements are inherently inequitable.

Because of its planned and coordinated character, and because of its unwillingness to relegate authority farther down
its bureaucratic hierarchy, the Soviet system is intrinsically
offensive-minded: It always prefers to take the initiative, inasmuch as he who initiates an action has better control of his
forces than he who responds to the actions of others. Time and
again, when it has been forced to respond to firm initiatives
(for example, the U.S. blockade of Cuba in 1962 or Israel's
preemptive strike against the Arabs in 1967) the Soviet government has reacted in a manner that suggested a mental state
bordering on panic. For this reason it is very valuable for the
Soviet Union to be aware at all times of its rivals' intentions.
The practice of regular U.S.-USSR consultations, instituted in
the past decade, works greatly to the advantage of the Soviet
leadership. The fact that the Soviet ambassador in Washington
has virtually free access to the president, and indeed has been
known to travel to Moscow on the same plane with the American secretary of state, assures the Politburo that it is reasonably
well informed of major American initiatives before they occur.
By terms of the U.S.-USSR [declaration of "Basic Principles
of Relations" of May 29, 1972, the signatories obligated themselves not to "obtain unilateral advantage at the expense of the
other, directly or indirectly"]. It is far from clear that the
Soviet Union kept its part of the bargain in early October 1973
having learned at least a few days ahead of time of the impending Egyptian-Syrian attack on Israel. At any rate, it was neither
commended nor criticized publicly by the U.S. administration
for its behavior on this occasion. Yet it is reasonably certain
that the Soviet Union would secure from the United States the
relevant information should the roles be reversed.

Although it sometimes threatens to seek the capital and
technology it requires in Western Europe and Japan, the Soviet
Union has no viable alternative to the United States because it is
only here that the capital and productivity it needs are available
in sufficient quantities. Furthermore, U.S. corporations control
worldwide rights to the most advanced technology. Part of the
strategy of détente is to exploit the need of the U.S. economy
for raw materials and markets so as to induce it to help with a
fundamental modernization of the economy of the Soviet

Union. Last but not least, because the United States is the only country able to deal with the USSR as an equal in any contest of wills, other potential investors (most notably Japan) have been reluctant to commit large sums in the USSR without U.S. participation for fear of ultimate expropriation—a fact which makes American economic cooperation doubly valuable to the Russians.

Toward Western Europe

It seems probable that the long-term objective of Soviet foreign policy is to detach Western Europe from its dependence on the United States, especially where defense is concerned, and to make it dependent on the USSR. It is difficult to conceive of any event that would more dramatically enhance Soviet power and tilt the "correlation of forces," so dear to its theorists, to its advantage. Russian military power resting on a West European economic base would give the USSR indisputable world hegemony—the sort of thing that Hitler was dreaming of when, having conquered continental Europe, he attempted to annex to it Soviet Russia's natural resources and manpower. However, the separation of Western Europe from the United States must not be hurried. The Soviet leadership has taken a measure of U.S. politics and knows (whatever its propagandists may say) that it faces no danger from that side. After all, if the United States had any aggressive intentions toward the USSR it would have made its moves in the late 1940s or early 1950s when its monopoly on nuclear weapons allowed it to do so with impunity. The U.S. forces in Western Europe present no offensive threat to the Soviet Union. Their ultimate removal is essential if the USSR is to control Western Europe, but their purely defensive character does not seriously inhibit Russia's freedom to maneuver. What the Soviet Union fears more is a German-French-English military alliance that might spring into existence should U.S. troops withdraw precipitately from Western Europe. The Russians are well aware that close to the surface of what appears to be a "neutralist" Western Europe there lurk powerful nationalist sentiments that could easily assume militant forms. Nor do they forget that England and France have nuclear deterrents that they could place at West Germany's disposal.

Hasty action on their part, therefore, could cause the emergence on their western flank of a nuclear threat probably much greater than that which they face in the east, from China, [as well as] from the United States. As long as the United States is in control of European defenses, this development is not likely to occur. Hence Soviet strategy is to hurry slowly.

If realized, the European security system for which the Russians have been pressing with moderate success for many years would give them a kind of veto power over West European politics, military affairs included. It would make them arbiters of West European defense and thus preclude the emergence of an effective West European military force equipped with nuclear weapons.

The Soviet Union is seeking to make the West European countries maximally dependent on the Eastern bloc, without, however, losing its own freedom of action. It tries to achieve this end by the following means: promoting heavy indebtedness of the Comecon countries; gaining maximum control of West European energy supplies (oil, natural gas, fuel for nuclear reactors); and promoting "cooperative" arrangements with West European business firms. For its part, the USSR (the other Comecon countries to a lesser extent) seeks to confine Western economic aid to "turnkey operations" and similar devices that minimize dependence on foreign sources. In their dealings with Western Europe, the Russians like to insist on very long-term arrangements, which would have the effect of tying Western economies to the Soviet economic plans. In some cases they even propose deals that would run for up to fifty years.[13] The effect of such economic relations would be increasingly to link the economies of Western Europe with those of Eastern Europe.

Toward the Third World

The Third World that interests the Soviet Union the most is that which adjoins its long and strategically vulnerable southern frontier. This perimeter is an area of primary importance and the theater of its most determined political, economic, and military activity. Suffice it to say that two-thirds of all foreign military and economic aid extended by the USSR between

1954 and 1972 went to six countries located in this region (India, Egypt, Iran, Afghanistan, Iraq, and Turkey). Africa and Latin America are of much smaller concern, and the same holds true of Southeast Asia.

On no political subject have Soviet theoreticians spilled more ink than on what strategy and tactics to adopt toward the underdeveloped countries. Analyzing Soviet behavior in this vast region, one can discern three consecutive strategic lines:

1. In the late 1950s, in the first flush of enthusiasm, the Soviet Union scattered its limited resources far and wide, helping any and all regimes that seemed ready to collaborate with it against the United States and the rest of the "imperialist camp." Much of this "water can" aid strategy ended badly, and a great deal of the investment went down the drain, in large part because the Russians were unfamiliar with the infinite variety of local situations, each calling for fine political and economic nuances.

2. To overcome this squandering of resources, in the early 1960s the theory of "national democracy" was pushed to the fore. This theory viewed the underdeveloped countries as in varying degrees of transition from feudal to socialist society and maintained that it was possible as well as desirable for them to bypass the capitalist phase. Soviet aid went to those countries which were prepared to expand the "public sector" at the expense of the "private," thereby eliminating Western influence, undermining the native bourgeoisie, and creating cadres of socialist functionaries hostile to capitalism. A prerequisite was political "democracy," by which was meant allowing Communist parties in these countries to surface and gradually to assume leadership of the "progressive" forces moving toward socialism. This policy too proved unsuccessful, in part because of the chronic instability of the governments of the "national democracies," and in part because most of these countries remained adamantly hostile toward their native Communist parties. By the late 1960s it became apparent that the Chinese, who had criticized this strategy from the beginning on the grounds that its net effect would be to promote in the Third World sturdy state capitalisms, may well have been correct.

3. Around 1970 the Soviet government began to adopt

another strategy toward underdeveloped countries, one based less on political or military and more on economic considerations. Aid at present is extended as part of a broadly conceived Soviet "complex" plan intended gradually to mesh the economies of the underdeveloped countries with those of the Comecon. Its hoped for result is a double effect of complementing Comecon economies (for example, with raw materials) and creating deep ties of economic (and ultimately, political) interdependence.

The common aim of the three consecutive Soviet strategies toward the Third World has been to cut off the capitalist countries from sources of raw materials and cheap labor, to deprive them of military bases, and ultimately to isolate them. The undertaking, however, is complicated and exacerbated by Russia's conflict with China. The Chinese are threatening the USSR from a flank which they had been always accustomed to regard as secure—namely, the political Left. They are trying to wean away the radical and nationalist constituency in the underdeveloped countries that since 1917 had been viewed from Moscow as a safe preserve. The Soviet Union cannot allow China to do this, least of all in regions adjacent to its own territory, and this fact compels it to take vigorous counteraction. From East Africa to Southeast Asia a bitter fight is being waged between Russia and China for hegemony over the local governments. Though little discussed in the press, it may well be the most significant political struggle in the world at large today. By means of military and economic aid programs, the cost of which must represent a heavy burden to their economies, the two powers contend for allies as each seeks to expel the influence of its rival.

Toward Communist China

Having tried every means at its disposal from appeals to sentiment to officially leaked rumors of a preemptive nuclear strike to bring China back into the fold, the Soviet Union appears to have settled on a patient strategy of containment. The immense military force concentrated on China's border (apparently defensive in posture) assures that China will not lightheartedly encroach on Soviet territory. The Soviet effort in the rest of

Asia, and among the left-wing, nationalist movements elsewhere, alluded to earlier has so far been successful in preventing the Chinese from seizing control of major territorial or political bases of potential use against the USSR. One of the greatest benefits of détente for the Soviet Union has been the unwillingness of the United States to exploit the Sino-Soviet conflict to its own advantage by pursuing more vigorously a "détente" with China. If détente with the United States had no other justification, this alone would suffice to keep it alive, as far as the Soviet Union is concerned.

The Soviet Union appears to have decided not to exacerbate further its relations with China, but to await opportunities for intervention in internal Chinese affairs, which are likely to open up after Mao's death. In the long run the USSR will probably strive for a breakup of China into several independent territorial entities. After the experience with Mao, even the emergence of a pro-Moscow successor government in Peking would not still Russia's long-term fears of China. A China separated by spacious buffer states (Sinkiang, Inner Mongolia, Manchuria) would be a far more comfortable neighbor to live with.

The political strategy we have outlined suffers from obvious contradictions. It seems odd, for instance, to urge multinational corporations to invest in the USSR while seeking to expel them from the Third World. Or to ask for economic assistance from the United States while building up a military machine directed against the same United States. Or to intervene in the internal affairs of other countries while denying anyone the right to interfere in its own. But each of the adversaries of this global policy tends to see only one of its facets at a time and to remain unaware of the whole picture, which facilitates the execution of what otherwise might have become an impractical line of conduct.

Soviet Tactics for Implementing Détente

At the very beginning of any discussion of Soviet methods of implementing détente, attention must be called to prudence as a feature common to all Soviet tactics. A certain paradox inheres in the Soviet Union: It is at the same time immensely strong and fatally weak. Its strength derives from the ability to marshal all its national resources in the service of any chosen cause; its weakness, from the necessity always to succeed or at least to appear to do so. The Soviet government lacks a legitimate mandate to rule and can never risk putting its credentials (that is, force) in question. Failure effectively to apply power abroad would at once raise doubts in the minds of Soviet citizens about the regime's ability to cope with internal opposition; and any loss of public faith in the omnipotence of the regime (and hence in the futility of resistance to it) might prove the beginning of the end. Thus the Soviet regime finds itself in the extremely difficult situation of having to create the impression of a relentless advance forward as it in fact moves very cautiously and slowly. It can act decisively only when it has a near 100 percent assurance of success, which, of course, occurs rarely.

Related is the habit of overinsuring by keeping open all options. The Soviet leadership by ingrained habit never places its eggs in one basket. It maintains some form of contact with all foreign political parties, from extreme Right to extreme Left; it builds up conventional forces as well as nuclear ones and simultaneously expands its naval arm—in all the service branches it accumulates masses of weapons, old and new, just to be on the safe side; in its economic drive, once the decision to seek help abroad had been taken, it sought to deal with everybody— the United States, Western Europe, Japan, and even such powers of second rank as Brazil. The lack of selectivity indicates insecurity lurking very close behind the airs of supreme self-confidence that Soviet leaders like to exude in public.

In our discussion of tactics we shall deal, successively, with political, military, and economic measures, concentrating on Soviet operations vis-à-vis Western Europe.

Some Political Tactics

The basic political tactic employed by the USSR on a global scale since its acquisition of nuclear weapons has been to try to reduce all politics to the issue of preserving the peace. The line it advocates holds that the principal danger facing humanity today is the threat of a nuclear holocaust, for which reason anything that in any way risks exacerbating relations between the powers, and above all between the United States and the

Soviet Union, is evil. This line (which happens to have been adopted by President Nixon and Secretary of State Kissinger) has two advantages from the Soviet point of view:

1. It offers it an opportunity to silence external criticism of the Soviet Union, for no matter what the Soviet Union may do or fail to do, good relations with it must never be jeopardized. A crass example of this tactic is to be found in arguments advanced by the USSR and echoed by certain Western politicians and commentators that the West should not support dissident movements inside the USSR, lest this exacerbate relations between the superpowers and thereby heighten the risk of war.

2. It allows the Soviet Union to avoid questions touching on the nature of the peace that is to result from détente. Peace becomes an end in itself. The issue of freedom is relegated to the margin, for once survival is at stake, who is going to haggle over the conditions?

As has been suggested earlier, the Soviet strategy for Europe is gradually to detach the Western half from the United States and bring it within the Soviet orbit. To achieve this end, the Soviet government works intensively to promote and make dependent on its goodwill parties and movements in the West that, whatever their motivation and attitude toward communism, happen at a particular time to further this end. Soviet support of de Gaulle represents a clear example of this tactic. Once the French leader had set himself earnestly to reduce American influence on the Continent, the USSR extended to him the hand of friendship, even though behind him stood the anticommunist Right. Very instructive, too, has been Soviet behavior in the 1974 French presidential election. Although Mitterand ran on a common ticket with the Communist party and in the event of victory was committed to put ministerial posts at its disposal, the Soviet government treated him with reserve. The reason behind this coolness seems to have been, not the fear of embarrassing the left-wing ticket and thus handing useful campaign ammunition to his opponent, but uncertainty about Mitterand's foreign policy views.[14] The same holds true of Moscow's behavior in the U.S. presidential election of 1972. On the face of it, Russia could have been expected to support Senator McGovern, because he advocated drastic cuts in the defense budget and reductions in American military commitments abroad, Europe included. But the Democratic candidate seemed to appeal to isolationist sentiments that at this juncture are not in Soviet Russia's interest. The policy of détente postulates a U.S. administration willing to assume certain global responsibilities (at any rate, in the immediate future); any other administration would be unlikely to favor the huge loans, investments, and sharing of technical knowledge that the Soviet Union seeks from the United States. Further, as noted, Moscow fears a precipitate withdrawal of U.S. troops from Europe, as advocated by McGovern, preferring such a withdrawal to proceed piecemeal and in the context of a European "security pact." For all these reasons Moscow preferred to back President Nixon.

Such tactics require Moscow to have friendly access to all kinds of political groupings, no matter what their ideology. It could well happen that a European party committed to anti-communism should also turn out to be very anti-American, in which case its attitudes toward the USSR could be temporarily overlooked. On the other hand, a Communist party in power might choose to pursue an independent foreign policy that was harmful to Soviet interests. It is not inconceivable, for instance, that in view of its advocacy of a "European" policy line, the Italian Communist party may appear in Moscow's eyes a less palatable alternative to the present Christian Democratic government than a fascist one. In general, Moscow does not seem all that anxious to promote at this time Communist parties in Europe, apparently preferring to deal with parties of the center and to the right of it. Direct cooperation with the West European "establishment" has proved very profitable. It is undoubtedly safer to exploit the "bourgeois" desire for profits and peace than to incite the Left and risk a backlash and possibly even open the door to Chinese penetration.

A persistent feature of Soviet policy toward Western Europe has been the effort to break up all political, economic, and military alliances, the very existence of which obstructs Soviet objectives. Originally, the Soviet Union did whatever it could to frustrate the creation of the Common Market (EEC). Later, it reconciled itself to the EEC's existence, although it continues to refuse to treat it as a juridical entity and by various means tries to bypass it. (For example, anticipating the establishment of EEC control over all foreign trade of its member states as of January 1, 1973, the Soviet Union has promoted bilateral "cooperative" arrangements with West European countries, which so far have remained exempt from central EEC management.) The difficulties that the EEC has experienced in recent years, including the breakdown of its unity during the October 1973 war, has certainly not been lost on Moscow.[15] There is also some reason to expect that the Soviet Union may ultimately succeed, as a result of the European "security pact" that it has avidly sponsored, in emasculating NATO.

The pursuit of Soviet strategy in the West entails a steady increase of Soviet intervention in the West's internal life. This effort, so far, has had very limited success, but it represents a development deserving greater attention than it ordinarily receives. In the United States, the Soviet Union has established a lobby that can reveal on occasion an astonishing degree of activity. Represented by diplomats, journalists, and occasional delegates from Eastern Europe, it operates on Capitol Hill, in business organizations, at universities, and in learned societies, and its purpose is the promotion of legislation favorable to the Soviet Union. Perhaps the lobby's most ambitious effort has been mounted against the amendment introduced by Senator Jackson to the Trade Bill which would deny the USSR and other nonmarket economies Most Favored Nation status until they accord their citizens the right of unrestricted emigration. Great pressures have been brought to bear upon Senator Jackson and the co-sponsors of his amendment to have it withdrawn in which, at various stages, the National Association of Manufacturers and some leaders of the Jewish community in the United States, acting in what they considered their constituents' best interests, were involved.

In the United States, these pressures to interfere with domestic politics have so far had little success. In Western Europe the Russians have been more fortunate. The idea is gaining acceptance in Western Europe that nothing must be done that could be interpreted in the USSR as endangering its security or challenging its prestige. An outstanding example of this is the willingness of Norway to prohibit international companies from exploring oil deposits under the waters along its northern sea-coast, where the Soviet Union is anxious to keep NATO away from the sea-lanes used by its naval units stationed at Murmansk. Negotiations in progress between the two governments seem to point to the recognition by Norway that oil exploration in this area will be carried out either by itself alone or in cooperation with the Soviet government.[16]

Pressures are being exerted on European governments and private enterprises to prevent the spread of literary works un-favorable to the Soviet Union and to isolate individuals and groups whom the Soviet government dislikes. (A telling instance is the report that the Czech Chess Master Ludek Pachman, who had been a political prisoner in Czechoslovakia following the Soviet invasion, has been unable after his recent emigration to Western Europe to gain admission to international tournaments; the Icelandic government has rejected a German offer to have him play as a member of the West German team on the grounds that this might annoy the Russians and prevent their participation.)[17]

In all, the results of these internal pressures leave much to be desired from the Soviet point of view, and one wonders whether they are worth the effort (and bad publicity) that they cost. The unexpectedly firm behavior of certain European delegations at the Geneva Security Conference in discussions connected with "Basket Three" and involving human cultural exchanges between East and West indicates that powerful sectors of Western opinion not only will not tolerate Soviet repression but insist on the right to bypass the Soviet government and establish contact with its citizenry. Still, the matter deserves close watch; certain forces in the West prefer conciliation at all costs and, willingly or not, help the Soviet government gain acceptance of the principle—from which it alone can benefit—that because of its awesome military arsenal it must always be placated.[18]

Military Policies

It is fair to say that the West has consistently underestimated the Soviet willingness and ability to pay for a large and up-to-date military establishment.[19] Western policymakers have always hoped that sooner or later their Soviet counterparts would conclude that they have enough weapons and decide to devote a growing share of their "national product" to peaceful purposes. This has not happened. The mistaken expectation rests in part on a misunderstanding of Soviet attitudes to military instrumentalities (the belief that they are primarily inspired by a sense of fear and insecurity) and partly from a stubborn faith in Soviet promises to raise Russia's living standards.

The most likely explanation for the relentless Soviet military drive is that nearly all communist expectations—except the reliance on the mailed fist—have been disappointed. The worldwide revolution that the Bolsheviks had expected to follow their seizure of power in Russia did not take place and, as early as the 1920s, had to be given up as a realistic objective. The economic crisis of the West on which they had counted did occur a decade later, but it failed to bring capitalism down. Communist ideology, having attained the apogee of its influence in the 1930s, has since lost much of its appeal and today attracts youth less than it had done before, the more so because it has to compete with anarchism and the Chinese variety of revolutionary doctrine. After its giant achievements in the 1930s, the Soviet economy has not been able to keep up with the pace set by the free economies; the Soviet economic model can hardly attract emulators after the USSR itself has had to seek help outside. In other words, had the Soviet government chosen to rely on the appeal of its ideology or the accomplishments of its economy, it would have consistently found itself on the losing side. Military might alone has never disappointed it. It won the Bolsheviks—in 1917, a tiny party—the Civil War that ensconced them in power. It saved the country from the Nazi invaders. It made it possible for Russia to occupy and retain Eastern Europe. Reinforced with a strategic nuclear arsenal, it has enabled the Soviet government to stand up to the United States and exact recognition as an equal. In short, military power has been the instrument by which a party once composed of a small band of émigré radicals gathered around Lenin had managed first to capture power in Russia, then to defeat the greatest war machine of modern times, and finally to rise from the status of a pariah nation to become one of the world's two superpowers. Merely to list these achievements is to gain an insight into the reason behind the single-minded obsession of Soviet leadership with military power. Anyone who counts on a deceleration of the Soviet military effort must be able to come up with some alternate instruments of international policy on which the Soviet leadership could rely with equal assurance of success.

The buildup of Soviet military forces in the 1960s and early 1970s has been phenomenal and, notwithstanding certain international agreements on arms limitations, shows no signs of abating. There is some disagreement among experts whether this buildup bears a measurable relationship to legitimate Soviet defense interests or has become an end in itself, a search for power for power's sake. There is no dispute, however, about the intensity of this effort, of the willingness of the government to allocate talent and money, of the dedication with which the armed forces maintain the martial spirit among the people. The Soviet leadership seems to strive to obtain a marked superiority in all branches of the military, in order to secure powerful forward-moving shields behind which the politicians could do their work. To reach this objective, the Soviet Union must have open to it all the options—to be able to fight general and limited conventional wars near its borders and away from them, as well as nuclear wars employing tactical and/or strategic weapons. The probability of this aim being given up is very low. Only effective pressure from below by a population fed up with seeing so much of the national wealth disappearing in the military budget could do so, but for this to happen, something very close to a revolution would have to occur in Russia. So far, the Soviet government has shown itself willing to limit the production or employment mainly of those weapons in respect to which it was bound to remain inferior to the United States or the further spread of which seemed counterproductive. A good test of its intentions would be to attempt negotiating limitations in the field of naval construction where the USSR is trying to attain parity with the United States. It is a safe prediction that should the U.S. government try to initiate such negotiations at this time it would run into a stone wall.

An interesting feature of Soviet military activity in recent years has been the practice of quietly establishing a presence in areas where, should hostilities break out, Soviet forces would already be in place and able to deploy for action. A case in point are Soviet incursions by air and naval units of NATO territories in the North Sea. Potentially even more dangerous are large Warsaw Pact maneuvers held in areas near major NATO troop concentrations. As is known, prior to the invasion of Czechoslovakia, Warsaw Pact troops had been put into a state of readiness in this manner. Something of the same tactic seems also to have been followed, possibly under Soviet guidance, by the Egyptians and Syrians in 1973 preparatory to their combined assault on Israel. The unwillingness of the USSR to agree to an exchange of warnings of such exercises more than a short time in advance indicates that its military leaders contemplate the possibility of using maneuvers as cover for preparing offensive operations against NATO.[20]

Finally, mention must be made of the tactic of "war by proxy." Détente cramps Soviet freedom to engage in military action, for it is a sine qua non of this policy that there must be no direct military confrontations between the United States and the USSR. To get around this limitation, the Soviet leadership seems to be systematically developing a technique of indirect military involvement. In regions where it has a strong need to expel hostile foreign influence (Western or Chinese), and yet fears direct involvement, it seeks to achieve its purpose by employing third parties. It provides its allies with arms and with diplomatic protection; in the event of disaster it undertakes an all-out effort on their behalf, but it does not commit to any appreciable extent its own forces. The use of this technique is especially evident in the Middle East, where the Soviet Union seems to have decided that the expulsion of Western political, economic, and military influence and the reduction of Israel to the status of an impotent minor power transcend its day-to-day relations with the Arab states. In an article written upon his return from an extended tour of the Middle East, the editor-in-chief of *Izvestiia*, Lev Tolkunov, has hinted that the Soviet Union had given the Arab countries in their conflict with Israel a blank check. The Arabs could be certain of Soviet backing regardless of the state of their relations with the USSR or the outcome of their initiatives:

The last war [October 1973] showed that the Soviet stand in the
Arab-Israeli conflict is not connected with the current state of affairs
in relations between the USSR and certain Arab countries. It was
not possible for this principled position to be affected by the artifi-
cially created negative factors which manifested themselves in respect to Soviet military experts in some Arab countries. To put it
more directly, they know in the Arab capitals that when the threat
of war hung over the Arab world, the Soviet Union proved in deed
the constancy of its policy of active support of the Arab states, by
sending arms both to Syria and Egypt.[21]

Those acquainted with the diplomatic history of Europe will
find in this policy a striking echo of the carte blanche given by
Imperial Germany to Austria-Hungary in July 1914, promising
unconditional support in its quarrel with Serbia, an assurance
generally regarded as a prime immediate cause of World War I.

The first major "war by proxy" was the Indian-Pakistani war;
the second, the October War, alluded to above. It seems entirely
possible that the USSR may attempt similar action in the future
(for example, Iraq and Afghanistan versus Iran, or India and
Afghanistan versus Pakistan).

Economic Policies

The main objective of Soviet economic policy abroad during
the era of détente is to modernize the Soviet industrial establishment. But, as noted, under the communist system economics
is never considered in isolation from politics, and every economic
policy is measured in terms of its likely political consequences.
Indeed, in recent years the economic weapon has been increasingly used to secure political benefits.

The principal political result desired is increased dependence
of the Western and Third World economies—and therefore, as
a corollary, of Western and Third World governments—on the
Soviet Union. We may single out three means by which this dependence can be accomplished: control of energy supplies,
indebtedness, and manipulation of West European labor.

The Soviet government seems to have realized earlier than
its Western counterparts how great had become the dependence
of modern economies on energy, especially oil, and to have
initiated steps to obtain control of this resource. The single-

minded persistence with which the USSR, its failures notwith-standing, has advanced its influence in the Middle East has had (and continues to have) as one of its prime motives the desire to establish control over the oil supplies of that region. Should the Soviet Union succeed in filling the military vacuum created by the British withdrawal from the Persian Gulf and sustained by American reluctance to commit forces there, it would be in a superb position to exercise a stranglehold on European and Japanese fuel supplies. The October 1973 war unmistakably demonstrated how low Europe would stoop to ensure the flow of its oil.

The Soviet Union has also been very active in seeking to establish itself as a major fuel supplier to the West. It already furnishes respectable amounts of oil and natural gas to Germany and Italy, and everything points to the further expansion of these deliveries. The recently concluded deal involving supplies of natural gas from Iran to the USSR to be matched by Soviet deliveries to Germany will further enhance Soviet control over West European energy requirements. The same applies to bids (consistently below those made by U.S. firms) to furnish enriched uranium to West European nuclear reactors. All this creates conditions of dependence that the USSR could exploit, should the need arise, much in the manner the Arab oil producers had done in the fall of 1973. It goes without saying that the am-bitious plans for U.S.-USSR cooperation in developing Siberian oil and gas fields would give the USSR similar leverage vis-à-vis the United States.

In monetary matters, the Soviet Union has traditionally pur-sued a very conservative policy. Its patient accumulation of gold reserves, at the time when the world offered more remunerative forms of investment, was part and parcel of the "bourgeois" approach to fiscal matters characteristic of communists. In re-cent years, however, the Soviet government appears to have thrown its traditional caution overboard and gone all out for foreign borrowing. The same applies to the "People's Democ-racies." The obligations assumed are onerous, because before long the Soviet Union will have to set aside a good part (per-haps one-half) of its precious hard currency earnings for debt servicing.[22] In part, this untypically risky policy may be influenced by the belief that inflation will cause a disastrous depreciation of Western currencies while enhancing the value of the raw materials that the Soviet Union is in a position to supply. (If this is indeed the case, this calculation leaves out of account the possibility that inflation could lead to a depression that would, in turn, severely curtail the demand for primary materials; but then, perhaps, the Soviet leaders assume that this time a worldwide depression would be followed by a collapse of the capitalist system, an event that would wipe out their debts altogether.) Another consideration may have to do with the psychology of the debtor-creditor relationship. Heavy Soviet indebtedness to Western governments and banks produces among the latter a vested interest in the preservation and well-being of the Soviet Union and improves the chances of the flow of credits continuing unimpeded.

Studies carried out by specialists in the field of East-West relations[23] indicate that the degree of economic interdependence so far achieved is not significant. But the danger is there; and should Moscow succeed in realizing its more ambitious plans for economic "cooperation" involving capitalist economies, the interdependence would attain a level at which political consequences of the most serious nature would be bound to ensue.

The steady growth of advanced modern economies and the difficulties of rationalizing production beyond a certain maximal point have resulted in a growing labor shortage; and that, in turn, has enhanced the power of organized labor. In some advanced industrial countries the trade unions have acquired a virtual veto power over government policies. It may be expected that (barring a depression) this power will continue to grow. This development induces the Soviet Union to try to heal the breach between those foreign trade unions that are communist-controlled, and therefore in some measure manipulable by it, and the free trade unions that either are directed by socialists, Catholics, or some other group or lack political affiliation entirely. One of the by-products of the American-Soviet détente has been to make communism respectable in labor circles and to weaken the resistance of democratic trade unionists to pressures for closer contacts and joint action with communist and communist-dominated trade union organizations. In the past two years, the Soviet Union has succeeded in partly healing the breach created in 1949 when the Communist World Federation of Trade Unions broke up due to the secession from it of democratic labor organizations. The quarantine on communist trade unionism, in effect during the past quarter of a century, seems to have broken down. With the active support of the British Trade Union Congress and the West German Federation of Labor, the recent head of the Central Soviet Trade Union Organization, A. N. Shelepin (a one-time KGB head!) has persuaded European labor leaders to agree to a joint conference. That meeting could well presage an era of collaboration and end up with free trade unionism falling under the sway of the better financed and centrally directed communist movements.[24] Further penetration of European labor, of course, would give Soviet leadership a superb weapon for influencing or even blackmailing West European industry.

Current Soviet Assessment of Détente

What, from Moscow's vantage point, has been the balance sheet of "peaceful coexistence" and détente to date?

On the *debit* side of the ledger two results deserve emphasis:

1. The dispute with China. The foreign policy pursued by the post-Stalinist leadership has served primarily the national interests of the Soviet Union, not those of the communist community at large. This had been the case even before 1953. As Stalin's words [see p. 74] assert, and as the historical record demonstrates, the guiding principle of Soviet foreign policy has always been national self-interest. But before Stalin's death, Soviet Russia had been the only major power with a communist regime, and until then one could argue with a certain logic that what was good for the USSR was good for communism. After all, the small East European regimes, put in power by the Red Army, hardly counted (except for Yugoslavia, which quickly fell out with Moscow). China, however, was a great power in its own right, and it would not tolerate a policy among whose primary objectives was an arrangement with the United States intended to elevate the USSR to the status of a superpower. Neither references to Lenin's lessons on strategy and tactics,

nor arguments based on expediency, nor threats achieved their desired result. The Chinese remained stubbornly convinced that the ultimate winner from détente would be either the Soviet Union or the United States, or both, but never China, and they reacted with the fury of the betrayed.

2. A certain degree of loss of internal control. For this, détente is only partly responsible. The abolition of indiscriminate terror and the intellectual "thaw" of the mid-1950s were principally inspired by the wish to reinvigorate the country and reinfuse it with enthusiasm for the communist cause. Détente, however, undoubtedly accelerated the process by which society in the USSR began to resist totalitarian controls. An authoritarian-demotic regime must have a threat with which to frighten the population into granting it unlimited powers: Napoleon had his "Jacobins," Lenin and Stalin their "counter-revolutionaries" and "interventionists," Hitler his "Jews" and "Communists." Détente in some measure de-Satanizes the external threat and thereby undermines the Soviet regime's claim to unquestioned obedience. To proclaim the cold war over—even while repeating ad nauseam that the struggle between the two systems must go on to the bitter end—is to put in question the need in Russia for a repressive regime. It makes it that much more difficult to justify tight controls over foreign travel and over access to information. Implicit in détente is also a certain respect for foreign opinion. To project the image of a country worthy of being a partner of the Western democracies, the Soviet regime cannot simply shoot people for holding seditious ideas. The presence of Western correspondents in the USSR has given Soviet dissenters a powerful weapon with which to neutralize the KGB—at any rate, where better-known public figures are concerned. All this is not without long-term dangers for the regime.[25]

On the *credit* side of the ledger there are the following achievements:

1. The USSR has indubitably achieved the status of an equal partner of the United States. As Gromyko publicly boasts in the passage cited at the beginning of this paper, all major international decisions are now acknowledged to require Soviet participation and acquiescence; no actions that seriously threaten Soviet interests are likely to be taken. The Soviet Union has at

long last become a world power. Russia's international prestige is greater than it has ever been in the country's history.

2. The USSR has succeeded in smashing the ring of alliances forged around it by the United States during the late Stalin era. NATO is in disarray; the other alliance systems lead only a paper existence. For its own part, the USSR has succeeded in establishing a strong political and military presence in the Middle East, where its good relations with the Arab countries and India have helped her in considerable measure to eject Western influence and establish the position of a regional patron. Countries that at one time had been solidly wedded to the United States— Germany, Japan, and the states of Southeast Asia, for example— find it increasingly necessary to conduct an "evenhanded" foreign policy.[26]

3. On the terms of détente, as laid down by the Brezhnev administration and tacitly accepted by President Nixon, the Soviet Union has not been seriously inhibited in carrying on its assault on the capitalist system. It has remained free to support national liberation movements (without risking similar actions against territories lying within its own orbit); it has been able to encourage "wars by proxy"; and it has been able to lobby and exert pressure abroad, without being obliged to grant the West corresponding rights in the communist bloc.

4. Détente has helped secure for the Soviet Union recognition, by West Germany, of its conquests in East Germany: It has legitimized the existence of two Germanys. The recently held Security Conference [in Helsinki] legitimized Russia's conquests of the rest of Eastern Europe. Such recognition is of great importance to Russia because it helps undermine whatever hope the peoples of Eastern Europe may still entertain of some day being freed of Soviet occupation armies and the regimes that these armies keep in power. It also makes it possible to begin to think of some day incorporating Eastern Europe into the Soviet Union.

5. Détente has already led to a considerable growth of Western investments in the Soviet economy and, if continued, should help the Russians overcome some of the most glaring deficiencies plaguing it. Especially attractive are long-term "cooperation" plans that tie the Western economies to the

Soviet, without creating undue Soviet dependence on the West.

It is thus fair to say that, on balance, détente has proved a profitable political strategy for the Soviet Union. It has vastly enhanced the international position of the Soviet Union and enlarged its room for maneuver, while, at the same time, legitimizing its conquests and strengthening its economy. The cost— alienation of China and internal restlessness—has been high, but apparently the Soviet leadership feels that it can prevent both dangers from getting out of hand. This explains why the Soviet leadership is vigorously pressing for détente to continue. There is every reason to expect that it will persist in so doing, no matter what the obstacles and frustrations, because as now defined and practiced, détente primarily benefits the Soviet Union.

Suggested U.S. Policy in the Age of Détente

There was a time in the United States when to question the country's policy of "containment" and the cold war exposed a person to the charge of disloyalty. Today, to question the readiness of the USSR to enter into a genuine détente with the West, or to criticize the manner in which relations with the Soviet Union are carried out, is to run the risk of being labeled a "cold warrior." Such labels are meaningless. The problem lies in finding not labels but policies. That can be achieved only if the motives of the critics of the present U.S. policy toward the Soviet Union are considered to be no less honorable than those of its supporters.

A sound policy toward the Soviet Union requires that the following objectives not be lost sight of:

1. *Its effect on the internal situation in the USSR.* Our policies must be so designed that they discourage those tendencies that make the Soviet government think and act in the traditional pike-carp fashion. This means, above all, doing everything within our ability to enhance the participation of the population in political and economic processes. A détente policy that relies exclusively on government-to-government relationships and therefore is subject to the slightest political vicissitudes is not only inherently unstable, but reinforces the centralist, authoritarian tendencies of the Soviet regime. To some extent such a

policy entails "intervention" in the internal affairs of the USSR; but then insofar as détente postulates that the world has become too small a place for countries to engage in classical nationalist policies, intervention—as long as it is not pursued by violent means—is right and proper, and in the fullest sense progressive.

2. *Its effect on the national interest of the United States.* Concessions to the Soviet Union, whatever forms they take (for example, recognition of East Germany, sale of wheat at subsidized prices, access to U.S. guarantees of foreign investments) should always be accompanied by a commensurate quid pro quo:—not pledges redeemable in an unspecified future, but instant political, military, or economic repayment. This practice is always sound because of the difficulty of foreseeing the future, especially in a country like the USSR, which lacks legitimate succession procedures and which can renege on its commitments with comparative ease. Instantaneous reciprocity or barter of concessions ought to lie at the heart of peaceful U.S.-USSR relations at all times.

It is also important in negotiating détente with the Russians to make certain that détente is not confined to those fields where an easing of tensions happens to suit the Russians, while allowing in all other realms of U.S.-USSR relations for war, both of the "cold" and "hot" variety, to rage unabated.

3. *Détente ought to be global and all-inclusive.* One should not tolerate the Soviet Union, while ostensibly engaging in "peaceful coexistence" with us, inciting its own population to "ideological struggles" against us, exhorting the underdeveloped countries to expropriate U.S. firms, or arming the Arabs to wage war against a small country to the survival of which we have a deep commitment. Either détente embraces all areas of U.S.-USSR relations, or it is a sham.

4. *In particular, détente is not compatible with an unabated Soviet military effort* for which no reasonable defense justification exists. As long as the USSR keeps on multiplying its arsenal and increasing the variety of military options open to it, its professions of peaceful intent must be viewed with skepticism. For as the Chinese strategist Sun Tzu warned in the fourth century B.C.: "When the enemy's envoys speak in humble terms, but he continues his preparations, he will advance."[27]

Notes

1. *XXIV S"ezd KPSS—Stenograficheskii otchet* [The 24th Congress of the Communist Party of the Soviet Union: Stenographic Record], I (Moscow, 1971), 482.

2. The historical evolution of this type of state authority is the theme of my book *Russia Under the Old Regime* (New York, 1975).

3. It is reported, for instance, that the Finnish government, which owing to Soviet pressures must pay nearly double the prevailing world price for the oil it imports from the USSR, is pressured not to reveal this unpalatable act to its citizenry (*Neue Zürcher Zeitung*, June 19, 1974). Similarly, in their dealings with private West European Banks, Russia and the "People's Democracies" are insisting, with apparent success, on a high degree of secrecy. See Christopher Wilkins in the *Times* (London), December 17, 1973.

4. Much evidence to this effect can be found in the pages of the periodical *USSR and the Third World*, published in London by the Central Asian Research Center.

5. Nor should it be forgotten that the officers who command Soviet Russia's military establishment are veterans of the most brutal war of modern history in which defeat would have spelled enslavement and eventual mass annihilation of their people.

6. J. V. Stalin, *Works*, XIII (Moscow, 1955), 308–309.

7. Malcolm Mackintosh in E. L. Dulles and R. D. Crane, *Détente: Cold War Strategies in Transition* (New York, 1965), 103–120.

8. See Brezhnev's views: "A scientific and technical revolution unprecedented in its rate and scope is now taking place in the world. And it is the communists, [those] who carried out the greatest social revolution, that should be in the front rank of the revolutionary transformations in science and technology. The CPSU believes that one of our most important tasks now is to accelerate scientific and technical progress, to equip the working people with modern scientific and technical knowledge, and to introduce as quickly as possible the results of scientific discoveries." L. I. Brezhnev, *Pravda*, November 13, 1968, cited in Foy D. Kohler et al., *Soviet Strategy for the Seventies: From Cold War to Peaceful Coexistence* (Coral Gables, Florida, 1973), 168.

9. *Frankfurter Allgemeine Zeitung*, May 24, 1974.

10. Speech of February 18, 1974, welcoming the President of Zambia, *USSR and the Third World*, IV, No. 2, 108.

11. *Osnovy Marksizma-Leninizma: Uchebnoe posobie* [The foundations of Marxism-Leninism: An education aid], 2nd ed. (Moscow, 1962), 359–360. Emphasis in the original.

12. Numerous citations to this effect can be found in Foy D. Kohler et al., *Soviet Strategy for the Seventies: From Cold War to Peaceful Co-existence* (Coral Gables, Florida, 1973).

13. D. Lascelles, *The Financial Times* (London), February 6, 1974.

14. H. Hamm, *Frankfurter Allgemeine Zeitung*, May 4, 1974.

15. See Brezhnev's speech of October 26, 1973, in which, in evident reaction to the EEC's gasoline shortages, he urged integrating its economy with that of the USSR.

16. C. Genrich, *Frankfurter Allgemeine Zeitung*, March 21, 1974, and H. Kamer, *Neue Zürcher Zeitung*, June 9, 1974. The USSR sees nothing wrong, however, in asking the very same international oil companies to help it conduct drilling off the coast of Soviet Sakhalin—*New York Times*, February 22, 1975.

17. *Frankfurter Allgemeine Zeitung*, January 31, 1974. There also exist reports that the movie *One Day in the Life of Ivan Denisovich* will not be shown in Japan, because the film distributor, Toho, fears Soviet objections.

18. An important subject in its own right is Soviet subversion in Western Europe (and elsewhere), the breadth and sophistication of which is depicted in *The Peacetime Strategy of the Soviet Union* (London, 1973).

19. Albert Wohlstetter, "Is there a strategic arms race?" *Foreign Policy*, No. 15 (Summer 1974), especially p. 5.

20. [The "Final Act" of the Conference on Security and Cooperation in Europe held in 1975 in Helsinki acknowledged this military loophole by providing that the "participating States . . . may, at their own discretion . . . notify their major military movements." Since no one on record has ever denied a sovereign state the right to notify other powers of its intended military moves, this clause, like so much else of the Helsinki accords, has something of a fairyland quality about it.]

21. *Izvestiia*, July 25, 1974. Lest these words be misread to apply only to defensive actions, Mr. Tolkunov insists in the same article that the October War had discredited the story that the USSR was supplying the Arabs only with "defensive" weapons, and preventing the Arabs from attacking Israel, arguing that the distinction between defensive and offensive weapons was quite arbitrary.

22. M. Kaser estimates (quoted in *Sowjetunion 1973*, Munich, 1973, 126, from *International Currency Review*, July–August 1973) Soviet foreign indebtedness for goods and services alone (that is, exclusive of capital borrowings) at $8.5 billion in late 1973. In his estimation, should Russia continue to accumulate obligations abroad at the same rate as recently, its external debt in 1980 would rise to $31 billion.

23. See, e.g., P. Hanson and M. Kaser, "Soviet economic relations with

Western Europe," and J. and P. Pinder, "Western European relations with the Soviet Union," in Richard Pipes, ed., *Soviet Strategy in Europe* (New York, 1976), 213–303.

24. Arnold Beichman, *The International Herald Tribune,* January 26–27, 1974.

25. It is in this light that one may interpret the dismissal of P. N. Demichev from the post of Secretary of the Central Committee for Agitation and Propaganda in November of 1974. Demichev, who had held his post since 1965, was responsible for the relatively "liberal" handling of dissidents. His dismissal has been immediately followed by repressive actions. See A. Solzhenitsyn in *Neue Zürcher Zeitung,* January 15, 1975.

26. In this connection it is interesting to note that polls conducted in recent years in West Germany and Japan have revealed a significant shift in the public's attitude toward the USSR. While Russia's popularity remains very low, a large part of the inhabitants of both countries have come to regard "good relations" with the USSR as essential to their security. In Germany some 19 percent of the persons polled thought good relations with the USSR to be more important than good relations with any other country, the United States included.

27. Sun Tzu, *The Art of War* (London, 1963), 119.

FIVE

Détente: A Discussion
with George R. Urban

George Urban is a most unusual interviewer: before he ap-
proaches the people he is going to interview, he reads their pub-
lished works. He is, therefore, in a position to confront them
with their past opinions, sometimes compelling them to admit in-
consistency or forcing them to articulate the unspoken premises
of their thoughts. George Urban's interview with me on the sub-
ject of détente went beyond the conventional political-military
boundaries of the topic to explore its ideological and psychologi-
cal dimensions.

Domestic Change in the Soviet Union

URBAN: Let [us discuss] the semantic differences that appear to
make any understanding between the Soviet *Weltan-*
schauung and our own—insofar as we have one—so difficult to come by. The problem boils down to the question whether, in our view, détente is exclusively about
inter-state relations or whether it is also predicated on
certain changes in the domestic conditions of the Soviet
Union. The semantic hurdles are, as we have already
seen, quite daunting. It is, in international politics, hard
enough for men of the same culture to understand each
other even though words have a shared meaning in their

This discussion, which took place in 1976, was published in part in George R. Urban,
Détente (London, 1977), 174–197. Part I, which duplicates some of my earlier writings that appear in this volume, is omitted. Part III, which Mr. Urban did not include
in his book, is published here for the first time, together with Part II.

vocabularies. But when neither of these conditions obtains, as in the case in Soviet-U.S. relations, isn't détente just an extremely costly way for us to underwrite the post-war gains and future stability of the Soviet Union? After all, we cannot even agree with the Russians on the meaning of the word "détente."

Let me quote a few examples from one authentic witness, Andrei Amalrik. "The idea of self-government, of equality under the law for all and of personal freedom—and the responsibility that goes with these—are almost completely incomprehensible to the Russian people." Amalrik writes in *Will the USSR Survive Until 1984?*: "The very word 'freedom' is understood by most people as a synonym of the word 'disorder' . . ."; "As for respecting the rights of an individual as such, such an idea simply evokes bewilderment"; ". . . 'justice' is motivated by the wish 'nobody should be better off than me' "; and so forth.

PIPES: As you know, I have myself written about these semantic barriers, and they are of course a great impediment. However, the purpose of détente is not so much to make Russia change its system of government as to reduce the threat which it poses to Europe. Now to some extent it is true that a freer and better informed Russia is less of a menace, and it is for that reason that we are calling for internal changes in Russia and Eastern Europe under "Basket Three" and through other channels. But a complete internal transformation is not really what we are after—we are after stability and peace, and if the Russians, even while maintaining their present system of government, can demonstrate that they are doing all in their power internally and externally to live in accord with us and their neighbors, then we would certainly not press them for any change in their system. It is not our way. Personally I wish that the system would change, but this is not a goal that a country can adopt as its foreign policy. It would be preposterous (as well as hopeless) for us to demand that the Soviet Union become a democratic country before we can talk peace with it.

URBAN: Let me quote you Amalrik again: "Collaboration takes for granted mutual reliance one on the other, but how can one rely upon a country [Russia] which over the centuries has been distending itself and disintegrating like sour dough?. . . Genuine rapprochement can be based on a community of interests, of culture, of tradition, and on mutual understanding. No such thing exists."

What strikes me as significant in this passage is that, in Amalrik's view, the external posture of the Soviet Union is a function of such elusive and definitely "domestic" factors as culture, tradition and understanding. Can therefore a minimalist conception of détente be anything more promising than a non-aggression pact?

PIPES: Détente implies no love relationship. The cultural and semantic barriers are of course there, but this need not affect state-to-state relations. After all, we have decent relations with countries which have totally different sets of values and traditions from our own—India and Japan, for example. Peaceful co-existence does not require that we all look alike and think alike. That would be an impossible demand; humanity lives at very different levels of development.

URBAN: You have not quite convinced me. I still feel—and I'll quote some more evidence in a moment—that a country's internal condition is a fair barometer of how we can expect it to behave in its external affairs, and that this is true for Russia par excellence. Consider Amalrik again, weighing up the character of Soviet Russia, and compare what he says with an observation of the Marquis de Custine writing well over a century earlier.

> *Amalrik:* What does this people with no religion and no morality believe in and what is it motivated by? It believes

in its own national strength which other peoples must fear and it is motivated by the realization of the strength of its own regime of which it is itself afraid.

The Marquis de Custine: This essentially conquering nation, greedy as a result of its hardships, atones in advance for the hope of exercising tyranny abroad by degrading submission at home; the glory and the wealth which the Russian nation expects distract it from the shame which it suffers at home; in order to clean itself of the ungodly sacrifice of all its public and personal liberties, the kneeling slave nation dreams of the domination of the world.

These two readings of the Russian national character are strikingly and depressingly alike: there is no glory to be had at home, hence aggrandizement is sought from adventure abroad—from Pan-Slavic nationalism in the nineteenth century, from proletarian internationalism in our own. How does all this augur for détente?

PIPES: I don't think there is a direct relationship between what the mass of people think and feel, and the international policies pursued in their name. The two operate on different levels—not totally different levels, I grant, but different levels all the same. In other words, we must not think of international relations as if they were human relations. If, for example, you went to Russia and tried to set up a business there, you would, I suspect, run into people—the ordinary people of Russia—who might make life very difficult for you. But if you are dealing at the international level, methods have been worked out a long time ago which make it possible for different civilizations to co-exist with each other in peace. That is what diplomacy is about. The rules of modern diplomacy were laid down at the end of the Thirty Years' War, in 1648, in the Treaty of Westphalia. The Treaty enshrined the idea that there can be a Catholic and a Protestant Europe, that the two can co-exist and have normal relations. This was a revolution in human thought, for until then it was always taken for granted that the condition of the survival of one was the extermination of the other. So, after 1648, you had a Protestant culture and a Catholic culture which—given the importance of popular religions at the time—were as different as ideologies are today and possibly much more important in the daily lives of the people. The diplomatic practices then established by these two, seemingly irreconcilable "camps" of Christianity, have made it possible to reconcile their interests—without abolishing their doctrines—in certain peaceful ways. We are the heirs to that tradition.

Therefore, while I agree with much of what de Custine and Amalrik have to say about the nature of Russian political culture, I don't think it follows that the Russian people must necessarily want to conquer the world, and even less do I believe that they will succeed in conquering the world. The tendency *is* there—the desire to show force abroad because there is weakness at home is clearly in evidence—but if you confront this with determined diplomacy in which sophistication is combined with force, you need not be overwhelmed.

URBAN: You are therefore keeping détente as a pursuit of foreign policy and détente as a device of cultural reconciliation in separate compartments, in which case you cannot wholly support the Jackson Amendment.

PIPES: Why? I approve of the Jackson Amendment. It is one of the very few tactical devices we have brought into being for making our economic support conditional on domestic reform in the Soviet Union. It fits in with my idea of barter, annual accounting, immediate returns, and so on.

URBAN: But it does not fit in with what you have just told me about the Treaty of Westphalia. Surely no Catholic ruler would expect a Protestant prince to make a concession on a point of dogma in order to qualify for a supply of linseed for his cattle.

PIPES: The Jackson Amendment, let me stress, did not touch
on Soviet dogma. Co-existence does not mean that you
accept the system as it is. Nor does it mean that, because
the Russians *are* aggressive and expansionist (and their
expansionism is attested by history), at no point shall
we be able to come to terms with them. We will—provided that we show half the determination in stopping
them that they show in trying to outwit us.

   We must remember that the Russians are immensely
responsive to power; they know how to use power but
they also know how to yield to it. To this day the entire mentality of the Soviet government is rooted in
peasant experience. If you study Russian history you
will find that the peasant was always surrounded by
force; he expected to bully or to be bullied. This is a
natural consequence of the virtual absence in Russia of
a legal tradition—where there is no law to adjudicate disputes, force inevitably replaces law. Here we have a great
asset which we have as yet not learned how to use. We
can make a very strong impression on the Russians at
both the personal and national levels provided that we
let it be known that we carry a sizeable stick. The Russians can recognize a superior adversary when they see
one, and they are very good at backing down without
feeling any shame—as we saw in Cuba and in our October
1973 alert. My point is that this healthy respect for
power makes it entirely possible for us to stop them
even in the face of everything you said and quoted about
the Russian character.

URBAN: But who, I ask you, is going to do the stopping?

PIPES: Ah, but that is an entirely different question. What I am
saying is that we *can* stop them if we want to stop them.
Proper leadership in the West could do it. The exercise
need not be futile—one could easily chart a whole series
of positions we could recapture from the Soviet Union
if we knew how to use the power we have and had made
the decision to use it.

URBAN: Khrushchev's memoirs bear out what you say. He makes the point time and again that during his incumbency the Soviet Union was, militarily and economically, terribly weak, but the weaknesses had to be covered up for otherwise the United States might do nasty things to Russia. Hence the bluffing, the thunder and fury of Khrushchev's peregrinating statesmanship. And, judging from the Soviet eagerness for détente, this may, certainly in the economic field, still be the case.

PIPES: Luckily for us, Khrushchev over-estimated both our willpower and our political sagacity.

URBAN: There is certainly no reason why we should not take the Russians at their word and agree with them that in matters of ideology there can be no peaceful co-existence. But as soon as *we* act on that understanding, up goes the cry of cold war, imperialism, and the rest. So the motto "in matters of ideology there can be no peaceful co-existence" is, in fact, interpreted by the Soviet side as meaning, "We are entitled to work for your destruction because we are on the side of history, but hands off the Socialist camp." However, there is, as I see it, also a deeper reason which prevents us from making a matching effort. Whether we agree with it or not, whether we think it is bogus or not—the Soviet Union *has* an ideology; we haven't. How do you put an ideological scaffolding around something as amorphous and fluid as "democracy"? I suspect, therefore, that even if we did have the will to take up the Soviet challenge, we'd be fighting with unequal equipment.

PIPES: I would not sell us that short. We do have an ideology, a very powerful ideology, much more powerful than those juvenile ideas, that sham religion which the Soviet Union promotes under the self-contradictory title of "Marxism-Leninism." I haven't the slightest doubt that if free elections were held around the world and people were to choose between, say, a set of values which

you and I put down on paper, and one that our opposite
numbers in the Soviet Communist Party did, we would
win hands down. The idea of law, the idea of freedom,
the idea of human dignity are extremely powerful ideas.
They have agitated humanity for centuries, and their
appeal is fresh and inexhaustible.

Our problem is: do we have the vision and the vigor
to pursue them? It is here that our principal weakness
lies. We haven't the will to use what we have. We are
being mesmerized by the sheer determination and (apparently) overwhelming self-confidence of the Soviet
side.

URBAN: Matched now by Soviet superiority in armed power too.

PIPES: That is of very recent origin and is even now not convincingly established. But we have allowed ourselves to
be hypnotized into lacking will even when we had complete armed superiority over the Soviets. And for this
we must not blame them—it is entirely *our* fault.

URBAN: We are now coming back to a problem we have already
discussed in a slightly different context: why are we unable to get a grip on ourselves in this battle of wits? You
said earlier we were too affluent, had too much to lose
and so forth. Is that, I wonder, the whole answer?

PIPES: It isn't, and the rest of the answer falls into two parts—
one has to do with Europe and the other with the United
States. The lack of determination is much greater in
Europe than in America and the reasons are straightfor-
ward. Two world wars have so debilitated the will both
of the European peoples and their governments that
they have become incapable of taking bold action of
any kind. There is a feeling in Europe—not always articulated but very prevalent—that almost any policy is
better than war, for war only destroys without settling
anything. Hence you choose the line of least resistance,
you conceal your impotence, above all from yourself,
by rationalizing your appeasement.

"The Russians," you will hear Europeans say, "are terrible people who run a detestable system, but they will mellow as they get into closer contact with Western civilization as all barbarians of the past have [allegedly!] done," and so forth.

The second factor, just as important, is the social revolution which Europe has undergone since the war. Until quite recently Europe was governed—by the yardstick of the United States, at any rate—by an upper class élite which ran foreign offices, military establishments and set the tone of government internally and externally. The private ethos of Europe was entirely upper bourgeois, and even those who had not climbed the ladder to bourgeois status aspired to it.

All this has radically changed. The lower middle classes and the working class have moved into positions of power and influence—they are Americanizing the whole social and ethical climate of Europe. Their materialism, their acquisitiveness, their ability to win for themselves in a few years possessions and living standards which would have been beyond the wildest dreams of their grandfathers, would put any American to shame. Moreover, these people are just not politically inclined—unlike their American counterparts, they have never been involved in the political process and they appear to have no desire to get involved. They are European isolationists in the same sense of the word as their cousins in America were American isolationists fifty years ago. They can see no point in standing up to the Soviet Union or even wasting time thinking of such problems when time could be usefully occupied in the football stadium or watching television.

To sum up: weariness and disillusionment with war and politics and, second, the pursuit of material wealth as a by-product of the social revolution have, between them, sapped the political will of Europe.

URBAN: I would have thought embourgeoisement and the acquisition of wealth would make people more rather than less conscious of the need to safeguard their new status and property, and that this awareness would call for an active foreign policy. After all, the officer who has come up from the ranks is always a greater stickler for respect and discipline than the man from West Point or Sandhurst. So, unless we have overnight turned into a continent of mindless sybarites, bourgeois status should have given us an extra stake in the political process rather than the reverse.

PIPES: You are right in saying that from the psychological point of view the nouveau riche should have more to worry about than those of established status. But here a third factor comes into play: for the past twenty-five years, and one might say for the past fifty years, the United States has assumed the military protection of Europe. If the various Berlin confrontations, the suppression of Hungary and the occupation of Czechoslovakia, for example, had been European happenings rather than moves on the Soviet-American chessboard, I am sure there would be a very different psychology in Europe. But as things are, the Europeans feel that their military power is so inferior to that of the Soviet Union that they could not begin to stand up to Russia, and that America's protective presence makes it unnecessary to do any such thing in the first place. So the new European rich go on concentrating on their personal ends, glutting themselves on the goods and the good life they have just discovered and leaving the rest to the Americans. This, to my mind, is the kind of thing that accounts for the paralysis of the political will of Europe.

Now this is not true of America. Of course, there is in America a sense of tiredness after twenty-five years or so of carrying the burden of world leadership. There is, in particular, fatigue after the Vietnam war, and there is confusion and bewilderment about the Watergate affair, Nixon's resignation and the state of the presidency. Nevertheless there is a very strong political sense which pervades the whole population—a sense of what freedom is about, what blessings we Americans enjoy because of our freedom. I am certain that if the United States were ever to be challenged on some issue that truly mattered to the future of America, the president of the United States would have no difficulty in rallying the American people. The will of America is not sapped.

I am not saying this in any spirit of vindictiveness: America, unlike Europe, did not suffer the ravages of two world wars on its territory; its losses were not comparable with those of the European countries and, also, the social revolution which has unhinged the European social order has been continuously with us for a century or so. For this combination of reasons, the average American is very conscious that America is a blessed land, that he owes America a great deal, and he is prepared to fight for it. The European, as I see it, isn't ready to fight for Europe. For the average European, politics have always been made by an élite or, in recent decades, by the Americans; hence he does not feel involved—a home, the box (television), and a holiday are as far as his horizons will stretch.

URBAN: This is, of course, precisely the picture we used to have of the average *American* during the period of isolationism—

PIPES: —and it was partly accurate. Now Europe has caught the disease and caught it with a vengeance. But while the United States is geographically so placed that it could (though it can no longer) indulge its short-sightedness, Europe cannot.

I'm not saying that the United States has no responsibility for European apathy; the flaccidity of Europe is indeed a measure of the success of American foreign policy, for we have given Europe too much of a good thing for too long. America ought to have started withdrawing from Europe in the late 1950s when EEC was being put together. Our attitude should have been: "You are building up your economic unity; we hope this will impel you towards political unity and the two will force you to have your own military capability. And just to make sure that all this does happen, we will start taking our troops out right now and complete our withdrawal over the next five or so years." This kind of thing would have given Europe a salutary shock.

URBAN: You would not obviously agree with M. Jobert (the former French Foreign Minister) that America was in Europe exclusively to protect its own, not Western Europe's, interests?

PIPES: I hardly think I could agree with anything M. Jobert might say. The United States has stayed in Europe because American foreign policy was beset by a sense of inertia—a fear that if we showed the slightest weakening of the United States' resolve to stay in Europe the Russians would at once take advantage of it. As always in history when you have a good thing going, the policy of least resistance is to keep it going. The American decision to stay was an understandable but costly long-term blunder.

URBAN: I can sense two flaws in your argument, and they may very well be flaws in my understanding of the points you have made. First, why is it that affluence and embourgeoisement have a way of making *our* nouveau riche lethargic, egocentric, and ineffectual but seem to have no such impact on comparable classes in the Soviet Union? You said earlier on that higher living standards and a greater sophistication would not change the militancy of the Soviet establishment; you claimed that only a lost war or some fatal rift in the party leadership could do that. This is an unusual judgement, for most Western observers believe that any liberalization of the Soviet system will occur for more or less the same reasons which—according to your analysis—account for our own apathy and our unwillingness to take part in the political process: the mellowing and enervating influence of the consumer society and the rising expectations it generates. If this were to be the case, apathy would be facing apathy, and détente might assume a more pleasing aspect than it does now. But this is not happening.

Is there any reason why the Soviet new class should be more resistant to the allurements of affluence than we are proving to be? Has that splendidly slothful figure, Oblomov, ceased to stand for the ruling vices of the Russian élite?

A Marxist might, of course, argue that the answer is very simple. He would claim that, having played out its role in the historical process, the European bourgeoisie, new and old, has lost its will to govern and is now propelling itself into the dustbin of history; not so the "new class" in the Soviet Union (my Marxist would, of course, never accept that term), where the proletariat is being carried forward, under the guidance of its "most progressive elements," by the wave of history.

PIPES: The two phenomena are totally unlike. Embourgeoisement in Western Europe is affecting virtually the whole population; the goods and gadgets and holidays are coveted by all and available to all. Embourgeoisement in Russia, insofar as it really exists, is the privilege of a relatively small élite which has never severed its umbilical cord with the state. Historical traditions play a role here, but without examining those in detail, let me simply state that the Russian élite shows a high degree of psychological continuity which manifests itself in nationalism and obedience, and especially obedience *to* nationalism, whatever other concepts may have been superimposed on that word in the name of ideology. I would go so far as saying that the Russian élite isn't a class or a pressure group in our sense at all. It resembles a self-perpetuating religious order rather than what one normally thinks of as a governing establishment. Your idea, therefore, that détente might produce a convergence of apathies which would make Europe and the Soviet Union comparably impotent, is not a contingency I would personally put my money on. But nor, I take it, would you.

URBAN: The second inconsistency (as I see it) concerns your
point that in the late 1950s, parallel with the building
up of EEC, the United States should have pulled out
some of its forces from Europe and signalled that, within
a few years, it would take out the rest. At the same time
you said that Russian governments have an immense
respect for power, and you also mentioned that, in the
official view prevailing in Washington in the late 1950s,
an American withdrawal from Europe would have entailed unacceptable risks. It is the latter point I want to
argue.

The Soviet leadership can be astonishingly unsophis-
ticated when trying to read and make sense of Western
political attitudes. We saw this in Korea, for example,
where one of Dean Acheson's casual remarks was interpreted by Stalin and his entourage as meaning that the
United States had ceased to regard Korea as being within
its sphere of interest, and this gave Stalin the green light
for the North Korean attack. Here is a very important
precedent, and my view is that, had the United States
gone home from Europe in the late 1950s or early 1960s,
Moscow might well have taken that for a sign of either
American weakness or an abdication of American responsibility or both. For what other reasons—Khrushchev
might have asked—would a great power give up something
it has got? If the Soviet leadership under Khrushchev was
foolish enough to believe that it could get away with
challenging the United States on its home ground in
Cuba, might it not have been tempted into an even
much more "hare-brained" adventure nearer home, once
the United States presence had been removed from
Europe? Khrushchev's tendency to project Soviet modes
of thinking on to the "enemy" was always evident and
is clearly attested by his memoirs.

PIPES: I don't agree. In the late 1950s the United States had a
very large nuclear superiority over the Soviet Union—
enough to make any Soviet move in Europe prohibitively
expensive. Russia's withdrawal from Cuba under deter-

mined American pressure was a sign of the size of the problem Russia was facing. Therefore if the United States had started moving out of Europe in those years of undisputed nuclear superiority (gradually, of course) it would have indirectly contributed to the aggregate power of the West by cajoling or pushing Western Europe into political unity and hence also into making a substantial military contribution of its own. So withdrawal would have ultimately strengthened our posture militarily *and* politically. It would have jerked Europe into pulling its weight more in accord with its economic power and geographic position. We could have prevented her from becoming a drop-out, which she now is.

URBAN: I grant you this is a convincing reading of what ought to have been done if our politicians of the time had known what we now know—for example about Khrushchev's inferiority complexes, the extent of his and his generals' bluffing to confound their adversaries and so on. But our politicians didn't, nor were they particularly far-sighted, nor did Europe want to abandon the Belloc principle: Better keep a hold of Nurse, for fear of getting something worse.

PIPES: Well, if this discussion has demonstrated anything it is that Europe has now landed itself both with "nurse" and "worse."

The Public Mood in the Soviet Union

URBAN: No evaluation of the chances of détente can be complete without some estimate being made of the public mood of the Soviet Union; but as there is no public opinion in Russia in the sense in which that term is used in countries enjoying a minimum freedom of expression, I propose to look at some of the prominent figures of Russian dissent to see whether anything resembling a public mood is articulated in their opinions.

We have in the persons of Alexander Solzhenitsyn and

Andrei Sakharov two outstanding and extremely courageous representatives of two originally nineteenth century trends in Russian life and letters: Slavophiles and
Westernizers. Solzhenitsyn may be said to be the heir to
a tradition stressing Russia's orthodox heritage, Christian
humility and a wary approach to European ideas.
Solzhenitsyn's affinity is with the early rather than the
late Slavophiles, because the latter were militant imperialists spreading by word and sword a Pan-Slavic racialism
and Messianism with which Solzhenitsyn has, of course,
nothing in common.

Sakharov, on the other hand, is heir to the wisdom
of that part of the nineteenth century Russian intelligentsia which believed that Western modes of thinking
and humane values would regenerate Russia's antiquated
social fabric once the obscurantism of Orthodox clerics
had been repudiated.

The extremes of Slavophile ideology and Westernizing thinking were perversely fused into unity in Stalin
and Stalinism. As Hugh Seton-Watson perceptively put
it: "The later Slavophiles degenerated into crude imperialists, trampling on the rights of other nations. The
later Westernizers became doctrinaire Utopians, thinking
no longer in terms of men and women but of abstractions like 'proletariat,' 'kulak,' 'middle peasant,' or
'village poor.' The worst features of both traditions were
united in the persons of Stalin and his helpers."

PIPES: This seems to me basically correct. One could also say
Solzhenitsyn is a conservative, Sakharov a liberal. I'm
not sure that I would call Solzhenitsyn a pure Slavophile.
He is a conservative and a nationalist. The Slavophiles
believed in the uniqueness of the Russian "soul" and the
universal mission of the Russian people, and I can't see
any of that in Solzhenitsyn. He loves Russia, instinctively and profoundly, but he does not romanticize
Russian culture and he never depicts the Russians as
racially or spiritually superior. Quite the contrary: in
August 1914 the Russian military appear as very second

rate compared to the Germans. Now any true Slavophile would have made the Germans look idiotic and the Russians ten feet tall and without blemish. Even Tolstoy, for example, although himself no Slavophile, showed a Russophile bias in *War and Peace,* where he depicted the German generals in a very damaging light. Solzhenitsyn simply believes that the Soviet regime has inflicted and is continuing to inflict enormous harm on the Russian nation. He is a conservative in the sense that he believes in strong government, but, like all true Russian conservatives, he also believes in law and order and freedom of speech. Remember that Russian conservatives have traditionally upheld the freedom of speech and freedom of opinion and were very far from being reactionaries.

URBAN: My impression is that there *is* a Slavophile element in Solzhenitsyn although not a very strong one. For example, in his *Letter to the Soviet Leadership* he says: "The catastrophic weakening of the Western world and the whole of Western civilization is by no means solely due to the success of an irresistible, persistent Soviet foreign policy. It is, rather, the result of an historical, psychological, and moral crisis affecting the entire culture and world outlook which were conceived at the time of the Renaissance and attained the acme of their expression with the eighteenth century Enlightenment."

PIPES: This is a Slavophile-Romantic view, I agree—the idea that the West began to rot the moment rationalism began to penetrate the medieval mind—but even if there is this element in Solzhenitsyn, he is a moderate, not a fanatical Slavophile. You can tell that he is not a true Slavophile because he is constantly urging the West to stand up to Russia. No Slavophile would have done that. No, Solzhenitsyn is a conservative nationalist very much in a Russian tradition which is older than the Slavophiles and goes back to the eighteenth century.

Now Sakharov represents, as you say, the liberal, Westernizing, pragmatic point of view. He is a scientist with a transnational conscience and a strong aversion to ideology, including Solzhenitsyn's.

URBAN: Between the two we have the Medvedev "heresy" as a third voice possibly representing yet another element in the public mood of Russia.

PIPES: The Medvedev brothers seem to me to be (I'm not sure they would agree with this characterization) essentially Leninists who believe that the Soviet system is basically sound. It has been perverted, they feel, by the wrong people having got hold of the levers of power, but this can be rectified. Now this is a view shared by quite a few people, inside and outside Russia, on the radical left of the Social Democrats. So if we call Solzhenitsyn a Conservative Nationalist and Sakharov a Western Liberal then the Medvedev brothers are Social Democrats who believe that you must have socialism but with a human face. The three types represent three major currents in the history of Russian social thought.

URBAN: There is a fourth, though, which may not represent a large section of Soviet society but is typically Russian in the stridency of its self-hatred and self-mortification— Andrei Amalrik. Here is a total attack on the people of Russia, and especially on the Russian intelligentsia, for their hypocrisy and cowardice.

PIPES: Amalrik's is a personal statement, hardly a political program. It goes back to Chaadaev—I can't think of any other kindred spirit in Russian intellectual history. Amalrik expresses a personal revulsion, as Chaadaev did and, in his own terms, Tolstoy did—not against Russia, but against the Russian government, and probably any government, although Amalrik's critique stands out by its radicalism. These are people who deliberately detached themselves from political parties and who regard it as their duty to observe and to criticize the mind and soul and physical condition of Russia from an Olympian height. This is an attitude much to be respected, but you cannot build a political platform on it.

URBAN: No, you can't, yet Amalrik's merciless exposure of the apathy and spinelessness of his own people has much to commend it. It has a ring of truth and integrity about it which surely carries the force of a political challenge in a country where both truth and integrity are at a discount.

Only a very profound love of Russia, and an implied hope that purification through self-hatred can improve the Russian people, could have induced Amalrik to write these lines: "It is not that the people do not change the government because the government is good but because we ourselves are bad. We are passive, ignorant, and fearful: we deceive ourselves with primitive myths and tangle ourselves with bureaucratic ways; we permit our most active citizens to be destroyed, and the majority of us do not understand our situation; our intelligentsia is venal, frightened, and deprived of moral criteria."

PIPES: It is a perceptive statement, but I doubt that a lot of people in Russia would choose to think of themselves in these scathing terms, no matter how much they might subconsciously agree with Amalrik.

URBAN: Leaving Amalrik aside, would you say that the three cases we have so far looked at represent the tips of the iceberg as far at least as the potentially opinion-making sections of the Russian people are concerned?

PIPES: Yes, I would, but I would add two further currents. One is the extreme Left, consisting of a number of undemocratic, anarchist, maximalist groups. The second, and much more important, is the extreme Right—a jingoistic, semi-fascist, blindly nationalistic movement, with pogroms, xenophobia, suspicion of intellectuals, and a special hatred and fear of the yellow races written on its banners.

If Russia were thrown open to free elections, you might well find that these five currents of opinion dominate the nation's politics. The relative strengths of these currents is naturally very difficult to estimate. My guess would be that the Solzhenitsyn-Sakharov-Medvedev type of movements would get an overwhelming majority of the vote, but how this vote would be split among them I would not venture to say. It is easier to suggest what kind of people would support each current. Sakharov would attract the technical, managerial, no-nonsense type of intelligentsia, who want to get things done rather as the Americans do and never mind the ideology. These people can see that an awful lot of things are wrong with Russia, and they believe that they can be put right by a level-headed, un-theoretical approach provided that there is freedom under the rule of law.

In addition to certain intellectuals, Solzhenitsyn might attract the educated peasants and the semi-intelligentsia who are Orthodox and patriotic and like to think that Russia is one up on every other nation (although Solzhenitsyn himself does not think so). This current might turn out to be a national peasant party or it might sail under some other patriotic flag. It might even be monarchist. The Medvedevs would probably have much less success because the notion that Leninism is basically sound—corrupted only in the execution—would not appeal to a great many people. After all Russia has seen fifty years of nothing but corrupt execution, so the virtues of an uncontaminated Leninism would remain to be demonstrated and I don't suppose the Russian electorate would want to expose itself to the risky business of another demonstration. Mind you, here and there the Medvedev heresy might appeal to young socialists, but the appeal would be very limited. If anything, the fascist-nationalist Right might have a bigger following, attracting (as the Nazis did) a lot of urban workers, some of the Lumpenproletariat, some of the disenchanted bureaucracy, the police, and so on. This would be an important force.

URBAN: I have my doubts whether the technical intelligentsia would prove the liberal force you expect it to be. In the second volume of his memoirs Khrushchev recounts with considerable dismay how the distinguished Russian physicist Pyotr Kapitsa refused to be harnessed to the Soviet nuclear program, and how Academician Sakharov tried to stop—without success—the Soviet hydrogen bomb testing program. Then come two sentences of momentous importance: "Despite such disagreements with some scientists, I believe that by the very nature of its activity the technological intelligentsia does not interfere in the more complicated spheres of social life, namely in ideology. A more difficult and slippery problem is posed by the creative intelligentsia. . . ."

In other words, what Khrushchev is saying is that the button pushers and machine minders will toe the line because they are not in the business of thinking, while the creative thinkers will, as he puts it "for ever be delving into questions of philosophy and ideology—questions on which any ruling party, including the Communist Party, would like to have a monopoly." And this strikes me as being entirely true—as true of Soviet Russia as it was of Nazi Germany.

PIPES: Technicians aren't scientists. Sakharov is a unique man, a great scientist and a man of immense courage. He has found within himself the spiritual resources to protest and take enormous risks. But of course I am not saying that the technical intelligentsia would *cause* any ideological trouble, and Khrushchev's reading of their intellectual temper agrees with mine. These people are either apolitical or politically submissive, and, despite all the noise our intellectuals make in the United States, I don't even find *them* a courageous lot. All I am saying is that, given the possibility of a free vote in Russia, the technological intelligentsia would swing towards Sakharov's position as the one best suited to their temper and interests. But I agree that they are not pathfinders or trouble makers.

I also agree with Khrushchev that the pressure for change always comes from the humanists, because the idea that you must have freedom at all costs isn't something that pops out of your work if you are a technologist. It isn't a very practical idea. It is something you feel, and you feel it more strongly the longer you have been associated with the study of human nature in one or several of its many manifestations. Now if you are a technologist and your problem is building an engine-room or improving the air-conditioning you have no particular urge to be free as an individual because in the small field in which you work you *are* free.

URBAN: A humanist is never free in the same sense, nor should he be, for part of his business is to question the assumptions of regimes, religions, and social orders and finally to immerse himself in the unanswerable problems of the human condition itself. And because he is unfree in this large sense, his struggle to carve out freedom for himself wherever he can is obstinate and unceasing.

PIPES: The only result that *I* have ever seen of the transfer of the scientific rationale from science to human affairs has been arrogance. Most scientists I have known, and they include Nobel prize–winners who won distinction in their field by virtue of a very rigorous sense of evidence, show none of this rigor when entering other fields of study. They sail into politics and economics blithely ignorant of what they are talking about. What is the psychology of this arrogance? When scientists have solved problems in some very intricate field of study, they assume they can solve others in what they regard as much less tricky fields at the drop of a hat. "Human relations—well, there is nothing there compared with studying molecules and genetic structure—these problems are simple." Scientists think of us as a bunch of lawyers who create problems that aren't really there. I can certainly not think of a single case where a scientist proceeded to extrapolate the rationale of science into a philosophy of human affairs and succeeded in creating one. There are a few distinguished scientists—Weizsäcker, for example, in Germany—who have become philosophers, but only by first abandoning science. In rare cases, a powerfully intelligent man may be able to do both, but there is no connection between one and the other.

URBAN: So you share Khrushchev's judgement.

PIPES: I do. Soviet scientists and technologists have, with the exception of Kapitsa and Sakharov, given the Soviet system little trouble.

URBAN: Even Sakharov, if we can believe Khrushchev's testimony, did not protest until after he had helped the Soviet government to build the hydrogen bomb. He inveighed against the testing program, but, at the time, he was not against military research.

PIPES: There is no question that among the dissidents, so-called, the scientists and technologists are entirely outnumbered by historians, writers, poets, and other humanists. I am nevertheless convinced that, given a free choice, the scientific intelligentsia is much more likely to rally behind the Sakharov type of liberal pragmatism than any other line. Incidentally, in a book I edited in 1960 I said that if there were to be a resistance movement in the Soviet Union, it would come from the creative intelligentsia, and I remember my reviewer in the *Times Literary Supplement* expressing disbelief. "No," he said, "it would come from the working class." Well, the Russian working class has not been heard from yet.

One must, of course, not exaggerate the numbers involved in Soviet dissent. True, there are many more dissidents than there were, say, fifteen years ago, and many more than one would then have believed possible. But dissent is still very much a mini-movement. When the movement was at its height, in 1968–71, there were still only about one thousand people sufficiently involved to put their names to documents. That, of course, demands great courage, for the consequences can be very unpleasant, and not many people are cast in the heroic mold. But suppose there stood behind each signature twenty or thirty or forty silent supporters who approved but were unwilling to stick their necks out. In a country of 250 million this would still be a conspicuously microscopic minority.

Moreover, the Russian intelligentsia is rather pessimistic. It has no faith in the possibility of changing the system. I would say that the majority of the intelligentsia, instead of trying to reform the regime, seek to escape it, and this "autonomization" may well represent the main form of critical movement in the Soviet Union. For every *intelligent* politically active, there must be ten escapists of this kind.

URBAN: "Internal emigration"—as the phenomenon is known in Central and Eastern Europe.

PIPES: All this may of course change, but until the majority of the intelligentsia can see that dissent is producing results, they are not going to take chances. Fortunately there are those one thousand brave souls who *will* stand up to be counted. Their commitment is so strong that the open defiance of the system is a categorical imperative for them. But the majority, even the most decent ones among them, will hesitate to put their careers and freedom at risk; they will sit on the sidelines, but once they perceive a genuine possibility of change, they will come into the movement in their tens of thousands. Whether one chooses to call this attitude self-preservation and prudence or, with Amalrik, opportunism and cowardice, it is a fact of life in the Soviet Union.

URBAN: But surely the privatization of life is itself an act of great political significance in a totalitarian state.

PIPES: It most surely is. Even under the ancien regime everything in Russia was politicized. In the Soviet Union the theory of "Art for Art's sake," for example, represents a constitutional statement. It is deeply subversive, for you are in fact saying that there are natural limits to the authority of the state. "This is my private universe," you are implying. "Keep off." The function of Russian literature has always been to reserve and preserve this private sanctuary. Pushkin, Herzen, Turgenev, Dostoevsky, Chekhov are, therefore, the most subversive intellectual challenge to the Soviet state.

URBAN: And yet, although all these subversive Russian classics are freely available in the Soviet Union and have, in fact, been incorporated in the secular culture, the over-spill into political action has been minuscule. In the Europe of 1848, a poem or an economic treatise was a call to political action and often led to direct political action. In 1956 and 1968, too, the works of Hungarian, Czech, and Slovak writers, poets, and economists had a direct impact on the shape of events. But in the Soviet Union, even Solzhenitsyn's *One Day in the Life of Ivan Denisovich* was published under official license, and when Solzhenitsyn went too far, the license was withdrawn.

PIPES: True, but, as I say, Russian literature is subversive in a different sense. With the possible exception of Dostoevsky, especially in his Pan-Slavic period at the end of his life, no great Russian writer was politically engaged in the sense of a Petöfi or Mickiewicz. The Russian classical writer is subversive because he is saying that man's spiritual private estate is autonomous and much more important than public thought or public activity. He believes that truth, integrity, the affirmation of the fragility of life and of the fallibility of human judgement are the best antidotes to lies. And a system which is, as Solzhenitsyn shows, permeated with lies, is extremely exposed to the subversive power of truth and civilized values.

In a book I have just finished writing I am quoting Chekhov's correspondence with the Conservative publicist A. S. Suvorin. Chekhov denies in one of his letters that it is the writer's job to press home [an ethical] message. He says: "It isn't. You don't judge. I describe horse-thieves," he writes to Suvorin; "Do you want me to tell the reader that stealing horses is immoral? He knows that without me. My business is to show that people steal horses not because they are poor, but because it is a cult with them—they can't live in any other way. And that is my function as a writer—not to be a conservative or liberal." Tolstoy says the same thing, and so does Pushkin: "Making political judgements— that's for you politicians and intellectuals; you fight it out. Our function is to describe things as we see them."

URBAN: But isn't this precisely what Amalrik is upbraiding the Russian intellectuals for when he accuses them of cowardice?: "People accustomed to thinking one thing, saying another and doing a third"—a cry that is as Greek in its simplicity as it is, alas, applicable to intelligentsias everywhere.

PIPES: Well, what do you want the Russian intelligentsia to do? Look at the conditions that exist in the Soviet Union! If you manage to maintain your human decency in that forcing house of corruption and brutality, if you can manage to keep your eyes open and not swallow the propaganda, you are doing all you humanly can short of joining the resistance and offering yourself for martyrdom. It is a very considerable achievement, and if enough people do it, the system is in trouble.

Unfortunately the regime can always call on an enormous reservoir of people untouched by Russian culture. These unread masses are not humanized in the way that makes the intelligentsia resistant to regime propaganda. But those who have been touched by classical Russian literature are difficult to handle. There are, of course, plenty of scoundrels in the KGB who know their

Pushkin by heart, just as there were many sensitive Beethoven lovers among the SS. Individual cases often escape generalization; but by and large I would stand by my judgement that the Russian classics perform an immensely humanizing and therefore subversive function.

One talks in Russia of two sovereigns—a sovereign of "bodies" and a sovereign of "souls"—the phrase is Pushkin's. Pushkin was a sovereign of the mind, Tolstoy was another, and, in our own day, Solzhenitsyn is a third, and that is why the Soviet Union could not tolerate him. But it would be a mistake to think, or to expect, that these Russian sovereigns of the mind incite to political action, revolution, or any other practical program. They are, rather, sensitizing the national culture, as Shakespeare did in England and Goethe in Germany, to those values which put the spirit before the body, truth before falsehood, beauty before the vulgar, and integrity before sophistry. It is the cultivation of these qualities that may make Russia ready for an overarching détente not only with the West but with her own past too.

SIX

Why the Soviet Union Thinks It Could Fight and Win a Nuclear War

When I wrote this essay in the spring of 1977 I thought I was stating the obvious, and so I was quite unprepared for the reaction that followed. It was extremely violent because my argument went to the very heart of a widely accepted nuclear doctrine, virtually axiomatic in American scientific circles, to the effect that there was only one rational strategy for dealing with nuclear weapons (the American one). I am glad to say that with the help of the Soviet military establishment, the opposition has gradually melted away. In August 1980 President Carter signed Presidential Directive 59, which postulates the possibility that the Soviet Union has a war-fighting, war-winning nuclear strategy and orders steps to protect the United States against it.

In a recent interview with the *New Republic,* Paul Warnke, the newly appointed head of the Arms Control and Disarmament Agency, responded as follows to the question of how the United States ought to react to indications that the Soviet leadership thinks it possible to fight and win a nuclear war. "In my view," he replied, "this kind of thinking is on a level of abstraction which is unrealistic. It seems to me that instead of talking in those terms, which would indulge what I regard as the primitive aspects of Soviet nuclear doctrine, we ought to be trying to educate them into the real world of strategic nuclear weapons, which is that nobody could possibly win."[1]

Reprinted by permission from *Commentary,* LXIV, No. 1 (July 1977), 21–34.

Even after allowance has been made for Mr. Warnke's notoriously careless syntax, puzzling questions remain. On what grounds does he, a Washington lawyer, presume to "educate" the Soviet general staff composed of professional soldiers who thirty years ago defeated the Wehrmacht—and, of all things, about the "real world of strategic nuclear weapons" of which they happen to possess a considerably larger arsenal than we? Why does he consider them children who ought not to be "indulged"? And why does he chastise for what he regards as a "primitive" and unrealistic strategic doctrine not those who hold it, namely the Soviet military, but Americans who worry about their holding it?

Be all that as it may, even if Mr. Warnke refuses to take Soviet strategic doctrine seriously, it behooves us to take Mr. Warnke's views of Soviet doctrine seriously. He not only will head our SALT II team; his thinking as articulated in the above statement and on other occasions reflects all the conventional wisdom of the school of strategic theory dominant in the United States, one of whose leading characteristics is scorn for Soviet views on nuclear warfare.

American and Soviet nuclear doctrines, it needs stating at the outset, are starkly at odds. The prevalent U.S. doctrine holds that an all-out war between countries in possession of sizable nuclear arsenals would be so destructive as to leave no winner; thus resort to arms has ceased to represent a rational policy option for the leaders of such countries vis-à-vis one another. The classic dictum of Clausewitz, that war is politics pursued by other means, is widely believed in the United States to have lost its validity after Hiroshima and Nagasaki. Soviet doctrine, by contrast, emphatically asserts that while an all-out nuclear war would indeed prove extremely destructive to both parties, its outcome would not be mutual suicide: the country better prepared for it and in possession of a superior strategy could win and emerge a viable society. "There is profound erroneousness and harm in the disorienting claims of bourgeois ideologies that there will be no victor in a thermonuclear world war," thunders an authoritative Soviet publication.[2] The theme is mandatory in the current Soviet military literature. Clausewitz, buried in the United States, seems to be alive and prospering in the Soviet Union.

The predisposition of the American strategic community is to shrug off this fundamental doctrinal discrepancy. American doctrine has been and continues to be formulated and implemented by and large without reference to its Soviet counterpart. It is assumed here that there exists one and only one "rational" strategy appropriate to the age of thermonuclear weapons, and that this strategy rests on the principle of "mutual deterrence" developed in the United States some two decades ago. Evidence that the Russians do not share this doctrine which, as its name indicates, postulates reciprocal attitudes, is usually dismissed with the explanation that they are clearly lagging behind us: given time and patient "education," they will surely come around.

It is my contention that this attitude rests on a combination of arrogance and ignorance; that it is dangerous; and that it is high time to start paying heed to Soviet strategic doctrine, lest we end up deterring no one but ourselves. There is ample evidence that the Soviet military say what they mean, and usually mean what they say. When the recently deceased Soviet Minister of Defense, Marshal Grechko, assures us: "We have never concealed, and do not conceal, the fundamental, principal tenets of our military doctrine,"[3] he deserves a hearing. This is especially true in view of the fact that Soviet military deployments over the past twenty years make far better sense in the light of Soviet doctrine, "primitive" and "unrealistic" as the latter may appear, than when reflected in the mirror of our own doctrinal assumptions.

*   *   *

Mistrust of the military professional, combined with a pervasive conviction, typical of commercial societies, that human conflicts are at bottom caused by misunderstanding and ought to be resolved by negotiations rather than force, has worked against serious attention to military strategy by the United States. We have no general staff; we grant no higher degrees in "military science"; and, except for Admiral Mahan, we have produced no strategist of international repute. America has tended to rely on its insularity to protect it from aggressors, and on its unique industrial capacity to help crush its enemies once war was under way. The United States is accustomed to waging

wars of its own choosing and on its own terms. It lacks an ingrained strategic tradition. In the words of one historian, Americans tend to view both military strategy and the armed forces as
something to be "employed intermittently to destroy occasional
and intermittent threats posed by hostile powers."[4]

This approach to warfare has had a number of consequences.
The United States wants to win its wars quickly and with the
smallest losses in American lives. It is disinclined, therefore, to
act on protracted and indirect strategies, or to engage in limited
wars and wars of attrition. Once it resorts to arms, it prefers to
mobilize the great might of its industrial plant to produce vast
quantities of the means of destruction with which in the shortest
possible time to undermine the enemy's will and ability to continue the struggle. Extreme reliance on technological superiority,
characteristic of U.S. warfare, is the obverse side of America's
extreme sensitivity to its own casualties; so is indifference to
the casualties inflicted on the enemy. The strategic bombing
campaigns waged by the U.S. Air Force and the RAF against
Germany and Japan in World War II excellently implemented
this general attitude. Paradoxically, America's dread of war and
casualties pushes it to adopt some of the most brutal forms of
warfare, involving the indiscriminate destruction of the enemy's
homeland with massive civilian deaths.

These facts must be borne in mind to understand the way the
United States reacted to the advent of the nuclear bomb. The
traditional military services—the army and the navy—whose
future seemed threatened by the invention of a weapon widely
believed to have revolutionized warfare and rendered conventional forces obsolete, resisted extreme claims made on behalf
of the bomb. But they were unable to hold out for very long.
An alliance of politicians and scientists, backed by the Air
Force, soon overwhelmed them. "Victory through Air Power,"
a slogan eminently suited to the American way of war, carried
all before it once bombs could be devised whose explosive power
was measured in kilotons and megatons.

The U.S. Army tried to argue after Hiroshima and Nagasaki
that the new weapons represented no fundamental break-
through. No revolution in warfare had occurred, its spokesman
claimed: atomic bombs were merely a more efficient species

of the aerial bombs used in World War II, and in themselves no more able to ensure victory than the earlier bombs had been. As evidence, they could point to the comprehensive U.S. Strategic Bombing Surveys carried out after the war to assess the effects of the bombing campaigns. These had demonstrated that saturation raids against German and Japanese cities had neither broken the enemy's morale nor paralyzed his armaments industry; indeed, German productivity kept on rising in the face of intensified Allied bombing, attaining its peak in the fall of 1944, on the eve of capitulation.

And when it came to horror, atomic bombs had nothing over conventional ones: as against the 72,000 casualties caused by the atomic bomb in Hiroshima, conventional raids carried out against Tokyo and Dresden in 1945 had caused 84,000 and 135,000 fatalities, respectively.[5] Furthermore, those who sought to minimize the impact of the new weapon argued, atomic weapons in no sense obviated the need for sizable land and sea forces. For example, General Ridgway, as Chief of Staff in the early 1950s, maintained that war waged with tactical nuclear weapons would demand larger rather than smaller field armies since these weapons were more complicated, since they would produce greater casualties, and since the dispersal of troops required by nuclear tactics called for increasing the depth of the combat zone.[6]

As we shall note below, similar arguments disputing the revolutionary character of the nuclear weapon surfaced in the Soviet Union, and there promptly came to dominate strategic theory. In the United States, they were just as promptly silenced by a coalition of groups each of which it suited, for its own reasons, to depict the atomic bomb as the "absolute weapon" that had, in large measure, rendered traditional military establishments redundant and traditional strategic thinking obsolete.

* * *

Once World War II was over, the United States was most eager to demobilize its armed forces. Between June 1945 and June 1946, the U.S. Army reduced its strength from 8.3 to 1.9 million men; comparable manpower cuts were achieved in the navy and air force. Little more than a year after Germany's surrender, the military forces of the United States, which at their peak had stood at 12.3 million men, were cut down to 3 million; two years later they declined below 2 million. The demobilization proceeded at a pace (if not in a manner) reminiscent of the dissolution of the Russian army in the revolutionary year of 1917. Nothing could have stopped this mass of humanity streaming homeward. To most Americans, peacetime conditions meant reversion to a skeletal armed force.

Yet, at the same time, growing strains in the wartime alliance with the Soviet Union, and mounting evidence that Stalin was determined to exploit the chaotic conditions brought about by the collapse of the Axis powers to expand his domain, called for an effective military force able to deter the Soviets. The United States could not fulfill its role as leader of the Western coalition without an ability to project its military power globally.

In this situation, the nuclear weapon seemed to offer an ideal solution: the atomic bomb could hardly have come at a better time from the point of view of U.S. international commitments. Here was a device so frighteningly destructive, it was believed, that the mere threat of its employment would serve to dissuade would-be aggressors from carrying out their designs. Once the Air Force received the B-36, the world's first intercontinental bomber, the United States acquired the ability to threaten the Soviet Union with devastating punishment without, at the same time, being compelled to maintain a large and costly standing army.

Reliance on the nuclear deterrent became more imperative than ever after the conclusion of the Korean war, in the course of which U.S. defense expenditures had been sharply driven up. President Eisenhower had committed himself to a policy of fiscal restraint. He wanted to cut the defense budget appreciably, and yet he had to do so without jeopardizing either America's territorial security or its worldwide commitments. In an effort to reconcile these contradictory desires, the President and his Secretary of State, John Foster Dulles, enunciated in the winter of 1953-54 a strategic doctrine which to an unprecedented degree based the country's security on a single weapon, the nuclear deterrent. In an address to the United Nations in

December 1953, Eisenhower argued that since there was no defense against nuclear weapons (i.e., thermonuclear or hydrogen bombs, which both countries were then beginning to produce), war between the two "atomic colossi" would leave no victors and probably cause the demise of civilization. A month later, Dulles enunciated what came to be known as the doctrine of "massive retaliation." The United States, he declared, had decided "to depend primarily upon a great capacity to retaliate, instantly, by means and at places of our choosing." Throughout his address, Dulles emphasized the fiscal benefits of such a strategy, "more basic security at less cost."

The Eisenhower-Dulles formula represented a neat compromise between America's desires to reduce the defense budget and simultaneously to retain the capacity to respond to Soviet threats. The driving force was not, however, military but budgetary: behind "massive retaliation" (as well as its offspring, "mutual deterrence") lay *fiscal* imperatives. In the nuclear deterrent, the United States found a perfect resolution of the conflicting demands of domestic and foreign responsibilities. For this reason alone its adoption was a foregone conclusion: the alternatives were either a vast standing army or forfeiture of status as a leading world power. The Air Force enthusiastically backed the doctrine of massive retaliation. As custodian of the atomic bomb, it had a vested interest in a defense posture of which that weapon was the linchpin. And since in the first postwar decade the intercontinental bomber was the only available vehicle for delivering the bomb against an enemy like the Soviet Union, the Air Force could claim a goodly share of the defense budget built around the retaliation idea.

Although the Soviet Union exploded a fission bomb in 1949 and announced the acquisition of a fusion (or hydrogen) bomb four years later, the United States still continued for a while longer to enjoy an effective monopoly on nuclear retaliation, since the Soviet Union lacked the means of delivering quantities of such bombs against U.S. territory. That situation changed dramatically in 1957 when the Soviets launched the Sputnik. This event, which their propaganda hailed as a great contribution to the advancement of science (and ours as proof of the failures of the American educational system!), represented in

fact a significant military demonstration, namely, the ability of
the Russians to deliver nuclear warheads against the United
States homeland, until then immune from direct enemy threats.
At this point massive retaliation ceased to make much sense and
before long yielded to the doctrine of "mutual deterrence."
The new doctrine postulated that inasmuch as both the Soviet
Union and the United States possessed (or would soon possess)
the means of destroying each other, neither country could
rationally contemplate resort to war. The nuclear stockpiles
of each were an effective deterrent which ensured that they
would not be tempted to launch an attack.

This doctrine was worked out in great and sophisticated
detail by a bevy of civilian experts employed by various government and private organizations. These physicists, chemists,
mathematicians, economists, and political scientists came to
the support of the government's fiscally-driven imperatives with
scientific demonstrations in favor of the nuclear deterrent.
Current U.S. strategic theory was thus born of a marriage between the scientist and the accountant. The professional soldier
was jilted.

*   *   *

A large part of the U.S. scientific community had been convinced as soon as the first atomic bomb was exploded that the
nuclear weapon, which that community had conceived and
helped to develop, had accomplished a complete revolution in
warfare. This conclusion was reached without much reference
to the analysis of the effects of atomic weapons carried out by
the military, and indeed without consideration of the traditional principles of warfare. It represented, rather, an act of
faith on the part of an intellectual community which held strong
pacifist convictions and felt deep guilt at having participated in
the creation of a weapon of such destructive power. As early
as 1946, in an influential book sponsored by the Yale Institute
of International Affairs, under the title *The Absolute Weapon*,
a group of civilian strategic theorists enunciated the principles
of the mutual-deterrence theory which subsequently became
the official U.S. strategic doctrine. The principal points made

in this work may be summarized as follows:

1. Nuclear weapons are "absolute weapons" in the sense that they can cause unacceptable destruction, but also and above all because there exists against them no possible defense. When the aggressor is certain to suffer the same punishment as his victim, aggression ceases to make sense. Hence war is no longer a rational policy option, as it had been throughout human history. In the words of Bernard Brodie, the book's editor: "Thus far the chief purpose of our military establishment had been to win wars. From now on its chief purpose must be to avert them. It can have almost no other useful purpose" (p. 76).

2. Given the fact that the adjective "absolute" means, by definition, incapable of being exceeded or surpassed, in the nuclear age military superiority has become meaningless. As another contributor to the book, William T. R. Fox, expressed it: "When dealing with the absolute weapon, arguments based on relative advantage lose their point" (p. 181). From which it follows that the objective of modern defense policy should be not superiority in weapons, traditionally sought by the military, but "sufficiency"; just enough nuclear weapons to be able to threaten a potential aggressor with unacceptable retaliation—in other words, an "adequate" deterrent, no more, no less.

3. Nuclear deterrence can become effective only if it restrains mutually—i.e., if the United States and the Soviet Union each can deter the other from aggression. An American monopoly on nuclear weapons would be inherently destabilizing, both because it could encourage the United States to launch a nuclear attack, and, at the same time, by making the Russians feel insecure, cause them to act aggressively. "Neither we nor the Russians can expect to feel even reasonably safe unless an atomic attack by one were certain to unleash a devastating atomic counterattack by the other," Arnold Wolfers maintained (p. 135). In other words, to feel secure the United States actually required the Soviet Union to have the capacity to destroy it.

*   *   *

Barely one year after Hiroshima and three years before the Soviets were to acquire a nuclear bomb, *The Absolute Weapon* articulated the philosophical premises underlying the mutual deterrence doctrine which today dominates U.S. strategic thinking. Modern strategy, in the opinion of its contributors, involved preventing wars rather than winning them, securing sufficiency in decisive weapons rather than superiority, and even ensuring the potential enemy's ability to strike back. Needless to elaborate, these principles ran contrary to all the tenets of traditional military theory, which had always called for superiority in forces and viewed the objective of war to be victory. But then, if one had decided that the new weapons marked a qualitative break with all the weapons ever used in combat, one could reasonably argue that past military experience, and the theory based on it, had lost relevance. Implicit in these assumptions was the belief that Clausewitz and his celebrated formula proclaiming war an extension of politics were dead. Henry Kissinger, who can always be counted upon to utter commonplaces in the tone of prophetic revelation, announced Clausewitz's obituary nearly twenty years after *The Absolute Weapon* had made the point, in these words: "The traditional mode of military analysis which saw in war a continuation of politics but with its own appropriate means is no longer applicable."[7]

American civilian strategists holding such views gained the dominant voice in the formulation of U.S. strategic doctrine with the arrival in Washington in 1961 of Robert S. McNamara as President Kennedy's Secretary of Defense. A prominent business executive specializing in finance and accounting, McNamara applied to the perennial problem of American strategy—how to maintain a credible global military posture without a large and costly military establishment—the methods of cost analysis. These had first been applied by the British during World War II under the name "operations research" and subsequently came to be adopted here as "systems analysis." Weapons' procurement was to be tested and decided by the same methods used to evaluate returns on investment in ordinary business enterprises. Mutual deterrence was taken for granted: the question of strategic posture reduced itself to the issue of which weapons systems would provide the United States with effective deterrence at the least expense. Under McNamara the procurement of weapons, decided on the basis of cost effectiveness, came in effect to direct strategy, rather than the other way around, as had been the case through most of military history. It is at this point that applied science in partnership with budgetary accountancy—a partnership which had developed U.S. strategic theory—also took charge of U.S. defense policy.

*   *   *

As worked out in the 1960s, and still in effect today, American nuclear theory rests on these propositions: All-out nuclear war is not a rational policy option, since no winner could possibly emerge from such a war. Should the Soviet Union nevertheless launch a surprise attack on the United States, the latter would emerge with enough of a deterrent to devastate the Soviet Union in a second strike. Since such a retaliatory attack would cost the Soviet Union millions of casualties and the destruction of all its major cities, a Soviet first strike is most unlikely. Meaningful defenses against a nuclear attack are technically impossible and psychologically counterproductive; nuclear superiority is meaningless.

In accord with these assumptions, the United States in the mid-1960s unilaterally froze its force of ICBM's at 1,054 and dismantled nearly all its defenses against enemy bombers. Civil-defense was all but abandoned, as was in time the attempt to create an ABM system which held out the possibility of protecting American missile sites against a surprise enemy attack. The Russians were watched benignly as they moved toward parity with the United States in the number of intercontinental launchers, and then proceeded to attain numerical superiority. The expectation was that as soon as the Russians felt themselves equal to the United States in terms of effective deterrence, they would stop further deployments. The frenetic pace of the Soviet nuclear build-up was explained first on the ground that the Russians had a lot of catching up to do, then that they had to consider the Chinese threat, and finally on the grounds that they are inherently a very insecure people and should be allowed an edge in deterrent capability.

Whether mutual deterrence deserves the name of a strategy at all is a real question. As one student of the subject puts it:

Although commonly called a "strategy," "assured destruction" was by itself an antithesis of strategy. Unlike any strategy that ever preceded it throughout the history of armed conflict, it ceased to be useful precisely where military strategy is supposed to come into effect: at the edge of war. It posited that the principal mission of the U.S. military under conditions of ongoing nuclear operations against [the continental United States] was to shut its eyes, grit its teeth, and reflexively unleash an indiscriminate and simultaneous reprisal against all Soviet aim points on a preestablished target list. Rather than deal in a considered way with the particular attack on hand so as to minimize further damage to the United States and maximize the possibility of an early settlement on reasonably acceptable terms, it had the simple goal of inflicting punishment for the Soviet transgression. Not only did this reflect an implicit repudiation of political responsibility, it also risked provoking just the sort of counterreprisal against the United States that a rational wartime strategy should attempt to prevent.[8]

I cite this passage merely to indicate that the basic postulates of U.S. nuclear strategy are not as self-evident and irrefutable as its proponents seem to believe; and that, therefore, their rejection by the Soviet military is not, in and of itself, proof that Soviet thinking is "primitive" and devoid of a sense of realism.

The principal differences between American and Soviet strategies are traceable to different conceptions of the role of conflict and its inevitable concomitant, violence, in human relations; and secondly, to different functions which the military establishment performs in the two societies.

In the United States, the consensus of the educated and affluent holds all recourse to force to be the result of an inability or an unwillingness to apply rational analysis and patient negotiation to disagreements: the use of force is prima facie evidence of failure. Some segments of this class not only refuse to acknowledge the existence of violence as a fact of life, they have even come to regard fear—the organism's biological reaction to the threat of violence—as inadmissible. "The notion of being threatened has acquired an almost class connotation," Daniel P. Moynihan notes in connection with the refusal of America's "sophisticated" elite to accept the reality of a Soviet threat.

"If you're not very educated, you're easily frightened. And not being ever frightened can be a formula for self-destruction."[9]

Now this entire middle-class, commercial, essentially Protestant ethos is absent from Soviet culture, whose roots feed on another kind of soil, and which has had for centuries to weather rougher political climes. The Communist revolution of 1917, by removing from positions of influence what there was of a Russian bourgeoisie (a class Lenin was prone to define as much by cultural as by socioeconomic criteria), in effect installed in power the *muzhik,* the Russian peasant. And the *muzhik* had been taught by long historical experience that cunning and coercion alone ensured survival: one employed cunning when weak, and cunning coupled with coercion when strong. Not to use force when one had it indicated some inner weakness. Marxism, with its stress on class war as a natural condition of mankind so long as the means of production were privately owned, has merely served to reinforce these ingrained convictions. The result is an extreme Social-Darwinist outlook on life which today permeates the Russian elite as well as the Russian masses, and which only the democratic intelligentsia and the religious dissenters oppose to any significant extent.

The Soviet ruling elite regards conflict and violence as natural regulators of all human affairs: wars between nations, in its view, represent only a variant of wars between classes, recourse to the one or the other being dependent on circumstances. A conflictless world will come into being only when the socialist (i.e., Communist) mode of production spreads across the face of the earth.

The Soviet view of armed conflict can be illustrated with another citation from the writings of the late Marshal Grechko, one of the most influential Soviet military figures of the post–World War II era. In his principal treatise, Grechko refers to the classification of wars formulated in 1972 by his U.S. counterpart, Melvin Laird. Laird divided wars according to engineering criteria—in terms of weapons employed and the scope of the theater of operations—to come up with four principal types of wars: strategic-nuclear, theater-nuclear, theater-conventional, and local-conventional. Dismissing this classification as inadequate, Grechko applies quite different standards to come up with his own typology:

Proceeding from the fundamental contradictions of the contemporary era, one can distinguish, according to *sociopolitical criteria,* the following types of wars: (1) wars between states (coalitions) of two contrary social systems—capitalist and socialist; (2) civil wars between the proletariat and the bourgeoisie, or between the popular masses and the forces of the extreme reaction supported by the imperialists of other countries; (3) wars between imperialist states and the peoples of colonial and dependent states fighting for their freedom and independence; and (4) wars among capitalist states.[10]

This passage contains many interesting implications. For instance, it makes no allowance for war between two Communist countries, like the Soviet Union and China, though such a war seems greatly to preoccupy the Soviet leadership. Nor does it provide for war pitting a coalition of capitalist and Communist states against another capitalist state, such as actually occurred during World War II when the United States and the Soviet Union joined forces against Germany. But for our purposes, the most noteworthy aspect of Grechko's system of classification is the notion that social and national conflicts *within* the capitalist camp (that is, in all countries not under Communist control) are nothing more than a particular mode of class conflict of which all-out nuclear war between the superpowers is a conceivable variant. In terms of this typology, an industrial strike in the United States, the explosion of a terrorist bomb in Belfast or Jerusalem, the massacre by Rhodesian guerrillas of a black village or a white farmstead, differ from nuclear war between the Soviet Union and the United States only in degree, not in kind. All such conflicts are calibrations on the extensive scale by which to measure the historic conflict which pits Communism against capitalism and imperialism. Such conflicts are inherent in the stage of human development which precedes the final abolition of classes.

Middle-class American intellectuals simply cannot assimilate this mentality, so alien is it to their experience and view of human nature. Confronted with the evidence that the most influential elements in the Soviet Union do indeed hold such views, they prefer to dismiss the evidence as empty rhetoric, and to regard with deep suspicion the motives of anyone who insists on taking it seriously. Like some ancient Oriental despots, they vent their wrath on the bearers of bad news. How ironic that the very people who have failed so dismally to persuade American television networks to eliminate violence from their programs, nevertheless feel confident that they can talk the Soviet leadership into eliminating violence from its political arsenal!

Solzhenitsyn grasped the issue more profoundly as well as more realistically when he defined the antithesis of war not as the absence of armed conflict between nations—i.e., "peace" in the conventional meaning of the term—but as the absence of all violence, internal as well as external. His comprehensive definition, drawn from his Soviet experience, obversely matches the comprehensive Soviet definition of warfare.

*   *   *

We know surprisingly little about the individuals and institutions whose responsibility it is to formulate Soviet military doctrine. The matter is handled with the utmost secrecy, which conceals from the eyes of outsiders the controversies that undoubtedly surround it. Two assertions, however, can be made with confidence.

Because of Soviet adherence to the Clausewitzian principle that warfare is always an extension of politics—i.e., subordinate to overall political objectives (about which more below)—Soviet military planning is carried out under the close supervision of the country's highest political body, the Politburo. Thus military policy is regarded as an intrinsic element of "grand strategy," whose arsenal also includes a variety of non-military instrumentalities.

Secondly, the Russians regard warfare as a science (*nauka,* in the German sense of *Wissenschaft*). Instruction in the subject is offered at a number of university-level institutions, and several hundred specialists, most of them officers on active duty, have been accorded the Soviet equivalent of the Ph.D. in military science. This means that Soviet military doctrine is formulated by full-time specialists: it is as much the exclusive province of the certified military professional as medicine is that of the licensed physician. The civilian strategic theorist who since World War II has played a decisive role in the formulation of U.S. strategic doctrine is not in evidence in the Soviet Union, and probably performs at best a secondary, consultative function.

Its penchant for secrecy notwithstanding, the Soviet military establishment does release a large quantity of unclassified literature in the form of books, specialist journals, and newspapers. Of the books, the single most authoritative work at present is unquestionably the collective study, *Military Strategy,* edited by the late Marshal V. D. Sokolovskii, which summarizes Soviet warfare doctrine of the nuclear age.[11] Although published fifteen years ago, Sokolovskii's volume remains the only Soviet strategic manual publicly available—a solitary monument confronting a mountain of Western works on strategy. A series called "The Officer's Library" brings out important specialized studies.[12] The newspaper *Krasnaia zvezda* ("Red Star") carries important theoretical articles which, however, vie for the reader's attention with heroic pictures of Soviet troops storming unidentified beaches and firing rockets at unnamed foes. The flood of military works has as its purpose indoctrination, an objective to which the Soviet high command attaches the utmost importance: indoctrination both in the psychological sense, designed to persuade the Soviet armed forces that they are invincible, as well as of a technical kind, to impress upon the officers and ranks the principles of Soviet tactics and the art of operations.

To a Western reader, most of this printed matter is unadulterated rubbish. It not only lacks the sophistication and intellectual elegance which he takes for granted in works on problems of nuclear strategy; it is also filled with a mixture of pseudo-Marxist jargon and the crudest kind of Russian jingoism. Which is one of the reasons why it is hardly ever read in the West, even by people whose business it is to devise a national strategy against a possible Soviet threat. By and large the material is ignored. Two examples must suffice. *Strategy in the Missile Age,* an influential work by Bernard Brodie, one of the pioneers of U.S. nuclear doctrine, which originally came out in 1959, and was republished in 1965, makes only a few offhand allusions to Soviet nuclear strategy, and then either to note with approval that it is "developing along lines familiar in the United States" (p. 171), or else, when the Russians prefer to follow their own track, to dismiss it as a "ridiculous and reckless fantasy" (p. 215). Secretary of Defense McNamara perused Sokolovskii and "remained unimpressed," for nowhere in the book did he find "a sophisticated analysis of nuclear war."[13]

The point to bear in mind, however, is that Soviet military literature, like all Soviet literature on politics broadly defined, is written in an elaborate code language. Its purpose is not to dazzle with originality and sophistication but to convey to the initiates messages of grave importance. Soviet policy-makers may speak to one another plainly in private, but when they take pen in hand they invariably resort to an "Aesopian" language, a habit acquired when the forerunner of today's Communist party had to function in the Czarist underground. Buried in the flood of seemingly meaningless verbiage, nuggets of precious information on Soviet perceptions and intentions can more often than not be unearthed by a trained reader. In 1958–59 two American specialists employed by the Rand Corporation, Raymond L. Garthoff and Herbert S. Dinerstein, by skillfully deciphering Soviet literature on strategic problems and then interpreting this information against the background of the Soviet military tradition, produced a remarkably prescient forecast of actual Soviet military policies of the 1960s and 1970s.[14] Unfortunately, their findings were largely ignored by U.S. strategists from the scientific community who had convinced themselves that there was only one strategic doctrine appropriate to the age of nuclear weapons, and that therefore evidence indicating that the Soviets were adopting a different strategy could be safely disregarded.

*   *   *

This predisposition helps explain why U.S. strategists persistently ignored signs indicating that those who had control of Soviet Russia's nuclear arsenal were not thinking in terms of mutual deterrence. The calculated nonchalance with which Stalin at Potsdam reacted to President Truman's confidences about the American atomic bomb was a foretaste of things to come. Initial Soviet reactions to Hiroshima and Nagasaki were similar in tone: the atomic weapon had not in any significant manner altered the science of warfare or rendered obsolete the principles which had guided the Red Army in its victorious campaigns against the Wehrmacht. These basic laws, known as

the five "constant principles" that win wars, had been formulated by Stalin in 1942. They were, in declining order of importance: "stability of the home front," followed by morale of
the armed forces, quantity and quality of the divisions, *military
equipment,* and, finally, ability of the commanders.[15] There
was no such thing as an "absolute weapon"—weapons altogether
occupied a subordinate place in warfare; defense against atomic
bombs was entirely possible.[16] This was disconcerting, to be
sure, but it could be explained away as a case of sour grapes.
After all, the Soviet Union had no atomic bomb, and it was not
in its interest to seem overly impressed by a weapon on which
its rival enjoyed a monopoly.[17]

In September 1949 the Soviet Union exploded a nuclear
device. Disconcertingly, its attitude to nuclear weapons did not
change, at any rate not in public. For the remaining four years,
until Stalin's death, the Soviet high command continued to
deny that nuclear weapons required fundamental revisions of
accepted military doctrine. With a bit of good will, this ob-
duracy could still have been rationalized: for although the
Soviet Union now had the weapon, it still lacked adequate
means of delivering it across continents insofar as it had few
intercontinental bombers (intercontinental rockets were regarded
in the West as decades away). The United States, by contrast,
possessed not only a fleet of strategic bombers but also numerous air bases in countries adjoining Soviet Russia. So once again
one could find a persuasive explanation of why the Russians
refused to see the light. It seemed reasonable to expect that as
soon as they had acquired both a stockpile of atomic bombs
and a fleet of strategic bombers, they would adjust their doctrine
to conform with the American.

Events which ensued immediately after Stalin's death seemed
to lend credence to these expectations. Between 1953 and 1957
a debate took place in the pages of Soviet publications which,
for all its textural obscurity, indicated that a new school of
Soviet strategic thinkers had arisen to challenge the conventional
wisdom. The most articulate spokesman of this new school,
General N. Talenskii, argued that the advent of nuclear weapons,
especially the hydrogen bomb which had just appeared on the
scene, did fundamentally alter the nature of warfare. The sheer

destructiveness of these weapons was such that one could no longer talk of a socialist strategy automatically overcoming the strategy of capitalist countries: the same rules of warfare now applied to both social systems. For the first time doubt was cast on the immutability of Stalin's "five constant principles." In the oblique manner in which Soviet debates on matters of such import are invariably conducted, Talenskii was saying that perhaps, after all, war had ceased to represent a viable policy option. More important yet, speeches delivered by leading Soviet politicians in the winter of 1953-54 seemed to support the thesis advanced by President Eisenhower in his United Nations address of December 1953 that nuclear war could spell the demise of civilization. In an address delivered on March 12, 1954, and reported the following day in *Pravda,* Stalin's immediate successor, Georgii Malenkov, echoed Eisenhower's sentiments: a new world war would unleash a holocaust which "with the present means of warfare, means the destruction of world civilization."[18]

This assault on its traditional thinking—and, obliquely, on its traditional role—engendered a furious reaction from the Soviet military establishment. The Red Army was not about to let itself be relegated to the status of a militia whose principal task was averting war rather than winning it. Malenkov's unorthodox views on war almost certainly contributed to his downfall; at any rate, his dismissal in February 1955 as party leader was accompanied by a barrage of press denunciations of the notion that war had become unfeasible. There are strong indications that Malenkov's chief rival, Khrushchev, capitalized on the discontent of the military to form with it an alliance with whose help he eventually rode to power. The successful military counterattack seems to have been led by the World War II hero, Marshal Georgii Zhukov, whom Khrushchev made his Minister of Defense and brought into the Presidium. The guidelines of Soviet nuclear strategy, still in force today, were formulated during the first two years of Khrushchev's tenure (1955–57), under the leadership of Zhukov himself. They resulted in the unequivocal rejection of the notion of the "absolute weapon" and all the theories that U.S. strategists had deduced from it. Stalin's view of the military "constants" was implicitly reaffirmed. Thus the re-Stalinization of Soviet life, so noticeable in recent years, manifested itself first in military doctrine.

*   *   *

To understand this unexpected turn of events—so unexpected that most U.S. military theorists thus far have not been able to come to terms with it—one must take into account the function performed by the military in the Soviet system.

Unlike the United States, the Soviet government needs and wants a large military force. It has many uses for it, at home and abroad. As a regime which rests neither on tradition nor on a popular mandate, it sees in its military the most effective manifestation of government omnipotence, the very presence of which discourages any serious opposition from raising its head in the country as well as in its dependencies. It is, after all, the Red Army that keeps Eastern Europe within the Soviet camp. Furthermore, since the regime is driven by ideology, internal politics, and economic exigencies steadily to expand, it requires an up-to-date military force capable of seizing opportunities which may present themselves along the Soviet Union's immensely long frontier or even beyond. The armed forces of the Soviet Union thus have much more to do than merely protect the country from potential aggressors: they are the mainstay of the regime's authority and a principal instrumentality of its internal and external policies. Given the shaky status of the Communist regime internally, the declining appeal of its ideology, and the non-competitiveness of its goods on world markets, a persuasive case can even be made that, ruble for ruble, expenditures on the military represent for the Soviet leadership an excellent and entirely "rational" capital investment.

For this reason alone (and there were other compelling reasons too, as we shall see), the Soviet leadership could not accept the theory of mutual deterrence.[19] After all, this theory, pushed to its logical conclusion, means that a country can rely for its security on a finite number of nuclear warheads and on an appropriate quantity of delivery vehicles; so that, apart perhaps from some small mobile forces needed for local actions, the large and costly traditional military establishments can be disbanded. Whatever the intrinsic military merits of this doctrine may be, its broader implications are entirely unacceptable to a regime like the Soviet one for whom military power serves not only (or even primarily) to deter external aggressors, but also and above all to ensure internal stability and permit external expansion. Thus, ultimately, it is *political* rather than strictly strategic or fiscal considerations that may be said to have determined Soviet reactions to nuclear weapons and shaped the content of Soviet nuclear strategy. As a result, Soviet advocates of mutual deterrence like Talenskii were gradually silenced. By the mid-1960s the country adopted what in military jargon is referred to as a "war-fighting" and "war-winning" doctrine.

Given this fundamental consideration, the rest followed with a certain inexorable logic. The formulation of Soviet strategy in the nuclear age was turned over to the military who are in complete control of the Ministry of Defense. (Two American observers describe this institution as a "uniformed empire."[20]) The Soviet General Staff had only recently emerged from winning one of the greatest wars in history. Immensely confident of their own abilities, scornful of what they perceived as the minor contribution of the United States to the Nazi defeat, inured to casualties running into tens of millions, the Soviet generals tackled the task with relish. Like their counterparts in the U.S. Army, they were professionally inclined to denigrate the exorbitant claims made on behalf of the new weapon by strategists drawn from the scientific community; unlike the Americans, however, they did not have to pay much heed to the civilians. In its essentials, Soviet nuclear doctrine as it finally emerged is not all that different from what American doctrine might have been had military and geopolitical rather than fiscal considerations played the decisive role here as they did there.

*   *   *

Soviet military theorists reject the notion that technology (i.e., weapons) decides strategy. They perceive the relationship to be the reverse: strategic objectives determine the procurement and application of weapons. They agree that the introduc-

tion of nuclear weapons has profoundly affected warfare, but
deny that nuclear weapons have altered its essential quality.
The novelty of nuclear weapons consists not in their destructiveness—that is, after all, a matter of degree, and a country like
the Soviet Union which, as Soviet generals proudly boast, suffered in World War II the loss of over 20 million casualties, as
well as the destruction of 1,710 towns, over 70,000 villages, and
some 32,000 industrial establishments to win the war and
emerge as a global power, is not to be intimidated by the
prospect of destruction.[21] Rather, the innovation consists of
the fact that nuclear weapons, coupled with intercontinental
missiles, can by themselves carry out strategic missions which
previously were accomplished only by means of prolonged
tactical operations:

> Nuclear missiles have altered the relationship of tactical, opera-
> tional, and strategic acts of the armed conflict. If in the past the stra-
> tegic end-result was secured by a succession of sequential, most
> often long-term, efforts [and] comprised the sum of tactical and
> operational successes, strategy being able to realize its intentions
> only with the assistance of the art of operations and tactics, then
> today, by means of powerful nuclear strikes, strategy can attain
> its objectives directly.[22]

In other words, military strategy, rather than a casualty of technology, has, thanks to technology, become more central than
ever. By adopting this view, Soviet theorists believe themselves
to have adapted modern technological innovations in weaponry
to the traditions of military science.

Implicit in all this is the idea that nuclear war is feasible and
that the basic function of warfare, as defined by Clausewitz,
remains permanently valid, whatever breakthroughs may occur
in technology. "It is well known that the essential nature of
*war as a continuation of politics does not change with changing
technology and armament.*"[23] This code phrase from Sokolovskii's authoritative manual was certainly hammered out with all
the care that in the United States is lavished on an amendment
to the Constitution. It spells the rejection of the whole basis
on which U.S. strategy has come to rest: thermonuclear war is
not suicidal, it can be fought and won, and thus resort to war
must not be ruled out.

In addition (though we have no solid evidence to this effect) it seems likely that Soviet strategists reject the mutual-deterrence theory on several technical grounds of a kind that have been advanced by American critics of this theory such as Albert Wohlstetter, Herman Kahn, and Paul Nitze.

1. Mutual deterrence postulates a certain finality about weapons technology: it does not allow for further scientific breakthroughs that could result in the deterrent's becoming neutralized. On the offensive side, for example, there is the possibility of significant improvements in the accuracy of ICBM's or striking innovations in anti-submarine warfare; on the defensive, satellites which are essential for early warning of an impending attack could be blinded and lasers could be put to use to destroy incoming missiles.

2. Mutual deterrence constitutes "passive defense" which usually leads to defeat. It threatens punishment to the aggressor after he has struck, which may or may not deter him from striking; it cannot prevent him from carrying out his designs. The latter objective requires the application of "active defense"— i.e., nuclear preemption.

3. The threat of a second strike, which underpins the mutual-deterrence doctrine, may prove ineffectual. The side that has suffered the destruction of the bulk of its nuclear forces in a surprise first strike may find that it has so little of a deterrent left and the enemy so much, that the cost of striking back in retaliation would be exposing its own cities to total destruction by the enemy's third strike. The result could be a paralysis of will, and capitulation instead of a second strike.

Soviet strategists make no secret of the fact that they regard the U.S. doctrine (with which, judging by the references in their literature, they are thoroughly familiar) as second-rate. In their view, U.S. strategic doctrine is obsessed with a single weapon which it "absolutizes" at the expense of everything else that military experience teaches soldiers to take into account. Its philosophical foundations are "idealism" and "metaphysics"— i.e., currents which engage in speculative discussions of objects (in this case, weapons) and of their "intrinsic" qualities, rather than relying on pragmatic considerations drawn from experience.[24]

Since the mid-1960s, the proposition that thermonuclear war

would be suicidal for both parties has been used by the Russians largely as a commodity for export. Its chief proponents include staff members of the Moscow Institute of the USA and Canada, and Soviet participants at Pugwash, Dartmouth, and similar international conferences, who are assigned the task of strengthening the hand of anti-military intellectual circles in the West. Inside the Soviet Union, such talk is generally denounced as "bourgeois pacifism."[25]

*   *   *

In the Soviet view, a nuclear war would be total and go beyond formal defeat of one side by the other: "War must not simply [be] the defeat of the enemy, it must be his destruction. This condition has become the basis of Soviet military strategy," according to the *Military-Historical Journal.*[26] Limited nuclear war, flexible response, escalation, damage limiting, and all the other numerous refinements of U.S. strategic doctrine find no place in its Soviet counterpart (although, of course, they are taken into consideration in Soviet operational planning).

For Soviet generals the decisive influence in the formulation of nuclear doctrine were the lessons of World War II with which, for understandable reasons, they are virtually obsessed. This experience they seem to have supplemented with knowledge gained from professional scrutiny of the record of Nazi and Japanese offensive operations, as well as the balance sheet of British and American strategic-bombing campaigns. More recently, the lessons of the Israeli-Arab wars of 1967 and 1973 in which they indirectly participated seem also to have impressed Soviet strategists, reinforcing previously held convictions. They also follow the Western literature, tending to side with the critics of mutual deterrence. The result of all these diverse influences is a nuclear doctrine which assimilates into the main body of the Soviet military tradition the technical implications of nuclear warfare without surrendering any of the fundamentals of this tradition.

The strategic doctrine adopted by the USSR over the past two decades calls for a policy diametrically opposite to that adopted in the United States by the predominant community of civilian strategists: not deterrence but victory, not sufficiency in weapons but superiority, not retaliation but offensive action. The doctrine has five related elements: (1) preemption (first strike), (2) quantitative superiority in arms, (3) counterforce targeting, (4) combined-arms operations, and (5) defense. We shall take up each of these elements in turn.

*   *   *

Preemption. The costliest lesson which the Soviet military learned in World War II was the importance of surprise. Because Stalin thought he had an understanding with Hitler, and because he was afraid to provoke his Nazi ally, he forbade the Red Army to mobilize for the German attack of which he had had ample warning. As a result of this strategy of "passive defense," Soviet forces suffered frightful losses and were nearly defeated. This experience etched itself very deeply on the minds of the Soviet commanders: in their theoretical writings no point is emphasized more consistently than the need never again to allow themselves to be caught in a surprise attack. Nuclear weapons make this requirement especially urgent because, according to Soviet theorists, the decision in a nuclear conflict in all probability will be arrived at in the initial hours. In a nuclear war the Soviet Union, therefore, would not again have at its disposal the time which it enjoyed in 1941-42 to mobilize reserves for a victorious counteroffensive after absorbing devastating setbacks.

Given the rapidity of modern warfare (an ICBM can traverse the distance between the USSR and the United States in thirty minutes), not to be surprised by the enemy means, in effect, to inflict surprise on him. Once the latter's ICBM's have left their silos, once his bombers have taken to the air and his submarines to sea, a counterattack is greatly reduced in effectiveness. These considerations call for a preemptive strike. Soviet theorists draw an insistent, though to an outside observer very fuzzy, distinction between "preventive" and "preemptive" attacks. They claim that the Soviet Union will never start a war—i.e., it will never launch a preventive attack—but once it had concluded that an attack upon it was imminent, it would not hesitate to preempt. They argue that historical experience indicates outbreaks of hostilities are generally preceded by prolonged diplomatic crises and military preparations which signal to an alert command an imminent threat and the need to act. Though the analogy is not openly drawn, the action which Soviet strategists seem to have in mind is that taken by the Israelis in 1967, a notably successful example of "active defense" involving a well-timed preemptive strike. (In 1973, by contrast, the Israelis pursued the strategy of "passive defense," with unhappy consequences.) The Soviet doctrine of nuclear preemption was formulated in the late 1950s, and described at the time by Garthoff and Dinerstein in the volumes cited above.

A corollary of the preemption strategy holds that a country's armed forces must always be in a state of high combat readiness so as to be able to go over to active operations with the least delay. Nuclear warfare grants no time for mobilization. Stress on the maintenance of a large ready force is one of the constant themes of Soviet military literature. It helps explain the immense land forces which the USSR maintains at all times and equips with the latest weapons as they roll off the assembly lines.

*   *   *

Quantitative superiority. There is no indication that the Soviet military share the view prevalent in the U.S. that in the nuclear age numbers of weapons do not matter once a certain quantity had been attained. They do like to pile up all sorts of weapons, new on top of old, throwing away nothing that might come in handy. This propensity to accumulate hardware is usually dismissed by Western observers with contemptuous references to a Russian habit dating back to Czarist days. It is not, however, as mindless as it may appear. For although Soviet strategists believe that the ultimate outcome in a nuclear war will be decided in the initial hours of the conflict, they also believe that a nuclear war will be of long duration: to consummate victory—that is, to destroy the enemy—may take months or even longer. Under these conditions, the possession of a large arsenal of nuclear delivery systems, as well as of other types of weapons, may well prove to be of critical importance. Although prohibited by self-imposed limitations agreed upon in 1972 at SALT I from exceeding a set number of intercontinental ballistic-missile launchers, the Soviet Union is constructing large numbers of so-called Intermediate Range Ballistic Missile launchers (i.e., launchers of less than intercontinental range), not covered by SALT. Some of these could be rapidly converted into regular intercontinental launchers, should the need arise.[27]

Reliance on quantity has another cause, namely, the peculiarly destructive capability of modern missiles equipped with Multiple Independently-targetable Reentry Vehicles, or MIRV's. The nose cones of MIRVed missiles, which both superpowers possess, when in mid-course, split like a peapod to launch several warheads, each aimed at a separate target. A single missile equipped with three MIRV's of sufficient accuracy, yield, and reliability can destroy up to three of the enemy's missiles—provided, of course, it catches them in their silos, before they have been fired (which adds another inducement to preemption). Theoretically, assuming high accuracy and reliability, should the entire American force of 1,054 ICBM's be MIRVed (so far only half of them have been MIRVed), it would take only 540 American ICBM's, each with three MIRV's, to attack the entire Soviet force of 1,618 ICBM's. The result would leave the United States with 514 ICBM's and the USSR with few survivors. Unlikely as the possibility of an American preemptive strike may be, Soviet planners apparently prefer to take no chances; they want to be in a position rapidly to replace ICBM's lost to a sudden enemy first strike. Conversely, given its doctrine of preemption, the Soviet Union wants to be in a position to destroy the largest number of American missiles with the smallest number of its own, so as to be able to face down the threat of a U.S. second strike. Its most powerful ICBM, the SS-18, is said to have been tested with up to 10 MIRV's (compared to 3 of the Minuteman-3, America's only MIRVed ICBM). It has been estimated that 300 of these giant Soviet missiles, authorized under SALT I, could seriously threaten the American arsenal of ICBM's.

*   *   *

Counterforce. Two terms commonly used in the jargon of modern strategy are "counterforce" and "countervalue." Both terms refer to the nature of the target of a strategic nuclear weapon. Counterforce means that the principal objective of one's nuclear missiles are the enemy's forces—i.e., his launchers as well as the related command and communication facilities. Countervalue means that one's principal targets are objects of national "value," namely the enemy's population and industrial centers.

Given the predominantly defensive (retaliatory) character of current U.S. strategy, it is naturally predisposed to a counter-*value* targeting policy. The central idea of the U.S. strategy of deterrence holds that should the Soviet Union dare to launch a surprise first strike at the United States, the latter would use its surviving missiles to lay waste Soviet cities. It is taken virtually for granted in this country that no nation would consciously expose itself to the risk of having its urban centers destroyed— an assumption which derives from British military theory of the 1920s and 1930s, and which influenced the RAF to concentrate on strategic bombing raids on German cities in World War II.

The Soviet high command has never been much impressed with the whole philosophy of countervalue strategic bombing, and during World War II resisted the temptation to attack German cities. This negative attitude to bombing of civilians is conditioned not by humanitarian considerations but by cold, professional assessments of the effects of that kind of strategic bombing as revealed by the Allied Strategic Bombing Surveys. The findings of these surveys were largely ignored in the United States, but they seem to have made a strong impression in the USSR. Not being privy to the internal discussions of the Soviet military, we can do no better than consult the writings of an eminent British scientist, P.M.S. Blackett, noted for his pro-Soviet sympathies, whose remarkable book *Fear, War and the Bomb*, published in 1948-49, indicated with great prescience the lines which Soviet strategic thinking were subsequently to take.

Blackett, who won the Nobel Prize for Physics in 1948, had worked during the war in British Operations Research. He concluded that strategic bombing was ineffective, and wrote his book as an impassioned critique of the idea of using atomic weapons as a strategic deterrent. Translating the devastation wrought upon Germany into nuclear terms, he calculated that it represented the equivalent of the destruction that would have been caused by 400 "improved" Hiroshima-type atomic bombs. Yet despite such punishment, Nazi Germany did not collapse. Given the much greater territory of the Soviet Union and a much lower population density, he argued, it would require "thousands" of atomic bombs to produce decisive results in a war between America and Russia.[28] Blackett minimized the military effects of the atomic bombing on Japan. He recalled that in Hiroshima trains were operating forty-eight hours after the blast; that industries were left almost undamaged and could have been back in full production within a month; and that if the most elementary civil-defense precautions had been observed, civilian casualties would have been substantially reduced. Blackett's book ran so contrary to prevailing opinion and was furthermore so intemperately anti-American in tone that its conclusions were rejected out of hand in the West.

Too hastily, it appears in retrospect. For while it is true that the advent of hydrogen bombs a few years later largely invalidated the estimates on which he had relied, Blackett correctly anticipated Soviet reactions. Analyzing the results of Allied saturation bombing of Germany, Soviet generals concluded that it was largely a wasted effort. Sokolovskii cites in his manual the well-known figures showing that German military productivity rose throughout the war until the fall of 1944, and concludes: "It was not so much the economic struggle and economic exhaustion [i.e., countervalue bombing] that were the causes for the defeat of Hitler's Germany, but rather the armed conflict and the defeat of its armed forces [i.e., the counterforce strategy pursued by the Red Army.] "[29]

Soviet nuclear strategy is counter*force* oriented. It targets for destruction—at any rate, in the initial strike—not the enemy's cities but his military forces and their command and communication facilities. Its primary aim is to destroy not civilians but soldiers and their leaders, and to undermine not so much the will to resist as the capability to do so. In the words of Grechko:

The Strategic Rocket Forces, which constitute the basis of the military might of our armed forces, are designed to annihilate the means of the enemy's nuclear attack, large groupings of his armies, and his military bases; to destroy his military industries; [and] to disorganize the political and military administration of the aggressor as well as his rear and transport.[30]

Any evidence that the United States may contemplate switching to a counterforce strategy, such as occasionally crops up, throws Soviet generals into a tizzy of excitement. It clearly frightens them far more than the threat to Soviet cities posed by the countervalue strategic doctrine.

*   *   *

Combined-arms operations. Soviet theorists regard strategic nuclear forces (organized since 1960 into a separate arm, the Strategic Rocket Forces) to be the decisive branch of the armed services, in the sense that the ultimate outcome of modern war would be settled by nuclear exchanges. But since nuclear war, in their view must lead not only to the enemy's defeat but also to his destruction (i.e., his incapacity to offer further resistance), they consider it necessary to make preparations for the follow-up phase, which may entail a prolonged war of attrition. At this stage of the conflict, armies will be needed to occupy the enemy's territory, and navies to interdict his lanes of communications. "In the course of operations [battles], armies will basically complete the final destruction of the enemy brought about by strikes of nuclear rocket weapons."[31] Soviet theoretical writings unequivocally reject reliance on any one strategy (such as the *Blitzkrieg*) or on any one weapon, to win wars. They believe that a nuclear war will require the employment of all arms to attain final victory.

The large troop concentrations of Warsaw Pact forces in Eastern Europe—well in excess of reasonable defense requirements—make sense if viewed in the light of Soviet combined-arms doctrine. They are there not only to have the capacity to launch a surprise land attack against NATO, but also to attack and seize Western Europe with a minimum of damage to its cities and industries *after* the initial strategic nuclear exchanges have taken place, partly to keep Europe hostage, partly to exploit European productivity as a replacement for that of which the Soviet Union would have been deprived by an American second strike.

As for the ocean-going navy which the Soviet Union has now acquired, it consists primarily of submarines and ground-based naval air forces, and apparently would have the task of cleaning the seas of U.S. ships of all types and cutting the sea lanes connecting the United States with allied powers and sources of raw materials.

The notion of an extended nuclear war is deeply embedded in Soviet thinking, despite its being dismissed by Western strategists who think of war as a one-two exchange. As Blackett noted sarcastically already in 1948-49: "Some armchair strategists (including some atomic scientists) tend to ignore the inevitable counter-moves of the enemy. More chess playing and less nuclear physics might have instilled a greater sense of the realities."[32] He predicted that a World War III waged with the atomic bombs then available would last longer than either of its predecessors, and require combined-arms operations—which seems to be the current Soviet view of the matter.

* * *

Defense. As noted, the U.S. theory of mutual deterrence postulates that no effective defense can be devised against an all-out nuclear attack: it is this postulate that makes such a war appear totally irrational. In order to make this premise valid, American civilian strategists have argued against a civil-defense program, against the ABM, and against air defenses.

Nothing illustrates better the fundamental differences between the two strategic doctrines than their attitudes to defense against a nuclear attack. The Russians agreed to certain imprecisely defined limitations on ABM after they had initiated a program in this direction, apparently because they were unable to solve the technical problems involved and feared the United States would forge ahead in this field. However, they then proceeded to build a tight ring of anti-aircraft defenses around the country while also developing a serious program of civil defense.

Before dismissing Soviet civil-defense efforts as wishful thinking, as is customary in Western circles, two facts must be emphasized.

One is that the Soviet Union does not regard civil defense to
be exclusively for the protection of ordinary civilians. Its chief
function seems to be to protect what in Russia are known as
the "cadres," that is, the political and military leaders as well as
industrial managers and skilled workers—those who could re-
establish the political and economic system once the war was
over. Judging by Soviet definitions, civil defense has as much to
do with the proper functioning of the country during and immediately after the war as with holding down casualties. Its
organization, presently under Deputy Minister of Defense,
Colonel-General A. Altunin, seems to be a kind of shadow
government charged with responsibility for administering the
country under the extreme stresses of nuclear war and its immediate aftermath.[33]

Secondly, the Soviet Union is inherently less vulnerable than
the United States to a countervalue attack. According to the
most recent Soviet census (1970), the USSR had only nine
cities with a population of one million or more; the aggregate
population of these cities was 20.5 million, or 8.5 per cent of
the country's total. The United States 1970 census showed
thirty-five metropolitan centers with over one million inhabitants, totaling 84.5 million people, or 41.5 per cent of the
country's aggregate.[34] It takes no professional strategist to visu-
alize what these figures mean. In World War II, the Soviet Union
lost 20 million inhabitants out of a population of 170 million—
i.e., 12 per cent; yet the country not only survived but emerged
stronger politically and militarily than it had ever been. Allowing for the population growth which has occurred since then,
this experience suggests that as of today the USSR could absorb
the loss of 30 million of its people and be no worse off, in terms
of human casualties, than it had been at the conclusion of
World War II. In other words, all of the USSR's multimillion
cities could be destroyed without trace or survivors, and, provided that its essential cadres had been saved, it would emerge
less hurt in terms of casualties than it was in 1945.

Such figures are beyond the comprehension of most Americans. But clearly a country that since 1914 has lost, as a result of two world wars, a civil war, famine, and various "purges," perhaps up to 60 million citizens, must define "unacceptable damage" differently from the United States which has known no famines or purges, and whose deaths from all the wars waged since 1775 are estimated at 650,000—fewer casualties than Russia had suffered in the 900-day siege of Leningrad in World War II alone. Such a country tends also to assess the rewards of defense in much more realistic terms.

*   *   *

How significant are these recondite doctrinal differences? It has been my invariable experience when lecturing on these matters that during the question period someone in the audience will get up and ask: "But is it not true that we and the Russians already possess enough nuclear weapons to destroy each other ten times over" (or fifty, or a hundred—the figures vary)? My temptation is to reply: "Certainly. But we also have enough bullets to shoot every man, woman, and child, and enough matches to set the whole world on fire. The point lies not in our ability to wreak total destruction: it lies in intent." And insofar as military doctrine is indicative of intent, what the Russians think to do with their nuclear arsenal is a matter of utmost importance that calls for close scrutiny.

Enough has already been said to indicate the disparities between American and Soviet strategic doctrines of the nuclear age. These differences may be most pithily summarized by stating that whereas we view nuclear weapons as a deterrent, the Russians see them as a "compellant"—with all the consequences that follow. Now it must be granted that the actual, operative differences between the two doctrines may not be quite as sharp as they appear in the public literature: it is true that our deterrence doctrine leaves room for some limited offensive action, just as the Russians include elements of deterrence in their "war-fighting" and "war-winning" doctrine. Admittedly, too, a country's military doctrine never fully reveals how it would behave under actual combat conditions. And yet the differences here are sharp and fundamental enough, and the relationship of

Soviet doctrine to Soviet deployments sufficiently close, to suggest that ignoring or not taking seriously Soviet military doctrine may have very detrimental effects on U.S. security. There is something innately destabilizing in the very fact that we consider nuclear war unfeasible and suicidal for both, and our chief adversary views it as feasible and winnable for himself.

SALT misses the point at issue so long as it addresses itself mainly to the question of numbers of strategic weapons: equally important are qualitative improvements within the existing quotas, and the size of regular land and sea forces. Above all, however, looms the question of intent: as long as the Soviets persist in adhering to the Clausewitzian maxim on the function of war, mutual deterrence does not really exist. And unilateral deterrence is feasible only if we understand the Soviet war-winning strategy and make it impossible for them to succeed.

Notes

1. "The Real Paul Warnke," *The New Republic*, March 26, 1977, 23.

2. N. V. Karabanov in N. V. Karabanov et al., *Filosofskoe nasledie V. I. Lenina i problemy sovremennoi voiny* [The philosophical heritage of V. I. Lenin and problems of contemporary war] (Moscow, 1972), 18–19, cited in Leon Gouré, Foy D. Kohler, and Mose L. Harvey, eds., *The Role of Nuclear Forces in Current Soviet Strategy* (Coral Gables, Florida, 1974), 60.

3. A. A. Grechko, *Vooruzhennye sily sovetskogo gosudarstva* [The armed forces of the Soviet state] (Moscow, 1975), 345.

4. Russell F. Weigley, *The American Way of War* (New York, 1973), 368.

5. [Recent studies indicate that original casualty figures for the Dresden raid had been grossly exaggerated.]

6. Matthew B. Ridgway, *Soldier* (New York, 1956), 296–297.

7. In Michael Howard, ed., *The Theory and Practice of War* (London, 1965), 291.

8. Benjamin S. Lambeth, *Selective Nuclear Options in American and Soviet Strategic Policy* (Rand Corporation, R-2034-DDRE, December 1976), 14. This study analyzes and approves of the refinement introduced into U.S. doctrine by James R. Schlesinger as Secretary of Defense in the form of "limited response options."

9. Interview with *Playboy*, March 1977, 72.

10. Grechko, *Vooruzhennye sily*, 347–348. Emphasis added.

11. *Voennaia strategiia* (Moscow, 1962). Since 1962 there have been two revised editions (1963 and 1968). The 1962 edition was immediately translated into English, but currently the best version is that edited by Harriet Fast Scott (New York, 1975) that renders the third edition while collating its text with the preceding two.

12. To date, twelve volumes in this series have been translated into English and made publicly available through the U.S. Government Printing Office.

13. William W. Kaufmann, *The McNamara Strategy* (New York, 1964), 97.

14. Garthoff's principal works are *Soviet Military Doctrine* (Glencoe, Ill., 1953), *Soviet Strategy in the Nuclear Age* (New York, 1958), and *The Soviet Image of Future War* (Washington, D.C., 1959). Dinerstein wrote *War and the Soviet Union* (New York, 1959).

15. Cited in J. M. Mackintosh, *The Strategy and Tactics of Soviet Foreign Policy* (London, 1962), 90–91. Emphasis added.

16. Articles in the *New Times* for 1945–46 cited in P.M.S. Blackett, *Fear, War, and the Bomb* (New York, 1949), 163–165.

17. We now know that orders to proceed with the development of a Soviet atomic bomb were issued by Stalin in June 1942, probably as a result of information relayed by Klaus Fuchs concerning the Manhattan Project, on which he was working at Los Alamos. *Bulletin of the Atomic Scientists*, XXIII, No. 10, December 1967, 15.

18. Dinerstein, *War and the Soviet Union*, 71.

19. I would like to stress the word "theory," for the Russians certainly accept the *fact* of deterrence. The difference is that whereas American theorists of mutual deterrence regard this condition as mutually desirable and permanent, Soviet strategists regard it as undesirable and transient: they are entirely disinclined to allow us the capability of deterring them.

20. Matthew P. Gallagher and Karl F. Spielmann, Jr., *Soviet Decision-Making for Defense* (New York, 1972), 39.

21. The figures are from Grechko, *Vooruzhennye sily*, 97.

22. *Metodologicheskie problemy voennoi teorii i praktiki* [Methodological problems of military theory and practice] (Moscow, 1969), 288.

23. V. D. Sokolovskii, *Soviet Military Strategy* (Rand Corporation, 1963), 99. Emphasis added.

24. See, e.g., *Metodologicheskie problemy*, 289–290.

25. Gouré et al., *The Role of Nuclear Forces*, 9.

26. Cited in *ibid.*, 106.

27. I have in mind the SS-20, a recently developed Soviet rocket. This is a two-stage version of the intercontinental SS-16 which can be turned

into an SS-16 with the addition of a third booster and fired from the same launcher. Its production is not restricted by SALT I and not covered by the Vladivostok Accord.

28. Blackett, *Fear*, 88. As a matter of fact, recent unofficial Soviet calculations stress that the United States dropped on Vietnam the TNT equivalent of 650 Hiroshima-type bombs—also without winning the war: *Kommunist Vooruzhonnykh Sil* [The Communist of the Armed Forces], No. 24, December 1973, 27, cited in Gouré et al., *The Role of Nuclear Forces*, 104.

29. Sokolovskii, *Soviet Military Strategy* (3rd ed.), 21.

30. A. A. Grechko, *No strazhe mira i stroitel'stva Kommunizma* [Guarding peace and the construction of Communism] (Moscow, 1971), 41.

31. *Metodologicheskie problemy*, 288.

32. Blackett, *Fear*, 79.

33. On the subject of civil defense, see Leon Gouré, *War Survival in Soviet Strategy* (Coral Gables, Florida, 1976).

34. [The 1979 Soviet census lists 18 cities with one million or more inhabitants, with an aggregate population of 33.1 million or 12.6 percent of the country's total. The comparable estimated figures for the United States for 1978 are 98.8 million or 45.3 percent.]

SEVEN

Soviet Global Strategy

One of the most difficult tasks in advising U.S. government officials on Soviet policy is to convince them that the Soviet government is not an ordinary great power, exploiting opportunities for aggrandizement as the latter present themselves. It is doubtful that any expansionist power in history has ever acted in such haphazard fashion; it is certain that the Soviet Union does not. A regime that from its earliest days has fused politics, economics, militarism, and ideology does not, indeed cannot, conduct its foreign policy in an entirely reactive manner, without an overall strategic conception. This paper is an expanded version of a lecture I delivered in January of 1979 in Lisbon as a guest of the Portuguese Ministry of Foreign Affairs.

In his State of the Union address earlier this year, President Carter at one point addressed himself to the Soviet leadership:

> The Soviet Union must answer some basic questions: Will it help promote a stable international environment in which its own legitimate, peaceful concerns can be pursued? Or will it continue to expand its military power far beyond its legitimate security needs, using that power for colonial conquests?

That the President could seriously raise such questions, with the record of over six decades of Soviet history at his disposal, sug-

Reprinted by permission from *Commentary*, LXIX, No. 4 (April 1980), 31–39.

gests that while he may have learned by now that the Soviet leaders prevaricate, he has yet to find out who they are and what they want.

A few evenings spent with a standard manual of Marxism-Leninism and a good history of the Communist party of the Soviet Union would help the President answer his questions and save him (and the rest of us) from some more costly mistakes. What he would quickly learn—for he is said to be an apt pupil—is that: (1) in the Soviet case, "legitimate" concerns are not synonymous with "peaceful" concerns or "defense"; (2) the Soviet leadership is unable, for sound ideological, political, and economic reasons, to "promote a stable international environment"; (3) its "legitimate security needs" do require "colonial conquests."

These facts are what they are, not because the Soviet leaders will them so but because they themselves are the victims of a system which they lack the power to alter—except at the risk of bringing the whole structure down. The sooner those in charge of our foreign policy abandon their unbearable moralizing and come to grips with the imperatives of the regime which fate has chosen to be our adversary, the better for all concerned. Here, then, are some rudimentary answers to the questions posed by the President.

To begin with the ideological factors behind Soviet foreign policy: Marxism-Leninism is by its very nature a militant doctrine, the child of the age of Social Darwinism, which views history as the record of uninterrupted class warfare and which advocates the continuation of class war as a means of abolishing, once and for all, classes and the exploitation of man by man. The kind of "stability" of which the President speaks and which he implies to be the desirable objective of all foreign policy can be attained, according to this doctrine, only *after* capitalism has been liquidated. The liquidation of capitalism, however, calls for a long period of instability, including international wars, which, according to Lenin, are an inevitable concomitant of capitalism.

Secondly, Marxism-Leninism is an international doctrine. As it perceives them, the phases in the evolution of mankind are global in scope and cannot be contained (except transitionally) within the limits of the nation-state or served by its "legitimate security needs." The fundamental international, or, rather, supranational, character of the doctrine is symbolized by Communism's permanent slogan since 1847, "Proletarians of all countries, unite!" In 1917, the Bolsheviks (and this held true of the Socialist Revolutionaries and Mensheviks as well) were not fighting for a change of regime in Russia, but for a world-wide revolution. It deserves note that one of the earliest declarations of the Petrograd Soviet (then still firmly in the control of "moderate" socialists), issued in March 1917, was addressed to the "Peoples of the Entire World" and called on them to rid themselves of their "ruling classes." This attitude was never repudiated by Lenin; nor has it ever been repudiated by his successors.

Now it is possible to minimize such ideological considerations with the argument that history is replete with instances of movements which, having laid claim to universality, nevertheless adjusted themselves to more modest roles: several religions, including Islam, provide good examples. But apart from the fact that accommodations of this nature have always occurred as the result of a universalist movement running into resistance that it could not overcome, Communism is not only a faith, it is also the program of a powerful secular government. It is precisely this fusion of a universalist historical doctrine with the most mundane aspirations of a great imperialist power that lends Communist Russia's global ambitions such force. For behind the lofty ideals of a classless society loom also the very vulgar interests of a ruling elite which finds in them a rationale for power and privilege.

The most painful reality that the Soviet leadership confronts every day of its existence is that it has no generally acknowledged mandate to rule. It lacks the legitimacy of ancient tradition; nor can it derive its authority from the personal charisma of a great living leader. This committee of colorless, self-perpetuating civil servants pretends to rest on a popular mandate and to this end every now and then stages mock elections, but the ritual of choosing without having a choice surely deceives only simpletons. Such mandate as the Bolshevik regime can reasonably lay claim to derives entirely from history, namely, from the assertion that it represents the vanguard of the majestic force of progress whose mission it is to accomplish the final social revolution in human history. Once this particular claim is given up—as it would be were the Soviet government to acknowledge the international status quo as permanent and accommodate itself within its present sphere of influence—the question of legitimacy would at once crop up. For indeed, who has given the Communist party of the Soviet Union the right to monopolize the country's political authority as well as its human and material resources?—none other than the goddess of history who has challenged it to the noblest mission ever assigned to man. The regime, therefore, must press onward and outward, it must win, or at least appear to win, incessant victories against "capitalism" so as to maintain the illusion of a relentless forward movement, commensurate with its mission. The alternative is to risk having its political credentials subjected to scrutiny and possible disqualification.

In addition to its universalist ideology and the ordinary political self-interest of the ruling elite, Soviet expansionism also has solid roots in Russian history. Because of the inherent poverty of Russia, due to adverse climate, soil, and other related factors, the country has never been able to support a population at a level of density common in more temperate zones. Throughout their history, Russians have colonized areas adjacent to their homeland in the northern taiga, sometimes peacefully, sometimes by conquest. Of all European countries, Russia has not only the oldest and most persistent tradition of imperial expansion, but also the record of greatest tenacity in holding on to conquered areas.

Thus, ideology, political survival, and economic exigencies reinforce one another, impelling Russia toward conquest. Each new territory acquired becomes part of the national "patrimony" and is, sooner or later, incorporated into the homeland. Each demands a "buffer" to protect it from real or imaginary enemies, until it, too, becomes part of the homeland, and, in turn, requires its own buffer.

*   *   *

The theory of détente, promoted by the Soviet regime since the mid-1950s, would seem to contradict the thesis that expansionism and international class war are indispensable to Russian Communism. As presented to the West (the matter is handled quite differently within the country), the theory, calling for peaceful coexistence between diverse social systems, seems to accept the prospect of a nonviolent evolution and a common, "convergent" end-product. In reality, détente is merely a tactical adaptation of a general strategy, which does not run contrary to the principles enunciated above. To explain why this is the case, one must say a few words about the essential characteristic of Communist politics as formulated by Lenin and elaborated upon by his epigones.

Lenin's historic achievement is to have militarized politics. It has been aptly said that Lenin stood Clausewitz on his head by making politics the pursuit of war by other means: war is the aim, politics a means, rather than the other way around. This being the case, the application of political strategy and tactics is determined by an essentially military assessment of what is known as the "correlation of forces." The latter, in Communist theory, embraces not only those factors which in Western terminology are included in the concept of "balance of power" but also economic capabilities, social stability, and public opinion, i.e., elements that, although not military in the strict sense of the word, nevertheless have considerable bearing on a nation's ability to wage war.

From this point of view, the decision whether to press one's offensive against the "class enemy," internal as well as external, or to hold back, must be based on a cool appraisal of the contending forces. In a speech delivered in May 1918, in which he reiterated that "final victory is possible only on a world scale," Lenin admonished his followers not to rush headlong into battle under all circumstances:

> We possess great revolutionary experience, which has taught us that it is essential to employ the tactics of merciless attack when objective conditions permit. . . . But we have to resort *to temporizing tactics, to a slow gathering of forces* when objective circumstances do not favor a call for a general merciless repulse.[1]

In the eyes of the Soviet leadership, the phenomena which in the West are labeled "cold war" and "détente" and perceived as antithetical are merely tactical nuances of one and the same strategy, alternately applied, depending on "objective circumstances." In the case of the détente policy launched in the mid-1950s, the decisive objective circumstance was the enemy's complete nuclear superiority which placed him in a position to destroy much of the Soviet Union at will. This particular circumstance did not in the least obviate the necessity of waging international class war, but it did call for the adaptation of one's battle plans: confrontation had to be avoided and indirect methods of combat given preference—at any rate, until such time as America's nuclear threat could be safely neutralized.

The end objective of Soviet global policy is, of course, a world from which private property in the means of production has been banished and the constituent states are, with minor variations, copies of the Soviet state. It is only in a world so fashioned that the elite ruling Soviet Russia would feel secure and comfortable.

This objective does not, as is sometimes thought, require that the USSR physically occupy the entire world, a task which is beyond even the capabilities of its large military and security forces. The term "hegemony" conveys very accurately the kind of international arrangement with which the Soviet leadership would be satisfied. The concept is of Greek origin and was originally coined to describe the dominance enjoyed by one or another city state, and especially the Macedonian kingdom, over Hellas. Possession of "hegemony" did not then and does not now entail physical conquest: rather, it signifies the ability of the hegemonial power to assert its interests within the area over which it claims hegemony by the threat of coercion, or, if that fails to produce the desired effect, by its actual application. Britain enjoyed hegemony over a good part of the globe in the nineteenth century; the United States had it between the end of World War II and its withdrawal from Vietnam. Germany launched two world wars in an unsuccessful attempt to obtain European hegemony. Andrei Gromyko, the Soviet Minister of Foreign Affairs, stated concisely the ultimate aspiration of Soviet policy in a speech to the 24th Congress of the

CPSU in 1971 when he boasted, somewhat prematurely: "To-day, there is no question of any significance which can be de-cided without the Soviet Union *or in opposition to it.*"[2] Implied in this statement is the rejection of the notion that Soviet in-terests are anything less than global in scope and can be confined within the boundaries of a national state or even a bloc of states. It goes without saying that the assertion of a similar claim by the United States would be rejected out of hand by the Soviet Union (as well as by American liberals) as a manifestation of the crassest imperialism. This is but one of many examples of the Soviet Union laying down the rules of international politics in a manner that entirely favors its own side.

If politics is warfare, then it requires strategic guidance. The strategy that one employs in the pursuit of global objectives cannot involve exclusively military weapons, but must embrace the entire spectrum of instrumentalities. Strategy of this type has been labeled "Grand" or "Total," and it suits a totalitarian country much better than it does a democratic one. The Soviet Union has indeed been organized by Lenin from the beginning for the waging of total war and it is to this end that the Soviet government has taken into its hands a monopoly of national powers and resources. There exists in the Soviet Union a mecha-nism of vertical and horizontal integration that not only enables but also compels the management of that giant political con-glomerate to attempt a coordinated national and international policy. The proprietors of the Soviet Union have to seek to inte-grate politics, economics, and propaganda (ideology) to an extent inconceivable in the West where each of these realms is controlled by different groups and tends to pull in separate directions.

*   *   *

Let us cursorily survey the ingredients of Soviet Grand Strategy. Space precludes any discussion of the many aspects and nuances of Soviet *political* strategy. Its guiding principle, however, can be succinctly defined: it is to rely not so much on the forces at one's own disposal (i.e., foreign Communist parties and their "fronts") as on allies one is able provisionally and temporarily to detach from the enemy's camp on individual issues (e.g., nationalism, "peace," "racism," "anti-Zionism," etc.). This technique, originated by Russian opposition groups in the Czarist underground, has proved very successful when applied to international relations. Its essence can best be conveyed in the words of Lenin himself. In 1920 the Communist leader was faced with unrest over his cautious foreign policy from hotheads in the Third International. These people wanted a direct assault on the entire capitalist West. To them Lenin said bluntly:

> The entire history of Bolshevism, both before and after the October Revolution, is *full* of instances of changes of tack, conciliatory tactics, and compromises with other parties, including bourgeois parties!
>
> To carry on a war for the overthrow of the international bourgeoisie, a war which is a hundred times more difficult, protracted, and complex than the most stubborn of ordinary wars between states and to renounce in advance any change of tack, or any utilization of conflict of interest (even if temporary) among one's enemies, or any conciliation or compromise with possible allies (even if they are temporary, unstable, vacillating, or conditional allies), is that not ridiculous in the extreme? . . .
>
> After the first socialist revolution of the proletariat, and the overthrow of the bourgeoisie in some country, the proletariat of that country remains *for a long time weaker* than the [international] bourgeoisie. . . . The more powerful enemy can be vanquished only by exerting the utmost effort, and by the most thorough, careful, attentive, skillful, and *obligatory* use of any, even the smallest, rift between the enemies, any conflict of interests among the bourgeoisie of the various countries and among the various groups or types of bourgeoisie within the various countries, and also by taking advantage of any, even the smallest, opportunity of winning a mass ally, even though this ally is temporary, vacillating, unreliable, and conditional.[3]

The success of this policy has been in large measure due to the fact that the "international bourgeoisie" not only refuses to acknowledge the manipulative intentions behind Soviet conciliatory policies but feels confident of its own ability to fish in the political waters of the Soviet Union by pitting nonexisting "doves" against equally spurious "hawks."

The Soviet *economic* arsenal is not rich enough to serve as a major weapon of Soviet global strategy. In its expansion, the USSR consequently relies much less on investments and trade as a means of spreading influence than was the case with the other great powers in the classical age of modern imperialism. Soviet economic leverage is exercised mainly through military and economic assistance carefully doled out to countries judged to be of strategic importance. Aid of this kind creates all kinds of dependencies, including the willingness of the recipient to host Communist administrative personnel. It is very instructive to analyze statistics of Soviet economic assistance to Third World countries because the figures give a good insight into the relative importance that Moscow attaches to them. On a per-capita basis, among the greatest beneficiaries of Soviet aid since 1954 have been South Yemen and Afghanistan. More recently, the USSR and its clients have poured vast sums of money into Turkey, a member of NATO, and Morocco. Significant increases in Soviet assistance are usually reliable indicators of Soviet strategic interests in a given area: judging by recent aid patterns, the Mediterranean enjoys very high priority in its mind.

In its relations with the advanced industrial powers, the Soviet Union is at a great disadvantage in attempting to exploit economic leverage, but even so it has had some success in making Western Europe and Japan dependent on its good will.

One form of leverage is the debts incurred in the West by the Soviet bloc during the period of détente. These are estimated today at [77.1] billion, one-quarter of it owed by the USSR, the remainder by the countries of Eastern Europe.[4] The external indebtedness of the Soviet Union cannot be considered excessive, given that country's natural resources and gold reserves, but the same cannot be said of the "People's Democracies" such as Poland, whose foreign obligations exceed those of its patron state. Western bankers have gladly lent vast sums to Eastern Europe on the assumption that any defaults would be made good by the Soviet Union. In so doing they have chosen to ignore official Soviet statements which repudiate any such obligation. Moscow's position on this issue, recently reiterated at an East-West conference held in Vienna, holds that "every

country must repay its own debts."[5] Loans of this magnitude
induce among Western bankers solicitude for the economic well-
being and benevolence of their Eastern European debtors, and
makes them beholden to détente, regardless of its political costs.

The other economic weapon is energy, of whose strategic
importance the Soviet leadership had become aware long before
it even dawned on Western politicians. In addition to placing
itself in a position to impede the flow of Middle Eastern oil (of
which more later), the USSR has sought to make Europe and
Japan dependent on direct Soviet energy supplies, especially
natural gas. To this end, it has established the practice of repay-
ing in gas the costs of transmission pipes supplied by foreign
concerns. West Germany [relies] already for 16 per cent] of
its natural gas on Soviet resources; and if negotiations now in
progress for further cooperation in this field are successful, its
dependence will increase further. What this development por-
tends became apparent during the October 1973 war when the
Soviet Union abruptly suspended gas deliveries to Veba, Germany's largest energy company, apparently in order to pressure
that country not to support Washington's pro-Israel policies.

A list of all the other instrumentalities which the Soviet
Union employs in its global strategy would be long and diverse.
Among them would have to be included such seemingly un-
political matters as family relations. The broadening of contacts
between relatives separated by the border between East and
West Germany which followed the [1970-71] accords, provides
the Communists with useful political leverage, the fear of their
disruption being often cited by Bonn circles as a strong reason
for preserving détente.

*   *   *

Of all the instrumentalities at the Soviet Union's disposal,
it is the military that occupies pride of place. Soviet imperialism
(this also held true of Czarist imperialism) is a military phenomenon par excellence, and in proportion as Soviet combat power
grows, both absolutely and in relation to the West's, it tends to
push into the background the political manipulation on which
the regime has had heavily to rely earlier. Increasingly, Soviet

spokesmen call attention to the shift in the military balance in Russia's favor as a decisive fact of the contemporary world, and boast of the ability it gives their country to frustrate America's attempts to respond to Soviet initiatives.

It is sometimes difficult for people who are told of the low living standards of the Soviet Union's population and of the inefficiency of its economy to believe that such a country can present a serious military threat to the West. They ignore the fact that wealth and technical inventiveness, in which the West has an indisputable lead, do not make for military might unless they are harnessed in the service of defense. They further ignore that, conversely, a relatively poor country, as long as it has more than a minimal industrial-technical base, can offer more than a military match for its neighbors once it decides to allocate the necessary resources for war. Japan is an industrial and technological power of the very first rank. Yet because it has chosen to rely for its defense on the United States and forgo a military establishment commensurate with its economic power, its armed forces are one-half in size and a fraction in effectiveness of those of Israel, a country with one-thirtieth of Japan's population and one-fortieth of its GNP. As concerns the Soviet Union's low living standards, it should be obvious that when a country with its huge industrial plant cannot satisfy its population's needs for consumer goods, the reason must be sought not in incapacity but rather in the deliberate diversion of industrial resources to other than consumer needs. In other words, the fact that its population suffers a low living standard attests not to Russia's inability to threaten us militarily but rather to the opposite.

Russia has always tended to devote a disproportionate share of its resources to the upkeep of the armed forces: in the reign of Peter the Great, for example, more than nine-tenths of the state budget was allocated for that purpose. A large military establishment helped conquer new territories for Russia's growing population as well as to maintain order within the empire. High Czarist functionaries were well aware how much of the international influence that imperial Russia enjoyed was due to its ability to threaten small and great powers along its immensely long frontiers.

The principal weakness of pre-1917 Russian armies was a low level of supporting industry and transport, and of all those other non-military factors that World War I revealed to be of decisive importance in modern warfare. The lesson was learned by the Bolshevik leaders who studied with admiration Germany's extraordinary performance in that war; as soon as they seized power they put into effect the home-front mobilization measures initiated by Germany but made even more effective in Russia by the abolition of private property and the introduction of the universal obligation to render state service. Stalin's Five Year Plans, for all the noise about constructing socialism, were as thoroughly military in their intent as were Hitler's Four Year Plans.

The conglomerate nature of the Soviet regime makes it eminently suitable for purposes of military mobilization. If the Soviet government so decides, it can lavish on the defense sector of the economy manpower and resources in the quantities and qualities required, and let the consumer sector fend for itself. The mightier the industrial base, the more rapid under these conditions can be the expansion of the armed forces, inasmuch as the allocations to the civilian sector can be kept relatively constant while the bulk of the growing surplus is turned over to the military. And, of course, there are no recalcitrant legislatures or inquisitive media to raise questions about the need for such heavy defense outlays.

Thus it happens that neither détente nor the arms-limitation agreements accompanying it, SALT I included, have produced a dent in the upward curve of Soviet defense appropriations. A recent study by William T. Lee, a specialist with long CIA experience, estimates that the share absorbed by the defense sector of the Soviet Gross National Product has grown from some 12-13 per cent in 1970 to perhaps as much as 18 per cent in 1980; and since the Soviet GNP during this decade has also kept on growing, the absolute amounts given to defense have risen yet more impressively.[6] Incidentally, in the same period (1970–79), U.S. defense expenditures as a share of the GNP have declined from 7.5 per cent to 4.6 per cent, and in constant 1972 dollars, from $85.1 to $65.0 billion.

*   *   *

Although the Soviet military seem determined to catch up to and surpass the United States in all the service branches, they assign the central role to strategic-nuclear weapons. These the Soviet military theorists regard as the decisive weapons of modern warfare. All the available evidence furnished by theoretical writings and observable deployments indicates that the Soviet General Staff does not share the prevalent U.S. view that nuclear weapons have no place in a rational strategy except as a deterrent. There exists a high degree of probability that in the event of general war the Soviet Union intends to use a part of its strategic arsenal in a devastating preemptive strike which would make an American retaliatory strike suicidal and possibly inhibit it altogether. The stress on large throw-weight combined with high accuracies of its ICBM's is a good indication that the Soviet Union intends to develop a first-strike capability.

The refusal of the American scientific community, which has been largely responsible for the formulation of U.S. nuclear strategy, to take seriously Soviet nuclear doctrine can charitably be described as an act of grave intellectual and political irresponsibility. Owing to it, in the coming decade the United States will find all three legs of its "triad" under growing threat which will not only make it difficult to respond to aggressive Soviet moves, but will also free the Soviet Union from those restraints which had inspired it to adopt the policy of détente in the first place. Once the nuclear balance will have become highly tilted, American crash programs will likely be discouraged by the same exponents of unilateral restraint who have helped bring the imbalance about, on the grounds that at this point any sudden moves would be "destabilizing" and could provoke the Soviet Union into a preemptive strike.

The strong Soviet commitment to the process of so-called "arms limitation" does not invalidate the contention that it operates on a first-strike doctrine. As has become evident since 1972, SALT I has had no significant influence on the development of Russia's strategic offensive forces. The same may be said of SALT II which, if ratified, would exert only a minimal effect on future Soviet deployments, while inhibiting and in some cases precluding important U.S. responses (such as long-range cruise missiles and protective shelters for the Minutemen missiles). Adopting for negotiating purposes the American "Mutual Assured Destruction" doctrine, the Soviet Union has been able to push through, at a relatively small price to its own deployments, severe restrictions on those of the United States.

Nuclear missiles, however, have not only a military utility: they are equally and perhaps even more useful as a means of political and psychological suasion. Russia's growing nuclear arsenal inculcates in influential Western circles a sense of all-pervasive fear which induces a spirit of accommodation. Once the view gains hold that there is no defense against nuclear weapons, it becomes not unreasonable to advocate avoidance of disagreement with another nuclear power as the highest goal of foreign policy. The following sentiments expressed by Congressman Jonathan Bingham of New York are quite typical of this body of opinion:

> *Above all*, we must remember that the Soviet Union remains the world's only other superpower—the only country in the world capable of destroying us. Maintaining good relations with the Soviet Union must be our *paramount* objective.[7]

I wonder whether Congressman Bingham has thought through the implications of his words. For he is, in effect, urging that we subordinate all our national interests as well as our ideals of freedom and human rights, and whatever else many of us regard as "paramount," to another criterion, namely, survival; and that in line with this criterion, we should seek accommodation with that country which can deny it to us. (Only we: there is nothing in this passage to suggest that the Soviet Union has a similar obligation toward us, the only country in the world capable of destroying it.) When this kind of thinking becomes prevalent, a nation loses the freedom to act in self-defense: psychologically, the white flag of surrender is up and sending unmistakable signals to the adversary. It takes little imagination to picture what effect this kind of thinking must have on the Soviet leaders: it virtually incites them to keep on increasing their nuclear preponderance, given that the greater their theoretical capability to destroy the United States, the louder the voices in the United States demanding that accommodation with the

Soviet Union be made the "paramount" objective of national policy.

*   *   *

Soviet global strategy is implemented by means of pressures exerted at various points of the globe in a bewildering succession of shifts that makes it difficult to discern patterns and causes some observers to interpret it as a mere exploitation of random opportunities. But this is not the case. Just as Soviet defense strategy calls for the disposition of forces around the Queen of the chessboard, namely, nuclear-tipped missiles, so its territorial strategy aims at the enemy's King, the United States. The latter is the only country with the wealth and power to frustrate Soviet intentions: the fall or even isolation of that "citadel of international imperialism" would allow the rest of the world to be picked up at will. A world in which the United States carries no weight comes automatically under Soviet hegemony. The reduction of the United States, therefore, is as essential to the Soviet Union as the elimination of Carthage was to Rome.

But this objective cannot quite be achieved by a succession of Punic wars: military conflict with its principal adversary is the least palatable of the alternatives open to Moscow because the U.S. nuclear arsenal can never be entirely suppressed and it is always able to inflict, no matter what the balance of power, devastating punishment. Hence, except in the realm of ideological warfare, to which the United States attaches no importance and where the most venomous hate campaign can be carried on with impunity, assaults on the U.S. must assume indirect forms that undermine America's security without appearing to do so.

This aim is best attained by detaching Europe and Japan from the United States and pulling them into the Soviet orbit: the addition of West European and Japanese industrial capabilities to those of the Soviet bloc would alter immediately and in a most dramatic manner the global correlation of forces in the latter's favor. Here economic statistics speak for themselves. The annual Gross National Product of the Warsaw Pact countries for 1977-78 was estimated at $1 trillion; that of the United

States at $2 trillion; that of Western Europe at somewhat above
$2 trillion; that of Japan somewhat under $1 trillion. By this
yardstick, the present correlation of economic forces is 5-to-1
in favor of the West; but it shifts to 4-to-2 in favor of the Communist bloc once Western Europe's and Japan's links with the
United States are severed. Even if one allows for a 50 per cent
decline in European and Japanese productivity as a result of
such a change (has it not been said that under Soviet domination the Sahara would promptly experience a shortage of
sand?), Moscow could still confront the United States as at least
an economic equal.

But an assault on Europe and Japan is risky, because they are
protected by forces with large U.S. contingents as well as by the
U.S. strategic deterrent. Hence, here too an indirect strategy is
preferable.

The Soviet Union may be said to be laying siege to Western
Europe and Japan in the same manner in which medieval castles
were blockaded prior to the introduction of gunpowder—that
is, by a systematic effort to cut off the flow of reinforcements
and supplies: reinforcements of manpower and material from
the United States, and supplies in the form of fuel and metals
from the Middle East and South Africa.

In the event of war, there would be activated a giant sea and
air lift pouring troops and material from the United States to
the European front. To disrupt this flow, the Russians have constructed a powerful ocean-going navy, centered on submarines
and concentrated in ports of the Kola peninsula. This navy
would have the task of penetrating the Iceland-Faroes-England
gap and striking at American convoys.

*   *   *

As political backing for this naval strategy, the Soviet government exerts relentless pressure on the Scandinavian countries,
sometimes directly, sometimes through the agency of Finland.
To relieve that pressure, Norway and Denmark have for a long
time refused the stationing of NATO troops and nuclear weapons on their territory; this act of self-denial has by now become part of the status quo which the Soviet Union jealously

guards and is unlikely to permit to change. [...] The construction in Finland of highways pointing in the direction of Norway strongly suggests that in the event of hostilities the Russians would strike fast to seize Norwegian ports and airfields, as Hitler had done in 1940. Sweden, not a member of NATO, is frequently harassed with accusations of violating its neutral status. It was apparently in response to Soviet browbeating that the Swedes consented to supply the USSR with a floating drydock capable of servicing a giant aircraft carrier presently under construction there. This Soviet activity in Scandinavia is given scant attention by the American media although its strategic implications for Europe are not much less than the more familiar Soviet challenge to the oil routes. Nine-tenths of U.S. war supplies to the European fronts would have to travel by sea, so that a serious Soviet threat to the North Atlantic sea lanes would be bound to have significant repercussions on the progress of European operations. (According to testimony by the recently retired commander of the Atlantic Fleet, Admiral Isaac Kidd, the Allied navies could maintain control of the North Atlantic sea lanes in face of this threat but only at a very high cost.)

The other Soviet pincer is directed toward the Middle East and aims at cutting off, in the event of hostilities, fossil fuels and minerals without which the economies of America's allies would not be able to function. The task here is much more difficult to accomplish than in the north, if only because the Red Army lacks naval and air bases in this area, but the intensity of the effort bespeaks the strategic design. Soviet forces have been positioning themselves over the years near three principal choke-points through which Middle Eastern oil supplies must travel en route to their destinations in Europe and Japan. One of these is the Strait of Bab el-Mandeb which guards access to the Red Sea and the Suez Canal. Soviet and pro-Soviet forces stationed in South Yemen and Ethiopia would undoubtedly attempt to seize this waterway in the event of war. To the east lies the Strait of Hormuz, at the entrance of the Persian Gulf. The Soviet Union has a long way to go to gain a stranglehold on these straits, but it should be noted that its occupation of Afghanistan has cut in half (from 1,100 to 550 kilometers) the distance Soviet planes must traverse to reach them. Finally, in Southeast Asia, where it has a friendly client in Vietnam, the Soviet Union is within reach of the Straits of Malacca, a major route for oil tankers on their way to Japan.

European and Japanese dependence on South African minerals, though less well known than their reliance on Middle Eastern oil, is nevertheless considerable. America's allies derive a high proportion of such industrial minerals as chrome, platinum, vanadium, and manganese from Rhodesia [Zimbabwe] and South Africa. The intense involvement of the Soviet Union in the so-called "national-liberation" movements in sub-Saharan Africa, the quick exploitation of opportunities offered by the dissolving Portuguese empire, indicate the intention to deny these resources to the West.

*   *   *

The flanking movement directed at Europe through Africa and the Middle East brings the USSR into contact with Third World countries and demands the formulation of a Third World political strategy. In the immediate post-Stalin years, the Soviet Union relied on alliances with so-called "national-bourgeois" movements, that is, movements that shared with the Soviet Union a common hostility toward the "capitalist" and "imperialist" West without being pro-Communist or socialist. They provided the kind of "temporary" allies whose utilization Lenin had recommended. The policy called for the exploitation of the anti-Western, anti-colonial sentiments of charismatic national leaders, some of them tainted with pro-Axis collaboration, as a means of eliminating the many strands of Western influence which remained in place even after formal colonial ties had been cut.

This strategy proved, by and large, disappointing. The Third World leaders whom the Soviet Union cultivated and supported with munificent aid turned out to enjoy too narrow a power base to serve as reliable allies: the sudden death of one or a successful coup against another could change the political climate in a given country overnight, turning it from a friend into an enemy and, in the process, sending billions of rubles' worth of aid down the drain. Such disagreeable reversals occurred in 1965 in Indonesia with the overthrow of Sukarno and a year later in Ghana with the removal of Nkrumah. Even worse were the consequences of the change in political orientation accomplished by Sadat after the 1973 war during which the Soviet Union had given him invaluable help. Once Sadat concluded that the concessions he desired from Israel could be procured for him by the United States but not by the Soviet Union, and that to qualify for U.S. support he needed to assume an anti-Soviet stance, the days of Soviet influence in Egypt were numbered. Moscow had to stand by helplessly while its immense investment in Egypt went to naught.

The defection of Egypt was the unkindest blow to Soviet policies in the Third World. Egypt was the linchpin of Soviet Middle Eastern strategy, the political-military base from which Moscow hoped to expand its influence both into East Africa and into the Arabian peninsula. It was the recipient of unstinting Soviet aid. To save its armies from impending disaster, the Soviet Union had engaged in a serious confrontation with the United States. And all this proved in vain once the "bourgeois-nationalist" dictator decided to reorient his foreign alliances.

Following Egypt's defection, Moscow seems to have undertaken a reappraisal of its Third World strategy, the results of which are becoming increasingly apparent. The new strategy calls for smaller reliance on "bourgeois-national" leaders like Sukarno, Nkrumah, and Sadat, in favor of minor political figures who owe their political status to Soviet backing. Such new Soviet friends in the Third World as the recently deceased Neto of Angola, Colonel Mengistu of Ethiopia, and Taraki and Karmal of Afghanistan are not national heroes with their own power base, however narrow, but small-time politicians dependent on Moscow's support. To place them in power—or to remove them from it once they have proven inconvenient—the Russians have not hesitated to resort to gangster-type "executions" by their military or security services. To buttress their influence, they bring in large numbers of permanent Soviet military "advisers," Cuban mercenaries, and security services from the USSR and Eastern Europe. Once these forces are installed, an infrastructure is created which is fairly impervious to

sudden changes in native leadership. Because of the presence
of Soviet, Cuban, and East European military and police personnel within their borders, it is unlikely that either Angola or
Ethiopia will slip out of Soviet control as easily as Indonesia
or Egypt had done. To solidify their hold further, the Russians
have assisted their hand-picked heads of state in carrying out
mass murders of the opposition: according to the late Amin,
the Taraki government in Afghanistan during its brief tenure in
office executed 13,000 political prisoners. Massacres on a similar scale have been perpetrated in Ethiopia.

*   *   *

Promising as the new Third World strategy is, it is not without drawbacks. In countries in which it intervenes so heavily,
the Soviet government assumes deeper commitments and finds
it even more difficult to accept with equanimity the prospect
of the area's slipping out from under its control, as its recent
actions in Afghanistan have demonstrated. Here even the advanced type of control—hand-picked candidate, surrounded by
Soviet military and police advisers, and made secure by extensive bloodletting of opponents—did not suffice and a full-scale
occupation was deemed necessary.

It is doubtful whether the Soviet Union would have dared to
intervene in the Caribbean as it is now doing were it not for a
fortunate accident. In 1962, in what he seems to have regarded
as a major diplomatic coup, President Kennedy agreed to guarantee Cuba from American invasion in return for the Soviet removal from there of its medium-range ballistic missiles. This
guarantee proved so valuable to the Soviet Union, by providing
it with a secure base for political subversion and military action
in the Western hemisphere, that one is tempted to suspect that
the USSR had planted the missiles in Cuba precisely in order
to wrest just such an agreement. Cuba provides limited but
potentially valuable air and naval bases to Soviet forces. It also
furnishes troops and political cadres to carry out Soviet missions
in the Middle East, Africa, and Central America. It is altogether
the most dependable Third World ally, headed by a megalo-

maniac whose self-defined historic mission requires him to lean heavily on Soviet assistance.

There remains China. In regard to that country, the Soviet Union seems to have settled, after a certain hesitation, on a defensive strategy. In the early years of their quarrel, some Soviet leaders seem to have desired a quick, preemptive strike against China, but in the end cooler heads prevailed. The prospect of fighting another totalitarian regime, thousands of miles away, in an area poorly served by transport, was not appealing to a regime which, if it is to fight at all, must win quick, decisive victories. Soviet forces presently deployed in the Far East are formidable, to be sure, but they do not appear designed for offensive operations. The Chinese military estimate that in order to present a credible threat to them, the Russians would have to mass along their frontier between 2 and 3 million troops, which is several times the number they have there at present. Soviet missiles, too, are deployed mainly against NATO.

* * *

To frustrate Soviet global strategy, it is necessary, first and foremost, to acknowledge that it exists. We must get rid of the notion, widespread among America's educated and affluent, that the Soviet Union acts out of fear, that its actions are invariably reactions to U.S. initiatives, and that it seizes targets of opportunity like some kind of international pickpocket. We are dealing with an adversary who is driven not by fear but by aggressive impulses, who is generally more innovative in the field of political strategy than we are, and who selects his victims carefully, with long-term objectives in mind.

Secondly, it is essential to overcome an attitude toward nuclear weapons which leaves us increasingly vulnerable to subtle forms of psychological and political blackmail. We once had a similar attitude toward cancer: it used to be thought that the mere mention of this disease brought it about. In fact, however, open discussion of cancer has led to early diagnosis and treatment, and appreciably reduced the danger of death from it. Nuclear weapons are a kind of cancer of the international body politic. Awareness of their actual (rather than imaginary) dangers can lead to sensible measures being taken to reduce the risk of nuclear war breaking out and to keep casualties low should it nevertheless happen. Unless we are prepared to confront this danger, the growing Russian preponderance in strategic weapons will leave us in a position where we shall have no choice but to capitulate to Soviet demands whenever they are backed with the threat of war.

Thirdly, we should take an honest look at our alliance system which has deteriorated to the point where its utility seems more psychological than real. For some time now NATO has been a one-way street: the United States underwrites the security of Western Europe against Soviet attack, but its West European allies feel no particular obligation to support the United States in its confrontations with the Soviet Union in any other part of the world. This holds true even of the Middle East where Europe's interests are, if anything, yet more directly involved. Such behavior encourages the Soviet leaders to act aggressively in the Third World, in the knowledge that here the United States will be confronting them alone, and that such confrontations serve to exacerbate America's differences with its allies.

Fourthly, we must correct as rapidly as possible the skewed military balance, especially where strategic and naval forces are concerned. If a commensurate effort is undertaken by Western Europe and Japan, and if the mutual obligations of our alliance are made more equitable than they now are, then Soviet expansion into the Middle East and Africa ought to prove costlier and therefore less attractive.

The ultimate purpose of Western counterstrategy should be to compel the Soviet Union to turn inward—from conquest to reform. Only by blunting its external drive can the Soviet regime be made to confront its citizenry and to give it an account of its policies. It is a familiar fact of modern Russian history that whenever Russian governments had suffered serious setbacks abroad—in the Crimean war, in the 1904–05 war with Japan, and in World War I—they were compelled by internal pressure to grant the citizenry political rights. We should help the population of the Soviet Union bring its government under control. A more democratic Russia would be less expansionist and certainly easier to live with.

Notes

1. V. I. Lenin, *Collected Works* (London, n.d.), XXVII, 373, 377. Emphasis added.

2. See Chap. 4, p. 63, note 1.

3. Lenin, *Collected Works*, XXXI, 70–71.

4. [This is the most recent estimate for Gross Debt provided by the Central Intelligence Agency: *Estimating Soviet and East European Hard Currency Debt: A Research Paper*, ER 80-10327, June 1980.]

5. *Neue Zürcher Zeitung*, October 10, 1979.

6. *Soviet Defense Expenditures in the Era of SALT*, United States Strategic Institute Report 79-1 (Washington, D.C., 1979), 10–11.

7. Victor C. Johnson, co-author, *Foreign Affairs*, Spring 1979, 919. Emphasis added.

EIGHT

Militarism and the Soviet State

A major element in that "mirror-imaging" which is the bane of American perceptions of the USSR is anti-militarism—the conviction that the Soviet leadership must realize that war is not "cost-effective" and that money spent on the military sector of the economy is money wasted. The corollary of this notion is the belief that if the Soviet Union nevertheless does spend an inordinate amount of money on defense, it does so out of fear of us. This idea, in turn, leads straight to the policy of unilateral restraint and even disarmament. My purpose in writing this paper was to show that militarism is deeply imbedded in Soviet theory and practice. Insofar as we are in a position to attenuate it, we must become militarily not weaker but stronger, because Soviet militarism, as all militarism, thrives on coercion and turns into a wasted asset if unable to carry out its mission.

History suggests that peace is a breathing space for war.
—*V. I. Lenin*[1]

This essay deals with the role of militarism in the Soviet system. It seeks to indicate how deeply imbedded militarism is in communist theory and practice and how broad is its scope. It is meant to counteract a notion widespread in the West that the Soviet Union, a country with a socialist ideology, acute internal problems, and a history of appalling losses from war,

Reprinted by permission from *Daedalus*, Vol. 109, No. 4 (Fall 1980), 1–10.

resorts to militarism reluctantly, out of fear of foreign invasions or encirclement. This view, in my opinion, is entirely erroneous. It rests on a superficial knowledge of Russian history as well as communist theory and practice, reflecting a more or less unconscious propensity of many Westerners to impose on Soviet Russia their own values and experiences. Militancy—that is, a commitment to violence and coercion—and its principal instrumentality, militarism, seem to me as central to Soviet communism as the pursuit of profit is to societies with market-oriented economies. This is so for sound reasons derived from Russian history, the ideology of communism, and the Soviet view of the nature of future war.

Historical Factors

Shortly before the outbreak of World War I, Sergei Witte, the retired prime minister, put down the following observation in his memoirs:

> In truth, what is it that has essentially upheld Russian statehood? Not only primarily, but exclusively the army. Who has created the Russian Empire, transforming the semi-Asiatic Muscovite tsardom into the most influential, most dominant, grandest European power? Only the power of the army's bayonet. The world bowed not to our culture, not to our bureaucratized church, not to our wealth and prosperity. It bowed to our might.[2]

Witte's statement is correct in two related senses: the explicit one, that Russia historically has owed its international influence to the armed forces; and the inferential one, that in order to support an armed force of this power in a country with a weakly developed economy, Russia has had to devote an extraordinary quantity of human and material resources to military purposes.

Because the study of Russia's past has never been integrated into secondary school or university courses on history taught in the West, most Westerners have an extremely sketchy knowledge of that country: exotic episodes (Catherine the Great, Rasputin), heroic tales of repelled invasions (Tolstoy's *War and Peace*, Eisenstein's *Alexander Nevsky*), novels of the revolutionary underground (Dostoevsky's *The Possessed,* Conrad's *Under Western Eyes*) combine to produce the prevalent stereotypes. The English novelist Hugh Walpole was not far off the mark when he said that his countrymen were taught to see in the Russian "a blessed sort of Idiot unable to read or write but vitally conscious of God," and in Russia, "a land of snow, ikons, mushrooms and pilgrims."[3] Ignorance of Russia places Western statesmen at a great disadvantage vis-à-vis their Soviet counterparts, who, emerging from the background of an international revolutionary movement, have always had a keen interest in Western societies.

To a historian of Russia, the assertion that throughout its history this country had undergone an extraordinary number of foreign invasions and as a consequence developed a collective paranoia simply does not hold water. It is true, of course, that during their thousand-year-old history the Russians have suffered three especially devastating invasions: by the Mongol-Tatars in the thirteenth century, by the French and Prussians in 1812, and by the Nazis in 1941. But are the people who trot out these facts aware of the number of times that the Russians have invaded and inflicted comparable traumas on their neighbors? After all, a country does not become the largest state in the world, as Russia has been since the seventeenth century, merely by absorbing or repelling foreign invasions. How many, apart from specialists, know of Russian aggressions, such as the sixteenth century offensive in the East that resulted in the subjugation of the Muslim principalities of Kazan and Astrakhan, the conquest in the seventeenth century of Siberia, the continuous offensives against the Ottoman Empire and the partitions of Poland in the eighteenth century, the conquest of Turkestan and the seizures of Chinese territories in the nineteenth century? It is by means of this relentless movement outward that Russia has expanded until she came to occupy one sixth of the earth's land surface. To recall this record is not to attribute to the Russians uniquely aggressive proclivities; it is merely to correct a widespread misperception of them as a uniquely defense-minded people.

Russia's traditional expansionism and the militarism to which it gave rise were primarily caused by economic factors. The

northern forest zone (*taiga*), which was the homeland of Russians in the formative period of statehood (thirteenth to sixteenth centuries), is an inherently poor area with a substandard
soil and an extremely brief agricultural season. Yields of grains
here are low: Russian cereal crops have traditionally yielded
three grains for each grain sown, a ratio one half to one third
that obtained in Western Europe.[4] A prominent nineteenth century German geographer has estimated that the natural conditions in a region like northern Russia permitted, on the average,
a population density of twenty-five inhabitants per square
kilometer, whereas the countries of industrial Western Europe
were able to support a density ten to thirty times as great.[5]
It is in consequence of mounting population pressures, and the
related tendency to cultivate the available soil to the point of
exhaustion, that the Russian people have exerted constant pressure on their neighbors. In respect to external policy, Russian
history between the sixteenth and eighteenth centuries was in
large measure preoccupied with conquering the vast territories
to the south and southeast of the *taiga*, lands covered with very
fertile black-earth soil but inhabited by hostile Turkic tribes.
Once this task had been completed, with the absorption in 1783
of the Khanate of the Crimea, the Russian state began to encroach on the lands of the Polish-Lithuanian Commonwealth.
That conquered, it moved into the Balkans, Central Asia, and
the Far East. But even this expansion was not sufficient, as on
the eve of World War I one fourth of the Great Russian peasantry
had no land to cultivate.

To carry out its conquests, Russia devoted a lion's share of
its national wealth to military purposes. In Muscovy essentially
the entire landed class served in the monarchy's armed forces,
and a large proportion of the peasantry had to be enserfed to
enable these servitors to bear arms. The national economy was
mainly geared to warfare. Under Peter the Great, with the introduction of a standing army based on conscription (the first such
force in Europe), the burden of militarism on society bore yet
more heavily. The armed forces created by Peter required the
nation to maintain three professional soldiers for every one
hundred inhabitants—a ratio three times higher than was considered advisable at the time by the much richer countries of

the West.[6] The burden was immense for a country as poor as Russia, and so it was no wonder that in some years virtually the entire national budget had to be turned over to the military. The Russian historian Kliuchevskii has shown convincingly that the reforms of Peter, which laid the foundations of modern Russia, had been dictated in the main by military exigencies.[7]

Space forbids discussion of the role of the military in post-Petrine Russia. Suffice it to say that, in order to maintain a credible military establishment, Imperial Russia had to continue to lavish a disproportionate amount of its resources on defense. It has been estimated that on the eve of World War I Russia's per capita national income was a mere $44, compared to England's $243, France's $185, and Germany's $146.[8] And yet, with only a fraction of West Europe's wealth at its disposal, the government had to spend on its military establishment sums fully comparable to those of the West. Indeed, because of its technical backwardness and the related slowness of mobilization, Russia had no choice but to maintain the largest standing army in the world. There is a tragedy in the vicious circle that permeates Russian history: poverty calls for conquests; conquests demand a large military establishment; a large military establishment saps the productive forces of the country, perpetuating poverty. In the entire history of Russia there was only one period—the late nineteenth century—when its government underfinanced the armed forces in an effort to balance the budget and build up the country's industries. As the experience of World War I was to show, however, the experiment proved unsuccessful, and it was not repeated by the successors to the tsars.

The military establishment provided one additional service to the Russian state, and that was political. Traditionally, in Russia the armed forces have been charged with the responsibility for ensuring internal order. Troops were regularly called upon to quell peasant unrest and urban rebellions. In times of widespread unrest army officers were given authority to impose martial law and sometimes to judge civilians and even sentence them to death by field courts. The Imperial armed forces strongly resented this role,[9] but it was crucial to the survival of the old regime: it was precisely the refusal on February 27, 1917, of units of the Petrograd garrison to fire at crowds mill-

ing in the streets in defiance of government orders that led the
next day to the collapse of the Imperial government.

So much for the historical background. The communist
state, although permeated with different ideas and aspirations,
inherited the same land with the same traditions and many of
the same problems: it would be surprising, therefore, had it
entirely discarded that or any other legacy of Russia's past.

The Ideology of Marxism-Leninism

The doctrines of Marxism, especially after having been re-
worked by Lenin, are the product of the age of Darwinism.
(Engels, it will be recalled, at his friend's graveside compared
his accomplishments in the social sciences to those of Darwin
in biology.) This is to say that Marxism is a theory permeated
with the spirit of merciless conflict—and, therefore, violence
and coercion—as a regulator of human affairs. In this respect it
contrasts vividly with prevailing nineteenth century liberalism,
in the eyes of which conflict, especially in the form of war,
was inherently irrational.[10] Lenin, who entirely lacked Marx's
admiration for the historic achievements of liberalism, intensified
the militant element in the socialist doctrine: it is fair to say
that he perceived all human relations in terms of confrontations
and life-or-death struggles.

As a theory founded on the premise of economic determinism, Marxism-Leninism cannot view events in terms of
"rational-irrational" behavior or in isolation from other historical factors. In its view, warfare is one of several manifestations
of that class conflict that inheres in the system of private
ownership of the means of production: that is, a particular expression of class war. In the Soviet political literature it is
indeed common to have war treated as one feature of the global
class struggle, and victory in war and revolution regarded, for
all practical purposes, as interchangeable. One of the stated
missions of the Soviet Army since the days of Khrushchev is
to fulfill its "duty" to revolutionary movements abroad by
rendering them assistance and support.[11] It would be a mistake
to regard this line of argument as merely a rationalization of
aggressive intentions (although this element is not entirely

absent). It is a whole way of thinking that must be taken very seriously.

Neither Engels, who liked to think of himself as a military expert, nor Lenin ever took a moralizing attitude toward war. As Lenin liked to put it, "There are wars and wars," meaning just and unjust ones, the former being waged on behalf of the socialist ideal, the latter deriving from the unalterable nature of the capitalist mode of production.

The remarks of Engels on warfare under conditions of the capitalist-socialist conflict are of interest in this connection. Having studied the record of nineteenth century military encounters, especially the Civil War in the United States and the Franco-Prussian War of 1870–71 in which the industrially more advanced parties had triumphed, Engels concluded that in modern times the decisive factor was not the quality of the armed forces but their economic-industrial base of support. Looking ahead, he predicted that a socialist army would be as different from those of the capitalist enemy as Napoleon's had been from the professional armies of the old regimes:

> The emancipation of the proletariat will also produce a special military expression, create a special, new method of waging war. *Cela est clair.* One can even now determine the material foundations of this new warfare.... The grandiose discoveries of Napoleon in the science of war cannot be done away with by a miracle. The new [proletarian] science of war must also be a necessary product of new social relations, as that created by the Revolution and Napoleon had been the necessary result of new relations produced by the Revolution. But as in the proletarian revolution the issue is not abolishing steam engines but multiplying them, so in the conduct of war the issue will be not to reduce the cohesion and mobility of the masses but to enhance them. The premise of Napoleon's war conduct was enhanced productive forces; the premise of all new perfection of the conduct of war must also lie in new productive forces.[12]

There is no way of telling whether Lenin read these particular remarks, but using the same methodology as Engels he arrived at identical conclusions. Close observation of the German performance in World War I, in which Germany had stood fast for four years against vastly superior enemy forces, persuaded

Lenin of the immense advantages of total national mobilization—not only for war in the ordinary sense of the word, but
also for class war, that is, revolution. In 1917 he asserted: "In
contemporary war, as everyone knows, economic organization
is of decisive importance."[13] The period of War Communism
(1918–1921), in the course of which were laid the foundations
of the communist state, represented a grandiose effort to mobilize and unite under a single management the entire human and
material resources of the country for the purpose of waging
war—both the Civil War then in progress and the projected long-
term war against international capitalism.

Although for its own convenience the Soviet government
began in the mid-1950s to attribute to Lenin the idea of peaceful coexistence between countries with different economic and
social systems, Lenin in fact had never entertained such a
notion. He was quite prepared out of deference to the "correlation of forces" to enter into a temporary armistice with the
class enemy, but he never contemplated that the ultimate defeat
of capitalism could be attained without its defeat on the field of
battle. In March 1919 he was castigated by Karl Kautsky, the
leader of the Second International, for maintaining a vast military establishment at a time when other countries were de-
mobilizing. Lenin could have answered, of course, that his
government had no alternative because it was in the midst of a
civil war, but this was not how he chose to respond to the
charge. Kautsky's words brought a smile to his lips, he said—
"As if there was ever in history even one large revolution which
was not connected with war. Of course not!" And then, in an
uncharacteristic outburst of candor, Lenin articulated his
vision of the future:

> We live not only in a state but also in a *system of governments* and
> the existence of the Soviet Republic alongside the imperialist states
> over the long run is unthinkable. In the end either the one or the
> other will triumph. And until that end will have arrived, a series of
> the most terrible conflicts between the Soviet Republic and the
> bourgeois governments is unavoidable. This means that the ruling
> class, the proletariat, if it only wishes to rule and shall do so, must
> demonstrate this also with its military organization.[14]

This view explains why, after it had won the Civil War and no longer faced any military threat, the Soviet government not only failed to disband its swollen armed forces, but entered into collaboration with the *Wehrmacht* also, conniving with it to circumvent the military restrictions placed on Germany by the Versailles Treaty. This collaboration, carried on for a while even after Hitler's advent to power, enabled the *Wehrmacht* to perfect the strategy and tactics of the blitzkrieg, for which the rest of humanity, and the Russians most of all, were later to pay such a heavy price. It also, however, materially assisted the Russians to prepare for the coming war.[15]

Next to its fundamental commitment to conflict and war as a means of resolving "class" differences, an essential ingredient of Soviet thinking about warfare is the importance it attaches to the economic factor. This idea, fundamental to Marxism-Leninism, has received reinforcement from the experience of World War I. The outstanding performance of Germany, the failures of Imperial Russia, as well as the literature published in the West subsequently on the lessons of the war, all have persuaded the Soviet leadership that in the future war, about whose advent they entertained no doubt, the critical factor would be industrial capability. In the early 1920s Soviet military specialists concluded that they had to prepare for a "war of machines." Accordingly, they formulated a variety of strategic and tactical doctrines for combat of this kind that displayed considerable originality as well as prescience.[16] Acceptance of this doctrine by the government, however, had its price: it meant that one began to view the country's economy as essentially a military resource. The older Russian military doctrine (that of Imperial Russia) had stressed the offensive spirit of the soldier as the greatest asset: in line with this thinking, the Imperial government not only took no steps to prepare the country's economy for the contingency of war, but even in the midst of the war carried out the mobilization of the home front half-heartedly, almost unwillingly. By contrast, because the Soviet doctrine emphasizes industrial productivity as the principal factor in victory, the Soviet regime has tended to subordinate its industrial plant to military requirements. One may say that, in the Soviet Union, militarism is not a by-product of industrialism, as had been the case, for example, in Wilhelmian or Nazi Germany, but, on the contrary, industrialism is a by-product of militarism.

*   *   *

To wage a "war of machines" the Red Army required the kind of equipment to which in the mid-1920s it had had no access. Commercial arrangements with several capitalist countries, notably Germany, provided it with a great deal of modern technology, considerably more than is generally realized;[17] still, no one could have reasonably expected to create an up-to-date armed force under conditions of heavy dependence on foreign suppliers.

There is much evidence, direct and circumstantial, to indicate that military considerations significantly influenced Stalin's decision to proceed with forced industrialization. First, there was the spurious "war scare" of 1927, when Stalin proclaimed out of the blue that the country was in danger of imminent attack by unspecified enemies. This campaign helped create an atmosphere propitious for the immense national effort required to launch the First Five Year Plan, if only by exposing its opponents, such as defenders of the millions of repressed peasants, to the charge of treason. Subsequently, in the discussions accompanying the preparations and implementation of the Plan, much attention was given to its military implications. Thus, for instance, the resolutions of the 1927 Plenum of the Party demanded that, in the drafting of the Plan, "maximum" consideration be given to those branches of the economy that in the event of war would help defend the country and ensure its economic stability. K. E. Voroshilov, then the Commissar for War, at the Sixteenth Party Congress held in 1930, accordingly emphasized the intimate connection between the industrialization drive then in progress and defense.[18] But even without these statements, which some may be inclined to dismiss as of primarily propagandistic intent, the military consequences of the First Five Year Plan were soon incontrovertibly in evidence. Beginning with 1930 the Red Army received a steady stream of equipment produced by Russia's new industrial plant: tanks and other motorized stock, heavy artillery as well as antiaircraft and antitank guns, all of which enabled Soviet generals to begin inserting in the midst of their primitive masses of infantry a solid core of mechanized units. In the opinion of some contemporary observers, thanks to this equipment, the Red Army became by 1935 the most modern in Europe.[19] At the same time, by having launched these preparations when no other country was rearming, the Soviet government must bear responsibility for setting off the great arms race of the interwar period.

*   *   *

From the point of view of our inquiry, the experience of World War II on the Eastern front had two significant consequences. First, it has reemphasized the supreme importance in modern warfare of the "home front." The Soviet Union was able in the end to defeat Germany because it had forestalled a collapse of the administration and kept the defense industries going under the most adverse conditions imaginable. Even when the front was near collapse under the German onslaught, the rear held, and the recollection of this experience has served to enhance in the mind of Soviet leaders the importance of the rear as a factor in warfare. The phenomenon loosely referred to in Soviet literature as "morale" eventually came to occupy a position second only to industrial might as an essential ingredient of victory.

Second, World War II had provided the first and so far only occasion in the history of the Soviet state when the government and the population at large cooperated in a genuine partnership to defeat an invader bent on destroying both communism and the Russian people. This bond, sealed in blood, has been an immense asset to the Soviet regime, to whom the lack of a credible claim to legitimacy has always given all manner of difficulties. Its abstract assertion of legitimacy, derived from communism's historic mission, has for most of its subjects far less reality than the legitimacy the Soviet regime actually earned for itself by organizing the country to repel the Nazis. This helps explain the government's insistence on keeping the memory of the "Great Patriotic War" alive among the population: even citizens thoroughly disaffected with the communist system cannot help to concede, however grudgingly, that the regime, whatever its faults, did save Russia. By making the regime's political appeal depend so heavily on war experience, this further encourages Soviet militarism.

The Soviet View of Contemporary Warfare

The brief survey of current Soviet military doctrine that follows is intended to convey how inextricably it is linked with nonmilitary factors—in other words, how deeply and broadly Soviet peacetime thinking about victory in war touches every aspect of political, economic, and social life, and how intensely militaristic, as a consequence, is its outlook.

In the Soviet Union, military doctrine is treated with utmost seriousness. A network of academies, which have no exact equivalent in the West, prepares cadres of high-ranking specialists in all the branches of warfare. The most prestigious of these is the Military Academy of the General Staff named after K. E. Voroshilov. One of the seven "higher" (*vysshee*) military academies, it enrolls generals and admirals: its two-year course concentrates on strategic and operational subjects.[20] Out of these and related institutions issues a steady stream of military publications that offer a comprehensive view of Soviet military doctrine—more comprehensive, at any rate, than the corresponding literature on the American side, where the plethora of non-authoritative pronouncements must prove very confusing to Russian observers.[21]

To a Westerner, the most striking quality of current Soviet military doctrine is its comprehensiveness, that is, its tendency to reach far beyond the limits of what in the West is recognized as the proper province of military thought. This derives from the fact that Soviet theorists draw a basic distinction between what they call the "art of war" (*voennoe iskusstvo*) and the "science of war" (*voennaia nauka*), the former of which is seen as the latter's central, but subordinate, element. The art of war—subdivided into strategy, the art of operations, and tactics—corresponds to military science as understood in the West. The Soviet science of war is defined as a discipline that "studies the laws of war reflecting the dependence of the war's progress and outcome on politics, economics, [and] the relationship of the moral-political, scientific-technological and military potential of the warring parties."[22] Thus formulated, the science of war investigates the subject that in the Western literature is known as "Grand Strategy." The concept "correlation of forces" (*sootnoshenie sil*) frequently used in Soviet literature relates to the science of war by assessing not only the balance of power narrowly conceived to include troops and weapons, but also the entire panoply of nonmilitary factors that come into play when a modern country wages war. In line with this distinction, Soviet writers disparage Western military thought on the grounds that it treats the art of war as identical with the science of war.[23]

As a consequence of this approach, imbedded in Marxism-Leninism and strengthened by the memory of World War II, contemporary Soviet military doctrine places the economic and "moral" cohesion of the home front quite on par with the battle readiness of the military front. The armed forces must be prepared for combat long before the outbreak of hostilities, and so must be the civilian population. This mode of thinking, pushed to its logical conclusion, requires that the entire nation be kept in a state of readiness for war in peacetime, and that the line that in noncommunist societies separates the military from the civilian sectors be made much less distinct.

These considerations apply, of course, not only to defensive calculations, but also to offensive ones. Given the importance attached to industry, transport, communications, energy, and morale as factors that make for victory, Russian doctrine assigns urgent priority to strikes against these targets.

*   *   *

In this connection, nuclear weapons acquire particular relevance in Soviet thinking. In the West, horror of the consequences of nuclear warfare led early to the emergence of a school of thought that assumed nuclear weapons could have no military utility other than as a deterrent. Accordingly, Western doctrine for nuclear weapons has laid heavy stress on arms limitations agreements. Although, obviously, American military planners have had to concern themselves with force levels, targeting, limited strikes, and all the other aspects of nuclear conflict as if it were a genuine possibility, the theoretical underpinnings of these calculations have been neither elaborate nor intellectually impressive. To this day, the dominant strain in Western thinking about nuclear weapons is that they are weapons sui generis, exempt from the accepted norms of military science. The function of the home front is essentially to serve as hostage.

This attitude emphatically does not prevail in the Soviet Union.[24] After a period of hesitation following their acquisition of the hydrogen bomb in the late 1950s, the Russian leadership decided that nuclear weapons were a fact of life that could not be wished away. Whereas in the West their unprecedented destructiveness has produced the conviction that they have no rational application in an offensive mode, in the Soviet Union, by contrast, it was concluded that this very same quality makes them the decisive weapons of modern warfare. The Strategic Rocket Forces, formed in the winter of 1959-60, have been the centerpiece of the Soviet armed forces ever since. (Incidentally, they comprise not only "strategic," i.e., intercontinental, missiles, but all nuclear weapons with a range of over 1,000 kilometers, a fact that underscores the basic difference in our and their attitudes to nuclear weapons in general, and to the concepts of "strategic" and "medium range," or theater weapons, in particular.)

In the view of the Soviet military, nuclear missiles have revolutionized warfare even more than gunpowder and firearms had done in their day; and yet, like the latter, they have not subverted warfare's permanently valid laws. Their innovation consists in the fact that these weapons make it possible to secure directly strategic objectives (the destruction of the enemy's ability to resist) that in the past had been attainable only as a result of a sequence of individual battles: in other words, they make it possible to gain strategic objectives first and to treat tactical operations as mopping-up activities. Concretely, missiles can be used to annihilate the enemy's rear by disorganizing the twin pillars of modern war, the military complex and public morale.[25] According to an authoritative Soviet manual, it is the great value of nuclear missiles that they enable the armed

forces "more rapidly and effectively to realize the major part of
the goals of war" by reversing what had been the traditional
sequence of combat: "It is most probable that modern war may
begin with the defeat of military and economic objects, and ter-
minate with the destruction of the enemy's armed forces and
his unconditional surrender."[26]

The ability of nuclear missiles to accomplish directly the mission of destroying the home front—in itself a precondition for
the collapse of the enemy's armed forces—signifies in Soviet
doctrine that, more than ever, intelligent preparation for the
contingency of war requires that one's own "rear" be merged
with the front.

* * *

I have traced the causes of the intense militarism prevailing
in the Soviet Union, a country that, given the unique casualties
it has suffered over the past sixty-six years of revolution and
war, could be expected to be committed to disarmament and
pacifism. These reasons are partly economic and historical,
partly ideological in nature.[27] I have also stressed that the
philosophy of economic determinism, as reinforced by the experiences of World War I and World War II, has tended to erase
in the consciousness of Soviet leaders the line separating the
military and civilian sectors, with the civilian sector being increasingly regarded as an ancilla of the military.

The purpose of these observations is to suggest how much
more complicated than generally assumed are such undertak-
ings as arms limitations agreements and détente. For the United
States to increase or reduce its military commitment means,
essentially, either to raise or lower its defense expenditures.
This is not the case in the Soviet Union, where militarism is
imbedded in historical traditions, in ideology, in the country's
very political and economic structure. Here, significant changes
in military commitment would involve alterations in every aspect
of national life, indeed, in the system's "constitution." It is
therefore quite illusory to expect that a mere reduction of
U.S. defense appropriations or a freeze on certain weapon
deployments will elicit a corresponding response from the

Soviet Union. This fact has been amply demonstrated by the failure of détente, but it could have been forecast from an analysis of the Soviet system had such been undertaken when détente was first conceived.

Militarism is coercion on a mass scale: it is a denial of compromise on which all peaceful relations between individuals as well as societies must repose. To acquiesce to coercion, whether out of weakness or out of lack of will, is to confirm the basic premise of militarism and thereby to encourage it. Short of war—the ultimate test of coercive powers—the only effective way of frustrating coercions is to demonstrate one's willingness to stand up to the threat, that is, to persuade the military party that the application of force is not profitable. These observations may be trite, but then truth does not necessarily garb itself in innovative or highly complex theories.

In the case of the Soviet Union, dissuasion needs to be fashioned in terms that correspond to its own notions of "science of war" and "correlation of forces." It must challenge head-on the Soviet view of warfare in the age of strategic weapons as well as impress the Soviet High Command with our ability to meet its criteria of "politics, economics, [and] the relationship of the moral-political, scientific-technological and military potential of the warring parties." In other words, to neutralize Soviet militancy, the Western deterrent must coalesce into a Grand Strategy with operationally meaningful strategic capabilities as one of its components. "Web of interest," "unacceptable damage," and other such notions spun by Western theorists will not do in this context.

Thus thwarted, Soviet militarism may indeed be spurred on to even greater efforts: it is a risk that cannot be denied. But it is more likely that it will come under increased internal criticism as an unprofitable device for promoting national interests. Denial of success in the military competition probably will compel the Soviet government to turn inward, to confront its public opinion, and to start coping with its difficult internal problems. This end cannot be achieved, however, without a major and protracted effort: there simply are no cheap and easy ways to induce the Soviet government to alter its direction.

Notes

1. V. I. Lenin, *Sochineniia* [Works], 2nd ed. (Moscow-Leningrad, 1935), XXII, 328.

2. S. Iu. Vitte, *Vospominaniia* [Memoirs], Vol. 2 (Moscow, 1960), 380. Witte himself was a staunch antimilitarist, which lends his words special significance.

3. *Dark Forest* (New York, 1916), 17.

4. See my *Russia under the Old Regime* (New York, 1974), 5–12.

5. Friedrich Ratzel, *Anthropogeographie*, II (Stuttgart, 1891), 257–265. My figures represent a recalculation of Ratzel's, which are given in square leagues.

6. Cf. G. N. Clark, *The Seventeenth Century*, 2nd ed. (Oxford, 1947), 100.

7. V. O. Kliuchevskii, *Peter the Great* (London, 1958).

8. S. N. Prokopovich, cited in A. L. Sidorov, *Finansovoe polozhenie Rossii v gody pervoi mirovoi voiny (1914-1917)* [The financial condition of Russia during the First World War, 1914–1917] (Moscow, 1960), 131.

9. This topic is the subject of an unpublished doctoral dissertation by William Fuller, "Civil/Military Conflict in Imperial Russia, 1881–1914," Harvard University, 1980. The Soviet government, profiting from its predecessor's experience, has separated the military forces responsible for the maintenance of internal order into special units of KGB and border guards. These fully equipped forces number four to five hundred thousand, or more than one-tenth of the Soviet military effectives.

10. Even for a Social Darwinist like Herbert Spencer, warfare was "progressive" in the early phases of human history when it had served to eliminate the weak and "unfit," but it was no longer so in modern times when it diverted human labor and resources to the tasks of destruction: *Study of Sociology* (Ann Arbor, Michigan, 1961), 176–181.

11. See, e.g., I. S. Kardashev, *Internatsional'nyi dolg vooruzhennykh sil SSSR* [The international duty of the armed forces of the USSR] (Moscow, 1960).

12. "Bedingungen und Aussichten eines Krieges der Heiligen Allianz gegen ein revolutionäres Frankreich im Jahre 1852," Karl Marx, Friedrich Engels, *Werke*, VII (Berlin, 1960), 480–482.

13. Lenin, *Sochineniia*, XXI, 189.

14. *Ibid.*, XXIV, 122.

15. On this episode, see John Erickson, *The Soviet High Command* (London, 1962), 144–163 and 247–282.

16. Erickson, *The Soviet High Command*, 352–353 and passim. Skeptics who question the value of current Soviet publications on the prospects

of nuclear war would do well to ponder that in the 1920s leading Soviet military theorists, among them Frunze and Tukhachevskii, published in open literature strategic and tactical recommendations that were in large measure implemented by the Red Army in World War II.

17. This is the subject of Anthony Sutton's *Western Technology and Soviet Economic Development,* I (Stanford, Calif., 1968).

18. *Kommunisticheskaia Partiia Sovetskogo Soiuza v rezoliutsiiakh i resheniiakh s"ezdov, konferentsii i plenumov, 1898-1954* [The Communist Party of the Soviet Union in the resolutions and decisions of its congresses, conferences and plenums, 1898-1954], 7th ed., II (Moscow, 1953), 277; *XVI s"ezd Vsesoiuznoi Kommunisticheskoi Partii (b): Stenograficheskii otchet* [The 16th Congress of the All-Union Communist Party (Bolshevik): Stenographic Account] (Moscow-Leningrad, 1930), 282–289.

19. Max Werner, *The Military Strength of the Powers* (London, 1939), 40. John Erickson (*The Soviet High Command,* 326) in referring to the immediate effects of the first Five Year Plan on Soviet armed forces speaks of a "technical revolution."

20. The remaining "higher military academies" are devoted to tactics, chemical warfare, artillery, transport, communications, and engineering. On them, see *Sovetskaia voennaia entsiklopediia* [The Soviet military encyclopedia], II (Moscow, 1976), 172 ff. The ordinary military academies concentrate on more technical and tactical subjects.

21. It is not uncommon to hear from Westerners unfamiliar with the Soviet system of government disparaging remarks about the value of Soviet publications on military doctrine. They assert that similar doctrinal pronouncements may be found in Western publications and that even if it is conceded that such opinions are prevalent among the Soviet military, they do not necessarily reflect the views of the political leadership. In response it must be noted that in the Soviet Union all publications, but especially those dealing with military matters, are most closely controlled by censorship; only authorized personnel can pronounce on matters of military strategy, and in that sense all published doctrine is authoritative, which, of course, is not the case in the West. As for the alleged distinction between the Soviet political and military establishments, this very notion constitutes an example of "mirror imaging." It is true that in some respects Soviet generals enjoy a great deal of independence, greater than their Western counterparts, in that they are fairly free from civilian supervision in *implementing* military plans. At the same time, in *formulating* military policies they are tightly controlled by the political authorities. The Soviet Council of Defense, headed by Brezhnev, who happens also to be a Marshal of the Soviet Union (as is his Minister of Defense, Ustinov), directs the military mobilization of both civilian and military sectors of Soviet society.

The Main Political Administration, a department of the Party's Central Committee (at present under A. E. Epishev) is an organ of Party control over the armed forces (including censorship of military publications). It taxes the imagination how, under these circumstances, there could develop in the Soviet Union two distinct military doctrines.

22. *Sovetskaia voennaia entsiklopediia,* II, 184.

23. S. N. Kozlov et al., *O sovetskoi voennoi nauke* [On the Soviet science of war] (Moscow, 1964), 67.

24. My thoughts on this subject were spelled out in "Why the Soviet Union Thinks It Could Fight and Win a Nuclear War," *Commentary,* July 1977, 21–34 (Chapter 6 in this volume). Since the article was written, the U.S. government has made publicly available runs of the Soviet classified journal *Voennaia mysl'* [Military thought], which contains many articles on the subject of nuclear warfare. On the basis of these materials, Joseph Douglass and Amoretta Hoeber have written *Soviet Strategy for Nuclear War* (Stanford, Calif., 1979). This book, in my opinion, disposes once and for all of the notion that the Soviet military share the American view of nuclear weapons.

25. "The power of nuclear weapons will be [N.B.] concentrated above all toward destruction of the military-economic potential, defeat of the groupings of armed forces, and undermining the morale of the population." Major General V. Zemskov, "Characteristic Features of Modern Wars and Possible Methods of Conducting Wars," *Voennaia mysl',* No. 7 (July 1969), cited in Douglass and Hoeber, *Soviet Strategy for Nuclear War,* 16.

26. Kozlov, *O sovetskoi voennoi nauke,* 338, 345. "Military objects" in the above citation can mean only the enemy's nuclear forces, given that they are contrasted with "armed," that is, conventional, forces. The statement thus implies a strategic first strike.

27. This list does not, of course, exhaust the reasons for Soviet militarism, which should also include such factors as the absence of legitimacy on the part of that country's leadership and the noncompetitive quality of the Soviet economy. See Richard Pipes, "Soviet Global Strategy," *Commentary,* April 1980, 31–39 (Chapter 7 in this volume). And, of course, it goes without saying that the greater the Soviet military preponderance, the greater the temptation to rely on military threats and coercion; that is, militarism encourages more militarism, quite apart from other considerations.

Index

ABM. *See* Antiballistic missile
Absolute Weapon, The (Brodie),
   142, 143, 144
Accommodation, 184
Acheson, Dean, 38–39, 120
Afghanistan, 96. *See also* Soviet
   Union, and Afghanistan
Agitation and Propaganda,
   Secretary for, 80
Agitprop. *See* Agitation and
   Propaganda, Secretary for
Alexander I (tsar of Russia), 4
Alexander II (tsar of Russia), 68
Alexander Nevsky, 196
Allied Strategic Bombing Survey,
   162
Alliluyeva, S., 5–6
Altunin, A., 166
Amalrik, Andrei, 108, 109, 111,
   124, 125, 130, 132
Amin, Hafizullah, 190
Anarchists, 73
Angola. *See* Soviet Union, and
   Angola
Antiballistic missile (ABM), 145,
   165
Appeasement, 38
Arabs, 95–96
Arms Control and Disarmament
   Agency, 135
Arms limitation. *See* Strategic
   Arms Limitation Talks

Art of operations. *See*
   Operativnoe iskusstvo
Art of war. *See Voennoe*
   iskusstvo
Astrakhan, 197
Atlantic Community, 60
Atomic bombs. *See* Nuclear
   weapons
August 1914 (Solzhenitsyn), 47,
   122
Austria, 4, 20
Austria-Hungary, 96
Autonomization, 130
Aviation Day (1955), 30

Balance of power, 9, 11, 12, 13,
   14, 50, 51, 53, 57–58, 60, 76,
   81, 207
Baltic
   nationalities, 8
   states, 40
Bangladesh, 45
Basic Principles of Relations
   declaration (1972), 82
Basket Three, 92, 108
Behavioral response, 67
"Bei Russkogo, chasy sdelaet," 72
Belorussians, 8
Berlin. *See* East Berlin; West
   Berlin
Bessarabia, 40
Bingham, Jonathan, 184

215

Bison bombers, 31
Blackett, P.M.S., 162–163, 165
Bolsheviks, 28, 78, 93, 173, 182
  and Bolshevism, 178
Bombers
  B-36, 140, 152
  Soviet, 43. *See also* Bison
    bombers
Bombs. *See* Hydrogen bomb;
  Nuclear weapons
Bourgeoisie, 178. *See also*
  Meshchane; "National
  bourgeoisie"
Brandon, Henry, 52
Brazil. *See* Soviet Union, and
  Brazil
Brest Litovsk Treaty (1918), 41,
  53
Brezhnev, Leonid, 69, 71
British Trade Union Congress, 99
Brodie, Bernard, 143, 150
Bureaus. *See Prikazy*
Byzantium, 2, 3

Camp David meeting (1959), 31
Capitalism, 23, 174
Carter, Jimmy, 171
Castlereagh, Robert Stewart, 4
Catherine II (the Great) (empress
  of Russia), 9, 68, 196
Catholic Church, 2, 3
Catholics, 11
Caucasians, 8
Central Asian nomads, 8
Central Intelligence Agency (CIA),
  25
Central Soviet Trade Union
  Organization, 99
Chaadaev, Peter, 2, 124
Charles XII (king of Sweden), 70
Charter of the Nobility (1785), 9
Chekhov, Anton, 131, 132
China, 20, 42, 57, 58, 60, 73
  and Third World, 85
  See also Détente, and China;
    Soviet Union, and China

Chou En-lai, 78
Christian Democrats (Italy), 90
Chrome, 188
CIA. *See* Central Intelligence
  Agency
Civil defense, 165–167
Civil War (Soviet Union), 202,
  203
Class society, 10, 26, 173
Class war, 22–23, 147, 148, 172,
  175, 200
Clausewitz, Karl von, 23, 136, 144
  149, 156, 168, 175
Cobden, Richard, 7
Coercive powers, 210
Cold War, 29, 30, 73, 76, 102,
  103, 113, 176
Collective security, 58
Combined-arms operations,
  164–165
Comecon. *See* Council for Mutual
  Economic Assistance
Comintern, 11
Common Market. *See* European
  Economic Community
Communism, 11, 50, 52–53, 93,
  99, 173, 175, 195, 196
  and trade unions, 98–99
  See also Communist parties;
    Communist Party (Soviet
    Union); Soviet Union, and
    Communist negotiation;
    Soviet Union, and
    Communist Orthodoxy
Communist parties, 33–34, 42, 73,
  85, 90
  French, 89
  Italian, 90
Communist Party (Soviet Union),
  50, 72, 172, 174
  and art of operations, 23
  XVIth Party Congress (1930),
    204
  XVIIth Party Congress (1934),
    74
  XXIVth Party Congress (1971),

78, 176–177
Plenum (1927), 204
privileges, 9–10
tactics, 79
See also Politburo
Communist World Federation of
Trade Unions, 99
Concert of great powers, 49, 51,
52
Conference on Security and
Cooperation (1975, Helsinki),
101
Congo, 35
Conrad, Joseph, 197
Constantinople. *See* Byzantium
"Constant principles," 28, 152,
153
Consumerism, 81
Containment, 49, 50, 102
Convergences, 1, 2, 175
"Correlation of forces." *See*
Sootnoshenie sil
Cossacks. *See* Ukrainian Cossacks
Council for Mutual Economic
Assistance (Comecon), 84, 86
Counterforce, 162–164
Countervalue, 162, 166
"Country-busting," 29
Creative intelligentsia, 127, 129,
130, 132
Crimea, 8, 192, 198
Cuba. *See* Soviet Union, and
Cuba
Cuban forces, 189–190
Cuban missile imbroglio (1962),
27, 39, 41, 82, 120, 190
Cultural exchanges, 92
Custine, Adam Philippe, Marquis
de, 109, 111
Cyprus, 35
Czechoslovakia, 34, 57, 77, 92,
95, 116

Dal, 72
Darwin, Charles, 200
"Deeds not words," 20

Defense, 165–167
Defensor pacis, 35
de Gaulle, Charles, 89
Demichev, P. N., 80
Democratic intelligentsia, 5
Demonstrations, 34
Demoralization, 28
Denmark, 186
Depression, 98
Détente
and China, 86–87, 99–100, 102
and collaboration, 109
and foreign policy, 111
and internal affairs, 109–111
meaning of, 107–108
and military action, 95, 209
and Norway, 92
Soviet assessment of, 99–102,
176
and Soviet historical factors,
68–73
Soviet policy of, 66–67, 73–87,
92–99, 175, 180
Soviet reasons for, 53–54, 102
Soviet tactics for, 87–92
and stability and peace, 108
and Third World, 84–86
United States policy of, 65–66,
102–103. *See also* Jackson
Amendment
and Western Europe, 55–57, 60,
83–84, 89, 90
Deterrence. *See* Mutual deterrence
Dinerstein, Herbert S., 151, 160
Disinformation, 34, 43
Dissidents, 129, 130
Dissuasion, 210
Dostoevsky, Fedor, 131, 197
Dresden bombing casualties, 139
Dulles, John Foster, 44, 140, 141
Dvoriane. See Dvorianstvo
Dvorianstvo, 9–10

East Berlin, 40–41
Eastern bloc, 77, 84, 179

Eastern Europe. *See* Soviet
    Union, and Eastern Europe
Eastern Poland, 40
East Germany, 40, 41, 57
EEC. *See* European Economic
    Community
Egypt, 30, 36, 95. *See also* Soviet
    Union, and Egypt
Eisenhower, Dwight D., 20, 31,
    76, 140, 141, 153
Eisenstein, Sergei, 196
Élite
    European, 115, 117
    See also Russia, élites in;
        Soviet Union, élites of;
        United States, élites; Western
        élites
Emancipation of serfs (1861), 9
Embourgeoisement, 31, 115, 118,
    119
Engels, Friedrich, 21, 22, 23, 200,
    201
English liberalism, 6, 7
Equilibrium. *See* Balance of
    power; International
    equilibrium
Ethiopia, 187. *See also* Soviet
    Union, and Ethiopia
Europe
    Americanizing of, 115
    Catholic and Protestant,
        110–111
    and literature and political
        action, 131
    and Middle East, 192
    social democratization of, 59
    and world wars, 114–115, 117
    See also Élite, European; Soviet
        Union, and Eastern Europe;
        Soviet Union, and Western
        Europe; United States, and
        Europe; Western Europe
European civilization, 2, 6
European-East Asian military
    entente, 58
European Economic Community

(EEC), 34, 59, 90–91, 117,
    120
European security pact, 84, 90, 91
Extreme Left, 125
Extreme Right, 125, 126

Fear, War and the Bomb
    (Blackett), 162
Federal Republic. *See* West
    Germany
Finland. *See* Soviet Union, and
    Finland
Finno-Ugrian peoples, 8
Five Year Plans, 76, 182, 204
Foreign Directorate (First Main
    Administration), 24
Four Year Plans. *See* Hitler,
    Adolf, and Four Year Plans
Fox, William T. R., 143
France, 4, 32, 33, 59, 83, 199. *See
    also* Communist parties,
    French
"Free World," 14
Fusion bomb. *See* Hydrogen
    bomb

Garthoff, Raymond L., 151, 160
Geneva Conference (1955), 31
Geneva Security Conference, 92
German-French-English military
    alliance, 83
Germany, 13, 26, 45, 96, 199
    and World War II bombing,
        138, 139
    See also East Germany; Soviet
        Union, and Germany; West
        Germany
Ghana. *See* Soviet Union, and
    Ghana
Gladstone, William, 7
Goethe, Johann von, 133
Golden Horde, 71
Grand Strategy, 210. *See also*
    Soviet Union, Grand Strategy
Great Britain, 4, 7, 13, 32, 57, 83,
    199

Great Patriotic War, 205
Grechko, A. A., 137, 147, 148, 163
Greece, 56
Greek Orthodoxy. *See* Russia, and Byzantine Church
Grenzgebiet (adjoining areas), 23
Gromyko, Andrei, 24, 100, 176
GRU (Glavnoe Razvedovatelnoe Upravlenie), 24

Hayter, Sir William, 42
Hegemony, 75, 86, 176, 185
Herzen, Alexander, 131
Hiroshima bombing, 139, 163
Historical materialism, 39
Hitler, Adolf, 26, 27, 28, 29, 30, 32, 40, 70, 74, 83, 100, 159
and Four Year Plans, 182
Home front, 207. *See also* "Stability of the home front"
Human equality, 64
Humanists, 127, 128, 129
Hungary, 116
Hydrogen bomb, 30, 127, 129, 141, 163

ICBMs. *See* Intercontinental ballistic missiles
Iceland, 92
Iceland-Faroes-England gap, 186
Ideological war, 52, 54, 66, 76, 80, 103, 113–114, 185
IMEMO. *See* Institute of World Economy and International Relations
Imperialism, 23, 113
India, 58, 96, 109. *See also* Soviet Union, and India
Indian-Pakistani war, 96
Indochina, 20
Indonesia. *See* Soviet Union, and Indonesia; United States, and Indonesia
Inflation, 98
Inner Mongolia, 87

Institute of the U.S.A. (ISShA), 66, 158
Institute of World Economy and International Relations (IMEMO), 66
Intelligentsia. *See* Creative intelligentsia; Technical intelligentsia
Intercontinental ballistic missiles (ICBMs), 157, 159
Soviet, 30, 43, 161, 183
United States, 145, 161
Intercontinental bomber. *See* Bombers, B-36
Internal emigration. *See* Soviet Union, population mobility in
International diplomacy, "new era" of, 54. *See also* Nixon Doctrine
International equilibrium, 17. *See also* Balance of power
Interventionism, 12, 103
Iran, 96. *See also* Soviet Union, and Iran
Iraq, 35, 96. *See also* Soviet Union, and Iraq
Isolationism. *See* United States, and isolationism
Israel, 30, 181
and Syria, 35
See also United States, and Israel
Israeli-Arab war
1967, 27, 82
1973, 96, 97, 180
See also Israeli-Egyptian dispute
Israeli-Egyptian dispute, 36, 95
ISShA. *See* Institute of the U.S.A.
Italy, 33, 74. *See also* Communist parties, Italian; Soviet Union, and Italy
Izvestia, 95

Jackson, Henry, 91
Jackson Amendment, 111, 112

Japan, 5, 34, 40, 49, 58, 60, 109,
    181, 188, 192
  Gross National Product (GNP),
    186
  and World War II bombing,
    138, 139
Jews, 8
Jobert, Michel, 118
Juridical Dictionary. *See* Soviet
    Juridical Dictionary

Kahn, Herman, 157
Kalmuck prince. *See* Alexander I
Kapitsa, Pyotr, 127, 129
Karmal, Babrak, 189
Kautsky, Karl, 202
Kazan, 8, 57, 197
Kaznacheev, Alexander, 24
Kennan, George, 38
Kennedy, John F., 27, 39, 190
KGB (Komitet Gosudarstvennoi
    Bezopastnosti), 24, 25, 33,
    34, 43, 80, 100, 132
Khrushchev, Nikita, 26, 27, 29,
    30, 31, 76, 113, 120, 121, 127,
    128, 129, 153
Kidd, Isaac, 187
Kissinger, Henry, 48, 51, 52, 54,
    55, 89, 144
Kliuchevskii, V. O., 199
Koestler, Arthur, 22
Kola peninsula, 186
Korea. *See* North Korea; South
    Korea
Krasnaia zvezda, 150
Kurile Islands, 34, 40

Labor shortage, 98
Laird, Melvin, 147
Lasers, 157
League of Nations, 52
Lee, William T., 182
Left. *See* Extreme Left; New Left
Lenin, V. I., 22–23, 41, 52, 73,
    75, 93, 100, 147, 172, 173,
    175, 177, 178, 200, 201–202

  and Leninism, 22, 126
  and Leninists, 124
Leningrad casualties, 167
Letter to the Soviet Leadership
    (Solzhenitsyn), 123
Liberalism, 64. *See also* English
    liberalism
Liberal Protestantism, 7
List, Friedrich, 10
Little Russia, 8
Long-range cruise missiles, 183
Ludendorff, Erich, 21
Lumpenproletariat, 126

McGovern, George, 89, 90
McNamara, Robert S., 144, 150
Mahan, Alfred Thayer, 137
Malenkov, Georgii, 30, 153
Manchuria, 57, 87
Manganese, 188
Marx, Karl, 21, 22, 23, 31, 200
Marxism, 22, 147, 150, 200
  and model of class society, 10
Marxism-Leninism, 72, 79, 113,
    172–173, 200–204, 207
Massive retaliation, 141, 142
Material wealth, 115–116, 118
Medvedev brothers, 124, 126
Mengistu Haile-Mariam, 189
Mensheviks, 173
Mercantile class ethos, 6. *See also*
    United States, business ethos
    of
Meshchane, 71
Mickiewicz, Adam, 131
Middle East. *See* Egypt; Iran;
    Iraq; Israel; Oil, Middle East;
    Soviet Union, and Middle
    East; Syria; Turkey
Military Academy of the General
    Staff, 206
Military-Historical Journal, 158
Military Strategy (Sokolovskii),
    150, 156, 163
Minerals, 188
Minutemen missiles, 183–184

Minuteman-3, 161
MIRV's. *See* Multiple
    Independently-targetable
    Reentry Vehicles
Mitterand, François, 89
Modernity = peace equation, 52
Modernization, 65, 82
Morale of the armed forces, 28,
    152
Morocco. *See* Soviet Union, and
    Morocco
Moscow, sixteenth and
    seventeenth centuries, 3, 5, 7,
    9, 10, 39–40, 68, 198
Moslems, 8, 10, 197
Most Favored Nation status, 91
Moynihan, Daniel P., 146
Multiple Independently-targetable
    Reentry Vehicles (MIRV's),
    161
Murmansk, 92
Muscovy. *See* Moscow, sixteenth
    and seventeenth centuries
Mutual Assured Destruction
    doctrine, 184
Mutual deterrence, 141, 142, 143,
    144, 145–146, 154, 155, 157,
    158, 165
Muzhik, 71–72, 147

Napoleon Bonaparte, 28, 70, 100,
    201
National Association of
    Manufacturers, 69, 91
"National bourgeoisie," 75
    movements, 188, 189
National democracy, 85
National liberation movements,
    101, 188
NATO. *See* North Atlantic Treaty
    Organization
Natural gas, 97, 180
Nazi methods, 29, 38
Neto, Cuito Agostinho, 189
New Left, 7
New Republic, 135

Nitze, Paul, 157
Nixon, Richard M., 20, 48, 49,
    50, 51, 52, 54, 56, 57, 58, 90,
    101
    and concept of Soviet Union's
    tactics, 55, 89
    resignation of, 116
    visit to Moscow (1974), 69
Nixon Doctrine, 48, 49–51, 52, 60
Nkrumah, Kwame, 189
North Atlantic sea lanes, 187
North Atlantic Treaty
    Organization (NATO), 31,
    34, 57, 58, 92, 95, 101, 164,
    186, 191, 192
North Korea, 120
North Vietnam, 51, 188
Norway, 186, 187. *See also*
    Détente, and Norway
Novgorod, 57, 70
Nuclear blackmail, 30, 31, 42
Nuclear weapons, 29, 30, 35, 51,
    75–76, 81, 83, 94, 120–121,
    135, 138–139, 140, 141, 142
    151, 152, 156, 160, 191–192,
    207, 208. *See also*
    Counterforce; Hydrogen
    bomb; Soviet Union, nuclear
    doctrine; United States,
    nuclear doctrine

October Revolution (1917), 5, 178
October War. *See* Israeli-Arab
    war, 1973
Office of Ambassadors. *See*
    Posol'skii Prikaz
"Officers Library, The," 150
Oil
    embargo, 66
    as energy resource, 96–97, 180
    exploration, 92
    Middle East, 187
    See also Soviet Union, oil
Okinawa, 34
Old Right, 7

*One Day in the Life of Ivan
    Denisovich* (Solzhenitsyn),
    131
Operations research. *See* Systems
    analysis
Operativnoe iskusstvo, 21–25,
    41–42
Order of the Day (Stalin, 1942),
    28
Orthodox Christianity, 126. *See
    also* Russia, and Byzantine
    Church
Ottoman Empire, 57, 71, 197

Pachman, Ludek, 92
Pakistan, 45
Pan-Slavic nationalism, 110, 122,
    131
Passive defense, 157
Peace campaigns, 35, 88, 89, 103
Peaceful coexistence, 11–12, 25,
    41–42, 73, 74–75, 77, 99, 103,
    109, 112, 113, 175
Peasants. *See Muzhik*
Pentagonal world, 57–58
Persian Gulf, 187
Peter the Great (tsar of Russia), 4,
    181, 198–199
Petöfi, Alexander, 131
Petrograd Soviet, 173, 199–200
Philosophical Letters (Chaadaev),
    2
Pipes, Richard
    interviewed by George R.
        Urban, 107–133
Platinum, 188
Pluralistic world, 48
Poland, 57, 179, 197. *See also*
    Eastern Poland
Poles, Russian, 8
Polish-Lithuanian Commonwealth,
    11, 71, 198
Politburo, 24, 77, 79, 149
Political sociology, 31–33
Poslovitsky russkogo naroda
    (Dal), 72

Posol'skii Prikaz, 8
Possessed, The (Dostoevsky), 197
Potsdam Conference (1945), 151
Pravda, 153
Preemption, 159–160
Prikazy, 8
Privatization, 130–131
"Proletarians of all countries,
    unite!" 173
Protestant ethos, 147
Public opinion, 48, 121, 210
Pushkin, Alexander, 131, 132, 133

Quantitative superiority, 160–161

RAF. *See* Royal Air Force
Rand Corporation, 151
Rasputin, Grigori, 196
Realpolitik, 12
Reciprocity, 103
Red Army
    and Eastern Euorpe, 99, 154
    equipment, 204–205
    and Middle East, 187
    role, 153
    25th anniversary (1942) of, 28
    and Western Europe, 56
    in World War II, 159, 163
Red Sea, 187
Red Star. See Krasnaia zvezda
Rhodesia. *See* Zimbabwe
Ridgway, Matthew B., 139
Right. *See* Extreme Right; Old
    Right
"Rollback" threat, 44
Royal Air Force (RAF), 138, 162
Rus', 68
Russia
    and Byzantine Church, 2–3, 7
    and diplomatic relations, 3, 4–5,
        7–10
    eighteenth century, 4
    élites in, 4, 5, 7, 9–10
    empire-building in, 8, 10–11
    foreign policy of, 9–11

diplomacy, 22, 70, 110–111
and Eastern Europe, 11, 33, 57,
    59, 101
economy, 77–78, 82–83, 93,
    96–99, 179
and Egypt, 85, 96, 189
élites of, 7, 9–10, 24, 27, 32, 57,
    68–69, 71, 119, 147, 173, 176
and Ethiopia, 189, 190
expansionism, 26, 70–71, 112,
    174, 175, 179, 192, 197, 198
exports (1966–1973), 77
and Finland, 186, 187
foreign policy, 10, 22, 24–25,
    26–27, 38–42, 99: as extension
    of domestic politics, 67; *See
    also* Peaceful coexistence
and Germany, 20, 74, 162, 203
and Ghana, 189
gold reserves, 97
Grand Strategy, 177–180,
    185–192, 207
Gross National Product (GNP),
    182
historical view, 1–2, 5, 16, 57,
    64–65, 68, 72–73,
    197–200
indebtedness to the West, 98,
    179–180
and India, 85, 101
and Indonesia, 189
and industrialism, 203–204
intelligence services, 42–43
and internal pressure, 192–210
invasions of, 197
and Iran, 85
and Iraq, 85
and Italy, 97
and Japan, 82, 83, 88, 101,
    179, 180, 185. *See also* Kurile
    Islands
and literature and political
    action, 131–133
and Middle East, 97, 101, 187
militarism, 195–200, 203–210
and militarisms, 20–21

military force, 26, 83, 92–96,
    154–155, 180–185
military intelligence. *See* GRU
military policy, 149
military science degree, 149
Ministry of Defense, 155
Ministry of Foreign Affairs, 24,
    38
and Morocco, 179
national character of, 109–110
national policy of, 78–80
and navy, 58, 92, 94, 165,
    186
new class in, 119
nuclear doctrine, 136, 150–151,
    152–154, 158, 167, 183,
    208–209
nuclear parity, 53–54
and nuclear war, 156, 158,
    164–165, 167–168
oil, 97, 180
peace offensive, 60
per capita national income
    (1914), 199
and political security, 80
population density, 198
population mobility in, 69–70,
    130
and pragmatism, 53, 54–55
pressure on United States
    Congress, 69, 91
propaganda, 34–36
proprietary authority of, 68
proverbs, 64, 72
public mood of, 121–123
resistance in, 129, 132
and social sciences, 32, 33
and Southeast Asia, 101, 188
and South Yemen, 179, 187
strength, 87–88
and Syria, 96
and technology, 155
thaw in, 100, 102
and Third World, 69, 75–76,
    179, 188–191, 192. *See also*
    Détente, and Third World

imperial period of, 4, 8, 9, 199,
    203
Kievan state, 39
military doctrine of, 203
nation-building in, 8, 70
peoples of, 8
westernization of, 4–5
and xenophobia, 2
See also Moscow, sixteenth and
    seventeenth centuries; Soviet
    Union

Sadat, Anwar, 30, 189
Saint-Simon, Claude de, 52
Sakharov, Andrei, 122, 123, 124,
    125, 126, 127, 129
SALT I. *See* Strategic Arms
    Limitation Talks, I
SALT II. *See* Strategic Arms
    Limitation Talks, II
Santayana, George, 48
Satellites, 157
Saturation bombing, 163
Science of war. *See Voennaia
    nauka*
Scientists, 127, 128–129
Second International, 202
Security Conference. *See*
    Conference on Security and
    Cooperation
Self-interest, 17, 99
Serbia, 96
Service class. *See Dvorianstvo*
Seton-Watson, Hugh, 122
Shakespeare, William, 133
Shelepin, A. N., 99
Siberia, 8, 97, 197
Sinkiang, 87
Slavophiles, 4, 122, 123
Smart weapons, 56
Smith, Adam, 10
Smuts, Jan Christiaan, 52
Social Darwinism, 64, 147, 172
Social Democrats (Russia), 75
Socialism, 23, 124
Socialist Revolutionaries, 173

Social revolution, 115, 117
Soft strategy. *See* Peaceful
    coexistence
Sokolovskii, V. D., 150, 156, 163
Solzhenitsyn, Alexander, 47, 121,
    122, 123, 124, 125, 131, 133,
    149
Sombart, Werner, 6
Sootnoshenie sil, 26, 42, 53, 83,
    202, 207, 210
South Africa, 188
Southeast Asia. *See* Soviet Union,
    and Southeast Asia; *names of
    individual countries*
South Korea, 20. *See also* United
    States, and South Korea
South Vietnam. *See* United States,
    and South Vietnam
South Yemen. *See* Soviet Union,
    and South Yemen
Sovereigns of bodies and souls,
    133
Soviet Juridical Dictionary, 29
Soviet Union
    and Afghanistan, 85, 179, 187,
        189
    agrarian economy of, 16
    and Angola, 189, 190
    armaments, 80–81, 88, 103, 114
        141
    armed forces, 160, 196, 198,
        199, 207. *See also* Red Army
    and Brazil, 88
    and Central Powers, 41
    cereal crops, 198
    and China, 44–45, 53, 57, 71,
        86, 191, 197. *See also*
        Détente, and China
    climate and topography, 69, 70
    and commerce, 16–17
    and Communist negotiation,
        19–20, 41
    and Communist Orthodoxy, 5,
        21, 41. *See also* Communist
        Party
    and Cuba, 190

and threats, 29–31
and Turkey, 85, 179
and United States, 36–38, 41,
   75, 76, 81–83, 88, 90, 99,
   100–101, 185
urban population, 166
weakness, 88
web of interests, 49, 66, 210
Western correspondents in, 100
and Western Europe, 41, 56,
   82, 88, 91, 179, 185. *See also*
   Détente, and Western Europe
Western investments in, 101–102
Westernizers in, 122, 123–124
and West Germany, 57, 97, 101,
   180
working class, 129
as world power, 100–101
World War II losses, 156, 166,
   167
and xenophobia, 5, 125
and Yugoslavia, 99
See also Balance of power;
   Communist Party; Détente;
   Russia; United States, and
   Soviet Union
Spain. *See* United States, and
   Spain
Spencer, Herbert, 52
Splitting the half, 37
Sputnik, 30, 141
SS-18, 161
"Stability of the home front," 28,
   152, 205
Stalin, Joseph, 5, 11, 25, 28, 30,
   38, 40, 73–74, 99, 100, 120,
   140, 151, 152
   and German attack, 159
   purges of, 71
   and Stalinism, 122
   and war scare (1927), 204
Stateinye spiski, 3
Strait of Bab el-Mandeb, 187
Strait of Hormuz, 187
Straits of Malacca, 188
Strategic Arms Limitation Talks

(SALT), 168, 209
   I (1972), 161, 182, 183
   II, 136, 183
   See also Quantitative superiority
Strategic bombing surveys. *See*
   Allied Strategic Bombing
   Survey; United States,
   Strategic Bombing Surveys
Strategic Rocket Forces, 164, 208
Strategy in the Missile Age
   (Brodie), 150
Struve, Peter, 22
Suez Canal, 187
Sukarno, 189
Sun Tzu, 103
Suslov, Mikhail, 6
Suvorin, A. S., 132
Sweden, 187
Syria, 35, 95. *See also* Soviet
   Union, and Syria
Systems analysis, 144

Taiga, 69, 174, 198
Talenskii, N., 152, 153, 155
Tannenbaum, Frank, 14
Tannenberg, 47
Taraki, Nur Mohammad, 189
Tatars, 8, 10
Technical intelligentsia, 127, 128
   129
Thermonuclear weapons. *See*
   Nuclear weapons
Third International (1920), 73, 178
Third World, 41, 42, 43, 44, 96.
   See also Détente, and Third
   World; Soviet Union, and
   Third World
Thirty Years' War, 110
Threats. *See* "Rollback" threat;
   Soviet Union, and threats
Times Literary Supplement, 129
Tokyo bombing casualties, 139
Tolkunov, Lev, 95
Tolstoy, Leo, 123, 124, 132, 133,
   196
Trade. *See* World trade

Trade unions, 98–99
Treaty of Westphalia (1648), 110,
    111
Truman, Harry S., 39, 151
Turco-Mongolian empire, 8
Turgenev, Ivan, 131
Turgot, Anne Robert Jacques, 10
Turkestan, 8, 197
Turkey, 35. *See also* Soviet
    Union, and Turkey

Ugroza (threat). *See* Soviet Union,
    and threats
Ukrainian Cossacks, 8, 10
Ukrainians, 8
Under Western Eyes (Conrad),
    197
Unions. *See* Trade unions
United Press International (UPI),
    30
United States
    Air Force, 138, 140, 141
    Army, 138, 139
    business ethos of, 14, 65, 147
    commercial economy of, 16, 37
    constitution, 14
    defense expenditures, 209
    Department of State, 25
    and diplomacy, 7
    élites, 146–147
    and Europe, 116, 117, 118, 121,
        122
    forces in Western Europe, 83,
        84, 118, 120
    foreign policy, 49, 50
    Gross National Product (GNP),
        185–186
    historical view, 1–2, 6–7, 16
    and Indonesia, 15, 16
    and isolationism, 6–7, 31, 90,
        117
    and Israel, 15, 16
    Jewish community, 91
    military strategy, 137–138,
        140
    navy, 140

    nuclear doctrine, 136, 137, 139,
        140–141, 142–143, 145–146,
        157, 183, 207–208
    and Protestant ethic, 37–38
    and South Korea, 14, 39
    and South Vietnam, 12, 14, 22,
        116
    and Soviet Union, 15, 25, 27,
        191–192
    and Spain, 14, 15
    and stability, 14, 15
    Strategic Bombing Surveys, 139
    Trade Bill, 91
    urban population, 91
    and vocabulary of mechanics,
        13–14
    and xenophobia, 7
    and Yugoslavia, 15
    See also Balance of power;
        Détente; Nixon Doctrine;
        Soviet Union, and United
        States
UPI. *See* United Press
    International
Uranium, 97
Urban, George R.
    interview of Richard Pipes,
        107–133
Urban petty bourgeois. *See*
    Meschane
Utopians, 122

Vanadium, 188
Veba, 180
Versailles *Diktat*, 38
Versailles Treaty (1919), 203
"Victory through Air Power," 138
Vietnam. *See* North Vietnam;
    United States, and South
    Vietnam
Voennaia nauka, 206–207, 210
Voennoe iskusstvo, 206, 207
Voice of America broadcasts, 54
Voroshilov, K. E., 204, 206
Vorotyntsev, Colonel, 47

Walpole, Hugh, 197
War and Peace (Tolstoy), 123, 196
War by proxy, 95, 96, 101
War Communism, 202
Warnke, Paul, 135, 136
War of the Polish Succession
   (1733–1735), 4
Wars, 148, 149, 167, 201. *See also*
   Civil War; Class war; Cold
   War; Soviet Union, and
   nuclear war; *Voennaia
   nauka; Voennoe iskusstvo*
Warsaw Pact (1955), 95, 164
   countries' Gross National
   Product (GNP) (1977-78),
   185
Watergate affair, 116
Weizsäcker, 129
West Berlin, 20, 40
Western élites, 33
Western Europe, 41, 49, 51, 58,
   59, 60, 192
   cereal crops, 198
   energy supplies, 84, 96, 188
   Gross National Product (GNP),
   186
   labor, 96
   population density, 198
   See also Détente, and Western
   Europe; Soviet Union, and
   Western Europe; United

States, forces in Western
   Europe
Western powers, 9, 96
West German Federation of
   Labor, 99
West Germany, 31, 40, 59, 83. *See
   also* Soviet Union, and West
   Germany
Wilberforce, William, 7
*Will the USSR Survive Until
   1984?* (Amalrik), 108
Wilson, Woodrow, 52
Witte, Sergei, 196
Wohlstetter, Albert, 157
Wolfers, Arnold, 143
World trade, 77

Xenophobia. *See* Russia, and
   xenophobia; Soviet Union,
   and xenophobia; United
   States, and xenophobia

Yale Institute of International
   Affairs, 142
Yalta agreement (1945), 11
Yugoslavia, 56. *See also* Soviet
   Union, and Yugoslavia;
   United States, and Yugoslavia

Zhukov, Georgii, 153
Zimbabwe, 188